THE BIG BOOK OF
Five Nights at Freddy's

THE DELUXE *UNOFFICIAL* SURVIVAL GUIDE

TRIUMPH
BOOKS

This book is available in quantity at special discounts for your group or organization.
For further information, contact:

Triumph Books LLC
814 North Franklin Street
Chicago, Illinois 60610
Phone: (312) 337-0747
www.triumphbooks.com

Printed in U.S.A.
ISBN: 978-1-63727-061-5

Content packaged by Mojo Media, Inc.
Joe Funk: Editor
Jason Hinman: Creative Director
Contributing Writers: Rob Talley, Monica Rasmussen, Liam Martin
Horror Gaming Expert & Screen Grab Technician: Jack Hinman

WHAT'S INSIDE

WELCOME TO FREDDY'S WORLD

When the first game first launched in 2014, neither creator Scott Cawthon nor anyone close to him could have imagined the juggernaut Five Nights at Freddy's would become in less than half a decade.

But in today's digital world a person, event, or great content can go viral through a multitude of traditional and social media platforms. In the case of Five Nights at Freddy's, it all started as a video game, but its now-famous jumpscares have made it a durable sensation among a generation of kids.

The FNaF franchise is still in the early stages of expanding into other forms of traditional media, including an on-again, off-again major Hollywood film that will certainly, eventually get made because this franchise is too great.

In any case, by any measure, FNaF has entered mainstream pop culture. There's a thrill in being scared, and Freddy and company have proven to be monstrous masters of mechanical mayhem. In this book, we'll help you get the most out of all of the games in the series, and even explore the frightening appeal and use of scariness!

Along the way, we'll touch on tidbits, tips, and trivia about the franchise, take a closer look at the roster of colorful characters, and even explore other games that can add a little fright to your fun.

Consider this your essential survival handbook for making it through yet one more night at Freddy's for every game so far, but also as a collectible keepsake of a franchise that will continue to evolve and eventually grow into a multimedia powerhouse.

FIVE NIGHTS AT FREDDY'S

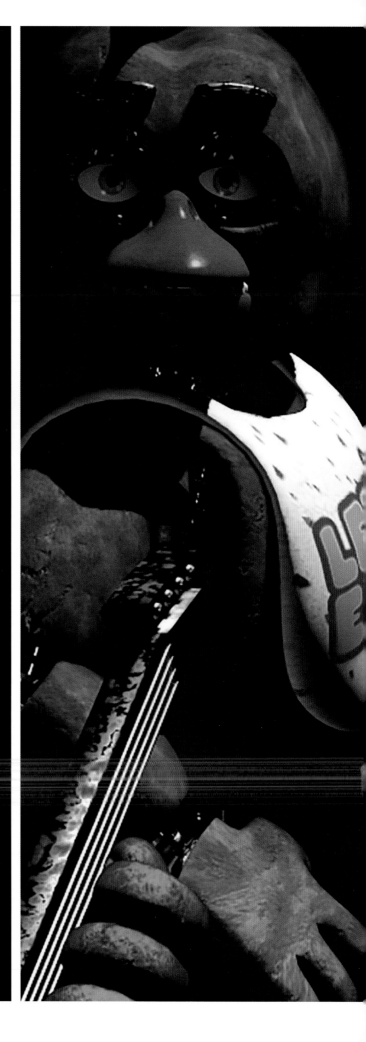

Before the pandemic, you may have been to one of those family restaurants or theme parks that feature crazy characters in costumes entertaining the kids. Chuck E. Cheese's and Walt Disney World come to mind when you're thinking of this kind of thing.

Workers dressed like oversized animals or cartoon characters, while friends and families gathered to play expensive games, eat bad pizza, and celebrate a birthday or special occasion.

Five Nights at Freddy's is the story of Freddy Fazbear's Pizza, where instead of actually hiring people to walk around in costumes all the time, the owners of the place decided to make the animals robotic so they can walk around and entertain the kids by themselves!

Somehow though, after the restaurant closes and all the customers go home, Freddy Fazbear and his fellow animatronic friends get confused when there aren't any kids running around for them to entertain.

You might think the owners of the restaurant would have paid to have Freddy and his friends looked at, or possibly repaired. But it turns out to be a lot easier on the wallet to just hire a security guard— in this case, you—to watch over them at night and make sure they don't get up to any mischief.

You're in charge of a lot.

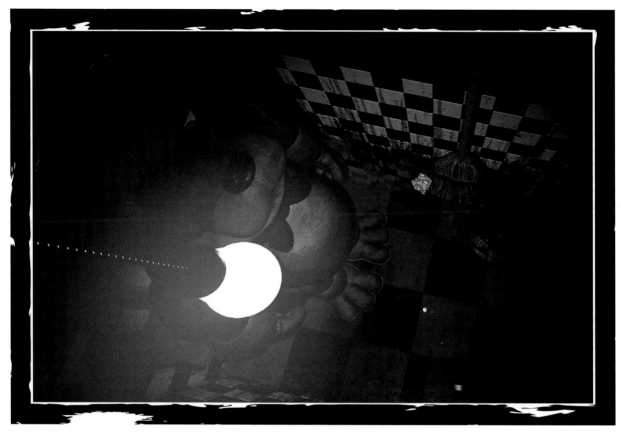

You've got your office, you've got your laptop to check in on all of the security cameras placed around the building, and you've got lights and doors on each side of your small office.

Now, we're not going to sugarcoat things— Freddy and his friends can get a bit irrational and most of your job is going to be checking on the security cameras to make sure that they're not getting in any trouble.

Each of the characters has its own spot to spend the night, so if you see through the security cameras that one or more of them have moved, it's time to be on your guard. These animatronic animals are designed to entertain people, and since you're the only person in the building at night, they'll be coming for you.

YOUR TOOLS AND HOW TO USE THEM

When you start the game the first thing you'll notice is your office. It's not very big but there are a couple of important things to pay attention to.

First off is your ability to turn your head— fancy that! When you scroll the mouse back and forth from the left to the right and back again, you'll be able to turn your head in both directions to check the doors on either side of the room.

Next up are the very obvious buttons you can see on both sides of the room. It'll be pretty easy to figure out what they do but just so you know beforehand, these buttons are for the door and for the lights in the hallway just outside. You're going to want to remember these buttons are there, even on your first night.

DYK? A CINEMATIC VARIATION ON THE FIVE NIGHTS AT FREDDY'S THEME IS THE 2006 COMEDY FILM, *NIGHT AT THE MUSEUM,* STARRING BEN STILLER. IN BOTH STORIES, THE PROTAGONISTS ARE OVERNIGHT SECURITY GUARDS WHO WORK UNTIL MORNING. THE ATTRACTIONS BEHAVE AS EXPECTED DURING THE DAY, BUT BECOME DEVILISHLY ANIMATED AT NIGHT.

Before we look at what you can do by pressing these buttons, let's scroll down to the bottom left of the screen where we can see a couple of very important "gauges."

The first gauge lets you know how much battery power you have left. Like we said before, the owners of this place aren't big on spending a lot of money so you've only got so much power every night.

Once the "Power left" gauge reaches zero, the other buttons for the door, the lights, and even the security cameras will stop working, so you have to be careful how much you use each of those gadgets.

The perfect way to make sure you're being careful is by checking the gauge right below the first one.

On this gauge, you're actually going to see some colors depending on the buttons you have pressed. The bigger that colored bar gets, as it goes from green to yellow to red, the more power you're using and the faster you're going to drain the battery.

The doors are your last line of defense and will either stay open or shut depending on the press of the button. When you see Freddy or another confused animatronic character just outside your door, you press the button and shut it as fast as you can. Just remember you can't keep them on all night—even keeping the doors closed will drain your battery—so you've got to be careful when you do it. How are you going to see them you may ask? It is night time after all, and things are very dark.

You're going to be able to see them with the lights on, of course, and they work just about the same way as the doors. You press the button to turn them on and press it again to turn the light off, whichever side you're on. Just remember not to keep too much on at a time or you'll lose all of your battery power.

In the middle of your in-game screen you'll see a white rectangle with a couple of arrow symbols in the middle of it. This is what brings up your laptop. On this laptop you're going to see a map of the building and where each of the security cameras are placed throughout.

Altogether there are 11 cameras you can check on throughout the night. It might be hard right off the bat to make sense of where everything is placed but try your best. The easiest way to make sense of it all is to start at the little square dot marked "you." If you've been to a mall and looked at one of those map displays they have to show people where all the different stores are, this probably looks familiar.

That little square dot is you, in your office. There are a couple of cameras just outside each door of your office so things are going to get serious if you see Freddy Fazbear or any of his malfunctioning friends hanging around there on either side.

Your last, and possibly the most important tool you've got, is your ears. Yes, you read it right, sounds play an important part in this game.

Whether you've got headphones in or have the sounds playing from a speaker system, one of the best ways to survive Five Nights at Freddy's is by listening for footsteps coming down the hallway toward your tiny office.

But it's not just footsteps you need to be listening for—there are a couple of different sounds that will let you know what might be happening when you're not looking through the lens of a security camera.

The thing about Freddy Fazbear and his animatronic family is that they're a little camera shy. As soon as they know you're looking at them on any of the security cameras, they freeze. So listening to them move is your best option most of the time if you want to know what they're up to.

Speaking of Freddy and friends...

CHARACTERS

Let's touch on just for a moment the subject of who to watch out for on your night-shift security job. There are four of these characters that switch from their daytime "entertain the kids" mode, to one where they just roam around the restaurant so they stay loose and limber and none of their robotic parts get rusty from not moving.

FREDDY FAZBEAR: Freddy's the main character and the mascot for "Freddy Fazbear's Pizza." He's the lead singer in the band—which you can tell by the mic in his hand while he's on stage—but he's really just a great big brown huggable bear. He's got a hat, he's got a big toothy smile, and sometimes his eyes glow in the dark when he's coming for you. Only sometimes. Watch out for Freddy making his way toward your office at night.

11

BONNIE THE BUNNY: Bonnie looks a lot like Freddy—he's big and cuddly, but pink and rather than a nice hat on his head he's got a red bowtie and when he's on stage he strums a guitar. He also doesn't have any top teeth or eyebrows. Even though he has a hard time making different expressions, it's not hard to tell what he's thinking as he wanders around at night with the rest of his animatronic bandmates.

CHICA: The third member in the band is Chica— she's a chicken and the backup singer. She's got eyebrows but like Bonnie doesn't have any top teeth. Then again, she's a bird so that kind of makes sense. One thing about her is that she's wearing a big white bib with the words "LET'S EAT" on the front in all capital letters. Chica hangs out in different rooms than the others at night. As you might be able to tell by her bib, they're usually rooms that deal with food, like the kitchen and the dining area.

FOXY: Foxy is a pirate. He's also a fox. When you're looking through the security cameras and you come to a scene with a big purple curtain, you're at Pirate Cove. Now, Foxy is the only animatronic animal who's currently broken down completely at the moment. The big purple curtain is even drawn during the day because Foxy isn't doing any more shows. However, if you ever see Foxy's face peeking through that curtain at night, back out of the security camera screen as quickly as you can and close both the doors. You're only going to see Foxy's face if he's coming for you, and he moves pretty fast.

GOLDEN FREDDY: There's one last character that you may or may not see during your five nights at Freddy's. He's called Golden Freddy and he's really just a dreamy version of Freddy with no eyes. It's rare to ever see him because there's a certain couple of things that need to happen first before he appears. Because he's so rare, however, if you ever do see him, it's game over. Golden Freddy will get you even if you've got both doors to the office closed. If he gets you, he does it so well that it will close the game altogether, forcing you to restart the whole game if you want to keep playing.

YOUR FIRST FIVE NIGHTS

Your First Night: You'll start with the phone call from the last security guard. Listen to what this guy has to say because he gives a lot of helpful hints as to how to deal with the different animatronic characters wandering around at night. The call will end around 2:00 am, and during the time that he's talking you should be pretty safe from Freddy and friends wandering around and coming for you. It's your first night after all, so it'll be the easiest.

Take this opportunity to explore your surroundings a little bit. We know there's not a lot to see but at least you can check on the security cameras and get familiar with where they're all located and what each one sees. Don't go too crazy though—remember, you've still got to watch out for your battery power down at the bottom left of the screen.

FYI ALTHOUGH WE DON'T KNOW FOR SURE WHAT YEAR THE GAME IS SET IN, YOUR PAYCHECK AT THE END OF THE GAME WAS THE MINIMUM WAGE IN THE EARLY 1990S.

The three main characters you have to watch out for always start out at the beginning of the night at the "Show Stage" (Cam 1A). During the day this is where Freddy Fazbear, Bonnie the Bunny, and Chica play their instruments and sing songs for the children coming to visit the restaurant. Normally this is where they should stay during the night. So this is the security camera you should be checking the most, as it's going to tell you who's out of place and moving around the building.

For the most part in Five Nights at Freddy's, there are really only about four different cameras you need to pay attention to the most. There's the Show Stage (Cam 1A), Pirate's Cove (Cam 1C), and the security cameras just outside the doors to the security office (Cam 2B and Cam 4B).

Check the "Show Stage" to see who's missing from the lineup and on the move, "Pirate's Cove" to see if Foxy is peeking out from behind his curtains, and lastly "W. Hall Corner" and "E. Hall Corner" to see if anyone's hanging right outside your doors.

You can follow Freddy Fazbear and the other animatronic characters as they wander through the other rooms of the restaurant but really it's only going to become your problem if they get too close to you. It's better to just keep an eye on who's missing from the stage and pay attention to who makes it too close to the office.

When you hear someone coming down one of the hallways and you're not completely sure who it is—maybe you missed them on the security camera or you're not checking every area on purpose—here are some good rules to follow depending on who shows up at your door:

• When Bonnie is coming for you, she'll usually show up at the door on the left.

IT'S ME

- If the purple curtains ever open up in Pirate's Cove and Foxy is on his way, then more often than not he's going to show up at the left door as well. (Sidenote: if the curtains are all the way open and Foxy's not behind them, you know he's on his way. Check security camera 2A and you'll see him running toward you. Shut that door!)

- The lead singer Freddy Fazbear comes through the door on the right most of the time when he's coming for you. Sometimes, but not very often, he will come through the left.

- Chica comes through the door on the right just like Freddy but this will be the only door that she comes through.

As we mentioned before, one of the most important tools you have to use is your ears—listen for the band members fumbling about in other rooms or wait to hear the footsteps coming down the hallway right outside your doors.

There won't be a lot of stuff happening during your first night—chances are you may not have to use the door-closing button more than once. Keep your guard up though—Freddy, Bonnie, Chica, or even Foxy can still surprise you at random.

A good strategy to use is to wait until you hear footsteps nearby. If you hear them at all, check the "Stage Floor" to see who it is, then quickly scroll through all the rest of the cameras to find out who it is and where they moved to. If you can figure out who's moving around the most, chances are that's going to be the one coming for you.

If you see through the door by using the light switch button that someone's about to come in and get you, close the door! Whoever it turns out to be is going to wait there a few moments before deciding to leave. If you want to check and see if anyone's still outside the door, turn on the light and you'll be able to see the shadow of whoever it is through the window. Other than that, just like when they're coming closer, you're going to be able to hear footsteps of Fazbear and friends as they walk away.

A good pro tip for when you think you hear someone coming down the hall is to quickly flash the lights on the side you hear the footsteps— chances are you'll catch whoever it is just before they rush in. It's a good strategy most players of Five Nights at Freddy's use—after all, that's what the lights are there for.

Stay brave and keep checking the right cameras and 6:00 am will roll around before you know it.

Your Second Night: Your second night is a lot like your first, but things are getting serious a little bit quicker than they did the night before. You're going to start hearing footsteps even before the phone call with your old night guard friend is done.

The trick from now on will be to keep an eye on where everybody is. So if you're hearing footsteps, try to locate who is making those sounds as quickly as you can. And check the map when you see Freddy Fazbear or any of his friends so you know where they are.

Keep the list of which character will pop up at which door handy while you're checking where all these characters are. Depending on which room you find Freddy, Bonnie, Chica, or even Foxy (he might be running down the hall towards you) in, you might have to worry less or you might have to worry more.

For the most part, keep up with the tactics you learned in the first night. Listen for footsteps, check the "Stage Floor" security camera to see who's been moving around, and prepare yourself to close the doors to the office at a moment's notice.

A new tactic you're going to want to get used to is flickering the lights on both sides of the room whenever you hear some footsteps getting closer. Sometimes Freddy Fazbear and his bandmates are sneaky and you might not always catch them on the security camera. You know they are coming for you, so flicking the lights to check is going to be your last chance to be warned someone's at the door. There's always a small window of time where they wait at the door before they pounce, and if you're quick enough you can turn off the light and slam the door fast enough to save yourself.

If you've managed to get the door down in time, and you're still alive, you're still not safe yet. These animatronic animals aren't going to go away just because the door was closed. Freddy and his friends are going to stick around just in case you want to open the doors again to check and see if the coast is clear.

Kind of clever, aren't they?

Well, you're clever too. If the door's open, you can use the light switch to check the area just outside it. But when the doors are shut, you can still turn on the light and just a little ahead you'll be able to see the light through the window into the hallway.

If someone's still waiting outside the door for you open it again, press the light-switch. Instead of just seeing light out in the hallway, whoever is standing in front of the light will cast a shadow, letting you know that either Freddy or one of his friends is still waiting for you.

This rule is different for each side of the room. When you turn on the light with the door shut on the left side, all you're going to see is either the shadow of whoever is blocking the light or just the regular lit up area where the light normally shines.

DYK? DURING A KICKSTARTER CAMPAIGN CREATOR SCOTT CAWTHON USED TO DEVELOP THE GAME IN 2014, FREDDY FAZBEAR WAS ORIGINALLY GOING TO BE NAMED FREDDYBEAR.

If we go over to the right side however, shutting the door and turning on the light will let you see whoever's in the hallway. For example, if Chica happens to show up at the right side of the room you're going to shut the door quickly, of course, but when the door is shut you can turn on the light and you will see her peaking in through the window.

The only one this isn't going to work for is Foxy. As soon as you close the door when Foxy is coming for you, he's gone almost right away, so you don't have to worry about checking with the hallway light. Remember that these guys are clever and sometimes you might shut the door for Foxy but he could be working together with any of the other characters roaming around the restaurant. So even if Foxy gets stopped by the door it might still be a good idea to use the hallway light and check for the shadow.

You know when Foxy's gone because he's going to knock on the closed door three times. As soon as he knocks that third time, you're safe from Foxy for now. But that doesn't always mean you're safe from everyone else.

Other than keeping those things in mind, just make sure to keep up with the regular stuff like watching your battery power. A good rule to follow for how much power you have left is to look at the clock and if half the night has ticked by and you're at about 50-70 percent battery power left, then you're managing your different tools well.

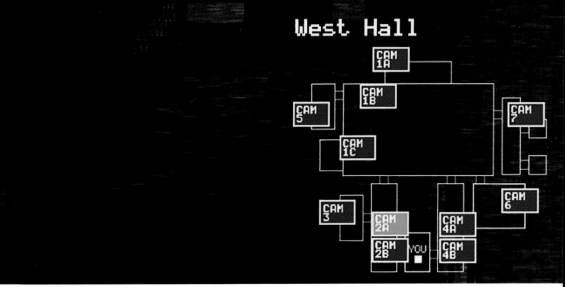

ower left: 83%

sage: ▌▌

As you get further into the game you're going to have to use the security cameras, the lights, and the doors more and more, so getting into the habit of using them smartly is helpful at the beginning of the game.

Your Third Night: The phone call on the third night is a lot less charming than it has been the last two nights, so now you know what's waiting for you if you let in Freddy or one of his animatronic band members. Don't sweat it, though!

There's going to be less information for us to give you as we get into the later nights. All you need to know is that as the game progresses further, things start to happen faster. So you might have noticed by now that after the first night, you can already hear footsteps moving around the building during your phone call. If you check the "Show Stage" security camera, chances are one if not all of the characters are already out of place and in different rooms.

Freddy, Bonnie, Chica, and Foxy are a lot more comfortable with you now and this is just going to keep getting worse the more nights you spend there.

At this point you might see that some of the security cameras are blacking out occasionally, only letting you hear what's going on rather than see anything. From the start of the game, this is the case only for the kitchen.

It's now all the more important to use your ears and listen for different sounds other than the footsteps. Do you hear what sounds like the rattling of dishes? Someone's probably in the kitchen, so you can check the map and see if there's anyone close by that area.

You might even hear Freddy start laughing occasionally. I'm not sure we really need to tell you that's not a good thing. We said before that Freddy shows up most often at the right door and only sometimes will be at the left door. When Freddy laughs, watch the left door because that's usually what lets you know he's coming and he thinks he's being funny trying to surprise you by showing up at the other door.

Another thing to watch out for now is the hallucinations. You might have seen a couple before, even some on your first night at Freddy's, but now they might be happening more often. Try to keep a cool head because in terms of gameplay they're not going to change much.

Your Fourth Night: Throw out most of what you've learned the three previous nights about the behavior of Freddy Fazbear and all of the other animatronic characters. Starting on the fourth night, things are going to get a lot more serious and the patterns and behaviors you've come to expect from all the characters you've grown to love will change.

That's fine though, because that just means you're going to have to change up how you play.

Foxy and Freddy have both had enough of you at this point and they're both really eager to grab you and stuff you into one of the spare character suits.

"FROM NOW ON YOU'RE GOING TO WANT TO START PAYING MORE ATTENTION TO FOXY BECAUSE A GOOD WAY TO GET HIM TO SLOW DOWN AND NOT CAUSE MISCHIEF IS TO KEEP AN EYE ON HIS PURPLE CURTAINS AT 'PIRATE'S COVE.'"

Foxy in particular is out to get you—he's not just going to go after you but now he'll start trying to do something about how much power you have left to use for the doors, lights, and security cameras. Like you weren't having a hard time worrying about that already!

From now on you're going to want to start paying more attention to Foxy because a good way to get him to slow down and not cause mischief is to keep an eye on his purple curtains at "Pirate's Cove."

When he does bust out, check to see if he's running down the hallway (camera 2A) and close the door. You'll hear him bang on it as usual but now it might be four knocks before he gives up. When he heads back you might even lose a percentage or two of battery power because of Foxy's tampering.

Foxy bangs on your closed door four times now. You want to save on battery power now more than ever, so a good trick is to open the door when you hear the first knock. The door will open and the knocks will keep happening but Foxy will already be gone and hiding back behind his curtains. It's a little glitch but all the power you save helps.

As a rule the other characters are going to take more of a back seat for the last two nights but it's random so you never know who might start working together. When you see all of Freddy Fazbear's bandmates on the security cameras now, you'll notice that they're no longer just standing still. Their heads start to twitch the longer the night goes on.

We covered Foxy—now you know that to keep him in check and react to him well enough is to keep checking on his purple curtains. Freddy, on the other hand, is just going to start laughing more and more on the last two nights.

When Freddy laughs, you have to be on your guard.

Listen to the footsteps in particular when you hear him laughing because while normal footsteps are going to be slow and steady, if Freddy's decided to come for you then you're going to hear fast shuffling steps moving pretty quickly in your direction. If that happens then you need to figure out where he's coming from as quickly as you can and shut the right door or your goose is cooked.

Other than that just keep your normal guard up for the rest of the characters and conserve your battery power as best you can. If you survive we can move on to the last night.

Your Fifth and Final(?) Night: It's crunch time everybody! By now you've played the game enough to know all the different buttons to press and what everything does, and you've probably got some good strategies ready to use. That's good because this is the night you're going to need them.

You've been checking security cameras and turning on the lights but now it's time to start zipping through them as fast as you can. Focus only on a couple of different security cameras, and the ones you do use, make sure to only keep them open for a split second—just long enough to check and see if anything's changed—then close it. The less time a security camera or light is on the less power you use up and the better chance you're going to have of surviving the night.

Foxy and Freddy are going to be your main targets and the most active out of all the characters, just like the night before, but now it's even worse.

You've been doing a good job keeping Foxy slow and behind his curtain for the most part by continuing to check up on him pretty often, but now it's time to start doing that for Freddy. Start checking the "Show Stage" security camera and try to keep Freddy from going about his business as much as you can.

Try to use the security cameras just to keep an eye on those two, and for everyone else turn up the volume and listen for any footsteps. If you think you might be about to get jumped by anyone else, then just use the hallway lights to check and see before closing the doors.

It's important now to only check on the other characters when you actually hear something.

It's time to develop a nice and steady rhythm, checking all the things you need to on the security camera about once every 3-4 seconds, then just rinse and repeat until something changes and you've got to act. Don't let any weird noises in other rooms or hallucinations distract you. Just keep up with your routine and you should be able to make it through the final night.

If you follow this strategy you'll be able to survive the fifth night and might even have some power left over by the time 6:00 am rolls around.

If you managed to make it through the five nights, congratulations! You collect your paycheck and are free to leave and go find a "normal" job... if that's what you really want. ●

FYI

Five Nights at Freddy's merch is produced mainly by two companies, Funko and Sanshee, and includes the typical products such as stuffed toys, action figures, posters, clothing, trinkets, and more. McFarlane Toys has also developed a series of Five Nights at Freddy's construction sets, and in October 2017, owner Todd McFarlane called the line "the single largest selling product, bar none, by a lot that I've done in 20-plus years," and contributed its success to the popularity of the game among kids.

FIVE NIGHTS AT FREDDY'S 2

Welcome back to Freddy Fazbear's Pizza! It's new, it's been redone, and you're going to see right off the bat that you're not back in your rinky-dink little office where you spent all your time in the first game.

Everything has been redone. The whole restaurant has been renovated almost from the ground up and things are better than they ever were before. You've got air vents on either side of your office instead of doors and the power system has been improved, so now you don't have to worry about wasting too much power at night when you're using the security cameras to keep an eye on things.

Be careful, though—just because you've got all the power you need to use the security cameras as much as you want, that doesn't mean you're safe. There's a whole team of new and poorly built animatronic characters prowling around at night looking for restaurant customers to entertain, and you're still the only one there.

The new location for the door to your slightly larger security office is directly in front of you. So if any of the usual crowd of animatronic animals want to come pay a visit, shine the flashlight straight ahead because a lot of the time this is where you're going to see them hiding in the dark.

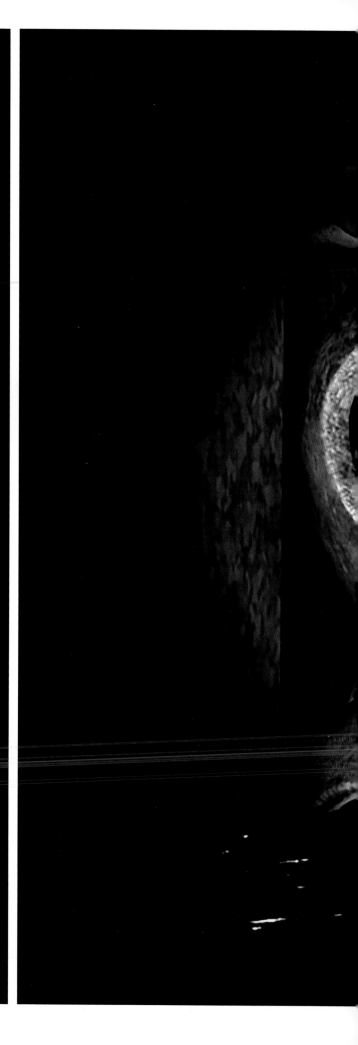

These new guys have been built a little differently—they've been programmed to recognize faces and have a whole library of different faces stored away to recognize any bad guys who might walk through the restaurant's doors. Unfortunately, they are still malfunctioning and it's going to be up to you to figure out how to survive again for all five nights.

Now in each room you can see into with a security camera you have the option to turn on the flashlight and light up any dark corners where things might be hiding. You're going to see your old pals Freddy Fazbear, Bonnie, and Chica, and even Foxy might still be around somewhere but now in a brand-new setting.

New party rooms for the kids, a new stage where all the characters perform for their audiences, and you've even got some security cameras that will see into the air vents in case something gets stuck in them.

Without further ado, let's take a look at the tools you have at your disposal to help you survive another five nights of fear.

YOUR TOOLS AND HOW TO USE THEM

The Security Cameras & Freddy Fazbear Head: If you've played the first game you're probably used to using the security cameras to have a look in all of the different rooms around the restaurant. We're in luck because those security cameras are back so if you were comfortable using them before, you're going to have no trouble getting used to these new ones.

If you're on your first night then the playful animatronic animals probably won't be wandering around too much, which means you've got the time to check your new office for a few minutes before things start to get scary.

DYK? IN OCTOBER 2019, TO MAKE THE MOST OF THE LATEST CELLPHONE TECHNOLOGY, THE MOBILE VERSION OF FIVE NIGHTS AT FREDDY'S 2 WAS REMASTERED AND IMPROVED TO LOOK LIKE THE PC VERSION.

When you're sitting at your office, take a look at the bottom of the screen. In the first game there was only one little bar you could mouse over that would open up your laptop, but now there are two.

Why are there two, you ask?

Well, it's really close to being the same as it was in the first game. The little bar on the right will bring up the map screen and show you where all of the security cameras throughout Freddy Fazbear's Pizza are. We'll go over that more in just a sec but for now let's focus on this new second bar that's on the left. You'll notice that it's red and when you mouse over it there is no map screen that comes up.

Introducing your very own Freddy Fazbear head!

First let's go back to taking a look at the map and what you can do with all of the security cameras that you couldn't do in the first game.

The rooms you'll see through the security cameras are going to be different because the owners of Freddy Fazbear's Pizza spent the money and got a newer, bigger restaurant. So while it's going to be unfamiliar, what you're going to remember is how the map screen actually looks.

Click on the different rectangles to see through the eyes of each particular camera. When you click on a camera you will see into that room and at the top of the map where all the rectangles are it will tell you the name of the room you're looking into.

You'll see a familiar room they've brought back from the first game—the "Show Stage" makes its return so Freddy and friends have a place to play their music for all the children who came to watch. Other than that, there's "Parts & Service," where you can see old broken robots stored to be worked on and fixed at a later date.

That's right, just like the old security guard on the phone at the beginning of the first night will tell you, they remembered that Freddy and all of the other animatronic characters are trying to get you and stuff you into an empty suit. They recognize faces (including yours) so the best way to avoid getting caught by them is to pull up this head and wear it over your own when someone gets too close.

You can keep it on and wear it for as long as you want. But beware!

This trick isn't always going to work—there are some characters that aren't going to be fooled by the fake head. We'll tell you just who isn't going to fall for the mask in just a little bit.

There's the "Main Hall," "The Game Area," and "Kids Cove," as well. You can even see a different view of "The Game Area" in "The Prize Corner." There are also four different "Party Rooms" that you might sometimes find Freddy Fazbear and his friends hanging out in.

Lastly, you can check the two different security cameras placed in each of the vents on both sides of your office. You never know what you might see crawling around in there.

Your Flashlight and the Battery Icon: Let's get out of the map screen and go back to your cozy little office. At the top left of the screen you'll see that there's still a battery icon in this game. Don't worry, it's not there to tell you how much time you have left to use the cameras—like we said earlier, the cameras never die. What this new battery icon does is tell you how long you have left to use your flashlight.

It may not seem like much but your flashlight plays an important role in this game. At the start of your first night you will see that to use your flashlight you press and hold the left control button on your keyboard. When you test it out for the first time you will see that it works right away by shining a beam of light right down the hallway in front of you.

Keep holding down the shift button as you scroll through all the different security cameras and you'll see that there's a dark spot in every room that your flashlight will light up, and if anyone's hiding in that darkness you'll be able to see them.

The Music Box: Check in on security camera 11 to have a look at the "Prize Corner." You'll see the counter where kids can come up and get prizes for the games they've been playing. The more important thing you're going to see is the little gray box slightly to the left of the map that reads "Wind Up Music Box." Underneath the box you can read, "Click and Hold."

You're going to hear the old security guard on the phone talk about this music box at the beginning of your first night. Remember when we mentioned there are some fun characters who aren't going to be tricked by the Freddy Fazbear head? This music box will keep that secret character calm the whole night as long as it keeps playing.

If you're good about keeping the music box wound up all the time you probably won't ever notice this, but there's going to be a small warning that appears if the winding ever gets too low. What this means is that if you forget or purposefully let the music box wind down without bothering to wind it back up, you'll see a small exclamation point appear in yellow at the bottom of your screen. If you let it go any longer it will go from yellow to red, and if it stays at red too long...well let's just say it's going to mean trouble.

Light Switches and the Time: The last important thing that you will see are going to be the light switches to the left and right of your office. Sometimes when the animatronic characters get sneaky and try to crawl through the vents to say hello, they're going to make it up into your office. You're not going to get any warning if this happens, either. It will be up to you to check these vents with the light switches to see who may or may not be hiding right in front of you.

The last thing you'll want to pay attention to is the clock at the top right of the screen. It doesn't work like a regular clock, something you're probably used to from playing the first game, and you don't get to see the minutes. It's only going to update every in-game hour until your night is over at 6:00 am and you're safe. Lastly, you'll be able to see what night you're on just above the clock—night 1 is going to be the easiest and it gets more and more difficult as you progress through each night, making night 5 the most difficult

Your Ears: That's right, noises make a comeback in this game and just like in the first Five Nights at Freddy's, the things you hear and how you react to hearing them could make or break this game for you. There are many more noises and creepy sounds to listen for and be afraid of now. You might even hear some giggling now and then or maybe the voice of a small child saying "Hello."

It won't be such a big deal at the start—the first couple nights are rather tame. Make sure to remember which sound means what early on as the last couple nights are pretty vicious. It gets to a point where you can't check the cameras fast enough and end up having to rely on only your ears to tell you what animatronic character is sneaking around and getting up to mischief.

Like footsteps in the last game, telling you who was coming closer to your office, in this game what you want to listen for is the bumps and thumps in the metal ventilation system. This is going to tell you who's crawling around in there and give you a heads up at who's planning to jump out at you from either side of the room.

THE NEW CHARACTERS

The same animatronic animals you know and love from the last game are still around, but the owners of the restaurant invested in getting some new versions made for the new restaurant.

Now, we won't be going over all of the old characters from the first game—if you've played it you should already know who they are and what they're about. They'll make appearances here and there in this game but the main focus during these five nights should be on the new characters. The new guys will be the ones coming for you so we're going to list them out in the hopes that you will at least recognize who's coming for you.

FYI WITH SIX ALL-NEW ANIMATRONICS JOINING DILAPIDATED VERSIONS OF THE ORIGINAL FIVE FROM THE FIRST GAME, 11 ANIMATRONICS NOW ROAM THE HALLS OUTSIDE YOUR OFFICE. OTHER FRIGHTENING NEW FEATURES INCLUDE THE LACK OF DOORS ON YOUR OFFICE (YIKES) AND THE ADDITION OF THE FREDDY FAZBEAR MASK.

These new characters are going to seem somewhat familiar—it's not your imagination. What the restaurant owners did was take the characters you already knew and loved and gave them a fresh new design so they'd be more appealing to the kids. To repeat, however, the old characters are still around, so keep that in mind when you play the game.

Toy Freddy: Our first new character is a spruced up version of the old Freddy Fazbear. This new version is more detailed and the color scheme is a lot better. Like the original Freddy you'll see that Toy Freddy is a bear, he's brown, and he carries a mic in his hand, because even in this game the "Freddy" character is still the lead singer in the band.

He's got rosy cheeks, whiskers, a top hat, and now even wears a nice little bowtie on his chest with some buttons below it. Watch out for his eyes—normally they're going to look just like everybody else's but if he makes it all the way into your office, that changes.

Toy Bonnie: Toy Bonnie looks a lot more like a rabbit in this game compared to the first Five Nights at Freddy's. We're sure you'll agree it won't be so easy to mistake him for Freddy anymore. A lot of the improvements are similar to how Freddy was improved himself. Things like the little whisker spots, the bowtie, and the rosy cheeks seem to be a popular change they made when the restaurant owners spent their money. He's also got a guitar just like the original Bonnie did when they were standing on the "Show Stage." In Five Nights at Freddy's 2, however, sometimes you might see Toy Bonnie walking around with it.

He's got a shiny new coat of paint, green eyes, and a buck-toothed grin to strike a happy feeling into the hearts of the audience.

Toy Chica: Out of all the new characters, Toy Chica probably looks the most like the original. She's still got her bib and she's still holding a cupcake just like in the last game. For some reason though you won't always see her beak.

Just like Bonnie she's got a shiny new coat of paint, with blushing cheeks and new eyebrows that let her show expression better than she ever could before.

What you'll notice about the paint jobs is that Freddy is the only one who is not shiny in this game. We can't tell you why that is—it might just be a design choice from the people who rebuilt these new improved versions—but just remember that if you see anyone shiny at all, chances are it's not going to be Freddy.

These first three animatronic characters all start each night on the "Show Stage," so right away when each new night begins if you check camera 9 that's where you'll find Toy Freddy, Toy Bonnie, and Toy Chica. The next set of animatronics are placed in other areas of the restaurant and it will be up to you to find them before they find you.

Mangle: If you remember Foxy from Pirate's Cove in the first game then just know that this new character looks almost nothing like him. Mangle once upon a time might have been a replacement for Foxy, as the original name for it was meant to be "Toy Foxy," but right now she—and we're not even sure if it is a she—is basically, well, she's mangled. We won't tell you where to find her (it shouldn't be too hard to figure out) but when you see her for the first time you'll see that Mangle is basically a broken animatronic lying in a heap on the floor. Curious to figure out why she's battered and broken? Make it to the third night and you'll find out.

Balloon Boy: There's a first for everything, and Balloon Boy is the first human animatronic ever featured in Freddy Fazbear's Pizza. Of course, that's not going to make much of a difference—this little stinker is definitely out to get you, too.

Just like the others, he's shiny, with rosy cheeks and a glassy stare that creeps you out. He wears a hat with a propeller on it and he's dressed in red and blue stripes. In one hand he's holding a balloon and in the other he's holding a sign that says "Balloons." Go figure.

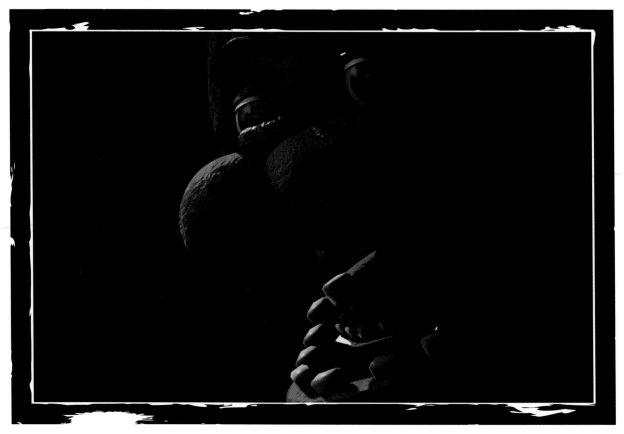

This little guy likes to crawl through the vents but he's not going to attack you directly—instead what he likes to do is mess with the lights. So if you let him have his way he'll make it so you won't be able to use the flashlight or the lights in the vents. If you let him get too far this light tampering will be permanent for the night, so you need to keep an eye on him.

He's creepy, he giggles, and he could spell disaster if you let him get too far into the office.

The Puppet: You heard us mention the music box before and on your first night you probably heard the old security guard on the phone tell you that keeping that thing wound up is a really important part of this job.

The Puppet is the reason why.

The only time you're going to see this guy in the game is if you've left the music box off for too long. He's tall—almost as tall as the ceiling—skinny, and almost completely black. His face is a white smiling mask with hollow black eyes and he's got three buttons on his chest.

It almost makes you wonder if he really is part of Freddy Fazbear's Pizza because he really doesn't look like an animatronic character at all. Especially not a kid-friendly one.

If you left the music box unattended for too long and the Puppet actually leaves the "Prize Corner" then it's game over. Just like Foxy in the last game leaving his curtain at Pirate's Cove, the Puppet will speed right towards you and not even the spare Freddy Fazbear head is going to fool him.

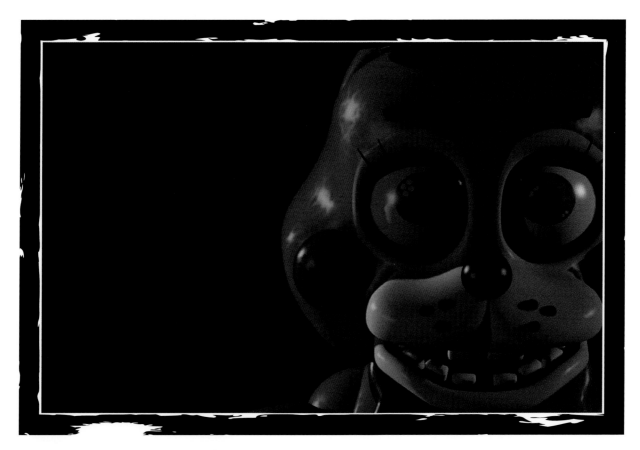

SURVIVING YOUR FIVE NIGHTS AT FREDDY'S, AGAIN

Night One: Your first night starts out just like you would expect from playing Five Nights at Freddy's. It starts out with a phone call from the senior security guard for Freddy Fazbear's Pizza. He's calling just like he always does to give you some warnings about things you're going to see and experience during your stay here. Isn't that nice of him?

As per usual the first night will be slow, so feel free to take some time and check out what all the new different features of your new office are for while you listen to the phone call. It should take a while, the guy has a lot to say.

Right off the bat you'll be able to check every security camera and see where all of the animatronic guys start each night and you can even start to crank the music box as well.

The music box will only start to really need cranking when the other security guard's call is done, however, and even that only happens on the first night. When the second night rolls around you have to worry about the music box right away.

Now that the security guard is done with his call you'll most likely be aware of all the things you need to worry about, if you didn't already know them before. Keep an eye on things with the security cameras, use your flashlight to peep into dark corners of each of the rooms, and pay attention to the music box to make sure that it stays wound up. Also keep an ear out for those bumps in the vents—it's only the first night but that doesn't mean someone isn't crawling through there looking to find their way towards you. Pay attention to the sounds getting closer or farther away and check on the security cameras if you need to. Most of all, remember how to protect yourself if anybody gets too close. (Hint: the empty Freddy Fazbear head.)

DYK? THOUGH THEY DON'T APPEAR IN THE FNaF 2 TRAILER TO CONCEAL THEIR IDENTITY, SHARP-EYED OBSERVERS MAY SPOT TOY CHICA ON SEVERAL POSTERS IN THE CAMERA FEEDS, WHILE THE PUPPET AND GOLDEN FREDDY APPEAR IN CHILDREN'S DRAWINGS IN THE BEGINNING OF THE TRAILER.

Don't worry so much about your flashlight battery power at this point—if you want to look around at all the areas with some light, you can. It's not as important to save as much power as you can during the first couple of nights.

In terms of how the animatronic characters are going to behave, we won't tell you the path each one takes as they make their way towards you but we will tell you where each one is going to pop up. It's most likely going to be a surprise anyway but we didn't want to give away too much in this book.

Turn to your left and look at the vent—you don't need to turn on the light but just be aware that Toy Chica, the bird, will be coming through this way when she's trying to get to your office. She's not the only one who's going to come through here but for the first night it'll just be her you have to watch out for. Toy Bonnie will be coming through the vent on the opposite side of the room when it's his turn to pop up and scare you, so have that empty Freddy Fazbear head ready!

While these two characters, and possibly others, can come through those vents it doesn't mean that they won't come straight through the doorway in front of you. It's random where they decide to go, so every once in a while it wouldn't hurt to back out of the security cameras and flash your light down the hall to see if anyone's there.

There's a particular noise you can listen for. It happens right before whoever is in the vents jumps out at you. It's a low kind of hum, kind of like the noise you might hear out of an old television tube when it first turns on. This is your cue letting you know that someone's about to pounce, so if you're in the middle of winding up the music box or searching through the other security cameras and you hear something like it, rush quickly to put on the empty Fazbear head and save yourself. The noise is accompanied by the lights flickering, so you can watch out for that as well as listening for the weird noise.

If you keep all these things in mind and are good enough about keeping up with them, the first night should be a breeze. Just don't panic and keep a cool head and things should turn out fine as we head into the second night.

Night Two: You're going to hate this, but in the second night things get amped up, a lot.

If you were thinking it was just going to be slightly more difficult than the first night, think again because the difficulty spikes a lot higher really fast and you've got to be on your toes the whole night long.

A pro tip for players from here on out is to turn up your volume—this helps you hear important noises that will tell you what's happening so you can prepare yourself for whoever might be coming at you. While we call this a pro tip, please realize that while it lets you hear things a lot better, if you mess up and Freddy Fazbear or one of his friends get you, it's going to be louder and it's going to be a lot scarier so dial up that volume at your own risk.

You were willy-nilly with your flashlight on the first night and that was fine but now is the time where you have to start watching how much flashlight power you use and to only use it when you really need to. These animatronic characters are going to be coming at you left, right, and center, and it's only through careful planning that you're going to stay alive.

Foxy from the first game makes a reappearance on the second night and he'll be there for the rest of the game. A good habit to get into doing is to use your flashlight only on the hallway in front of you to keep him at bay.

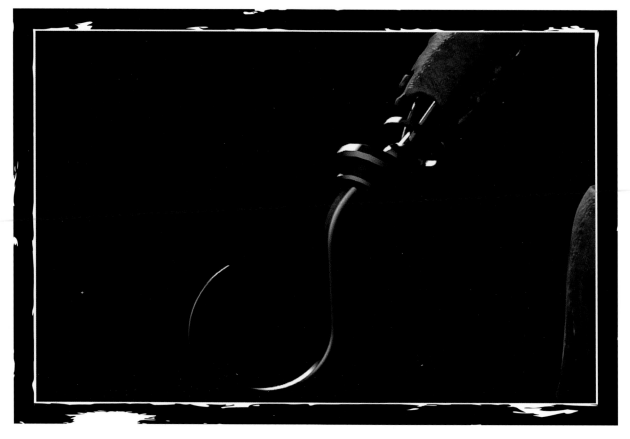

Mangle is also going to be on the prowl. She can come from anywhere so be prepared if you see her. Whether she's in the vents or down the hallway you have to be prepared for her because she's quick.

You've been listening to the noises before and from the second night onward the most important noises you have to listen for are the footsteps that tell you someone's walking down the hall directly towards your office, and the bumps in the vents that tell you someone's crawling in the vents. Get into the habit of listening to these two things right from the start and you should be golden.

The second night is also the night that Balloon Boy first makes his appearance. You may have noticed that on the first night he stayed in one spot the whole night long and didn't bother anyone. Well, that stops now and where you're going to find him trying to sneak into your office is through the vent on the left side.

Listen for the bumps and if you hear some giggling as well that's going to tell you that it's Balloon Boy crawling around in there rather than one of the other animatronic characters.

While the second night does ramp up the difficulty, it's still going to be a lot of the same stuff you experienced on your first night. Yes, the Balloon Boy will be new and you have to watch out for him, Foxy, and even Mangle, but the second night is really all about developing the right habits of how to play that will keep you alive for the nights to come.

Now if you want to look through the different cameras after hearing footsteps or movement of some sort, you really need to do it fast and barely flicker your flashlight in each room before moving on to the next. You've got until 6:00 am (yes, we know it's about 8-9 minutes, but still) so you have to conserve as much battery power as you can.

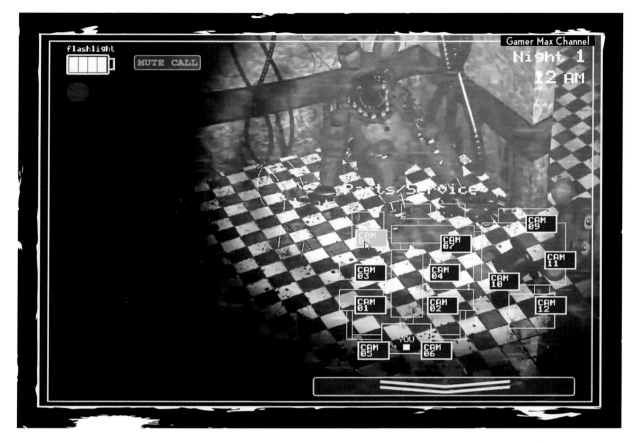

"THE MOST IMPORTANT NOISES TO LISTEN FOR ARE THE FOOTSTEPS THAT TELL YOU SOMEONE'S WALKING DOWN THE HALL DIRECTLY TOWARDS YOUR OFFICE, AND THE BUMPS IN THE VENTS THAT TELL YOU SOMEONE'S CRAWLING IN THE VENTS..."

Freddy Fazbear himself is now going to start marching around, that is if he didn't already during the first night. But by night two he's definitely on the move and more often than not you're going to see him directly in front of you down that long hallway. He might start off far back but he'll inch his way forward slowly. Keep using your flashlight as you keep an eye and ear out for the other guys but as soon as Freddy gets almost to the doorway to your office quickly put on the empty Freddy head and wait until he's gone. He might come at you right away or he might come at you after a couple of minutes or he might decide to leave you alone altogether, but keeping the mask on is always your safest bet. Just don't forget that the music box is still playing.

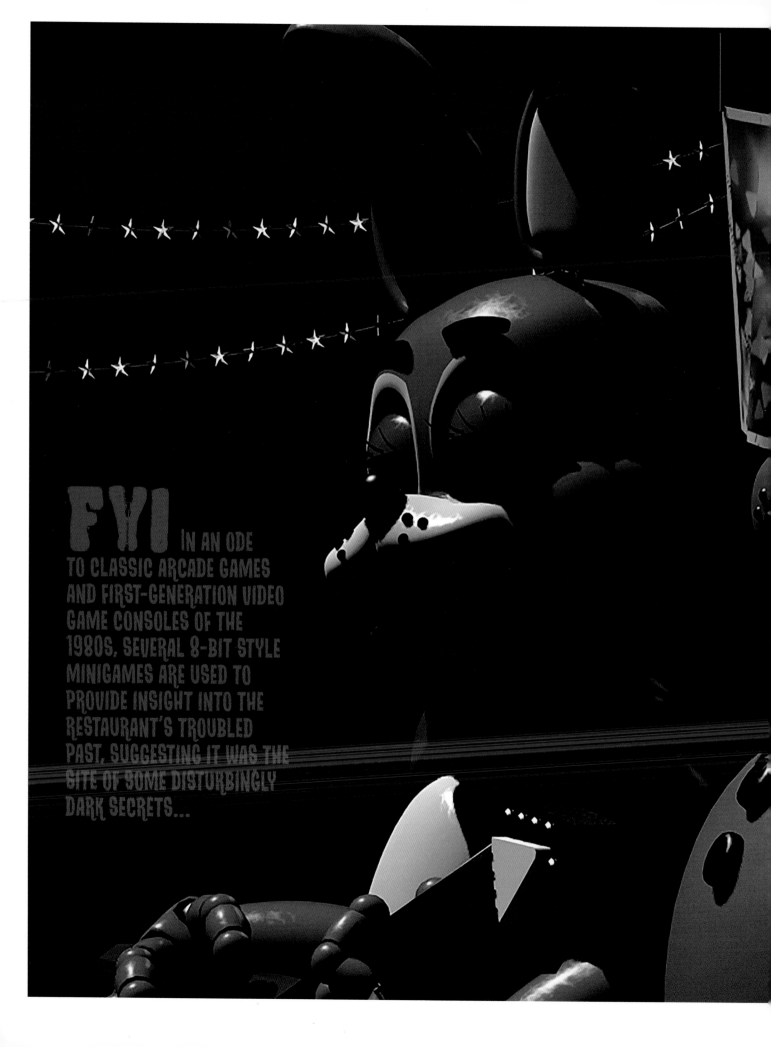

FYI IN AN ODE TO CLASSIC ARCADE GAMES AND FIRST-GENERATION VIDEO GAME CONSOLES OF THE 1980S, SEVERAL 8-BIT STYLE MINIGAMES ARE USED TO PROVIDE INSIGHT INTO THE RESTAURANT'S TROUBLED PAST, SUGGESTING IT WAS THE SITE OF SOME DISTURBINGLY DARK SECRETS...

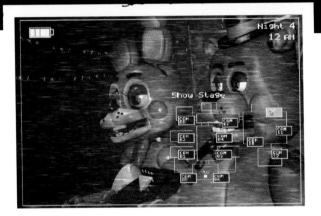

One more note about the music box is that if someone's right in your face and about to pounce but you need to wind that music box at least a little, you can. Whatever saves you time or however long you can get away with it before you need to put on the empty Fazbear head, take the time to wind up the music box or else it could be game over.

So to sum up, conserve your flashlight power as best you can. If you hear footsteps check the hallway—Foxy likes to hang out there, so if you see him flicker the flashlight in his face a bunch and he should leave. Foxy can get you even if you're wearing a Fazbear head so it's important to make him leave. If you hear something in the vents quickly check them. Keep that music box wound up, even if it's only a little bit at a time.

If you see anyone's face sticking out of the vent in your office, put on the empty Freddy Fazbear head right away and leave it on until they jump out and leave. Listen for the giggles and the "Hi" from Balloon Boy and don't let him mess around with your lights. Lastly develop good habits for where you're checking and how fast you can do it. The second night is all about learning the patterns that the different characters use when they're moving around the restaurant and using your tools properly to respond to them. Things are only going to get harder as we head into the third night.

Night Three: We're sure you're properly spooked after seeing that video from inside the Freddy Fazbear animatronic. We're not going to tell you what it means here, it'll be up to you to figure it out before the game is over.

It's starting to get really crazy now so we're going to suggest a few changes to the strategies you learned the night before.

Remember Foxy? When he appears in the hallway the best way to get rid of him is to shine the flashlight in his face. At this point though, if he appears too often you're going to waste too much power trying to get him to go away. If this keeps up you won't have enough to last you until 6:00 am, so now what you're going to do is to blink the flashlight at Foxy (if you see him in the hallway) five times for at least a half second each. This will still work to send him away and it takes as little amount of flashlight battery power that you can spare to do it.

Secondly, go over to the music box and wind it up, as you're holding down the "wind up" button say "One Mississippi" in your head. Did you do it? That's how long you should hold down the music box "wind up" button from now on, pretty much no more than a second, because you won't have time anymore to wind it up all the way. Every second you spend winding it is a second that someone can creep into your office and get you.

The old Five Nights at Freddy's characters are making their comeback now so you now have to watch out for all of the new guys and all of the old ones. If you happen to see any of the old animatronic characters make it into your office, put on the Freddy Fazbear head right away. You might not recognize them anymore—they're kind of broken and even scarier than they ever were before—but make no mistake these guys are fast and back with a vengeance. If you wait even a second too long it's game over so as soon as you see them that has to be your immediate reaction. This is also the rule whenever you see any of the old characters in the vents. Even if you see the original Bonnie crawling around the vent on the security camera, put on the mask right away. You only have a split second between seeing them and putting the mask on. These guys mean business.

As the night begins, start to practice winding the music box and quickly switching back to the security office. You need to be able to do this really fast from now on and almost every second thing you do should be to go back and wind up that music box, even a little.

Another thing to start doing regularly is to check the security cameras in the vents—there are going to be more and more people popping up in them and the more time you give yourself to prepare for them, the better.

Are you hearing that weird echoing, creepy music that happens every so often? If you do, that usually means someone is in the dark hallway right in front of you. It could be anyone but more often than not it's going to be Foxy. Remember what we said about the flashlight flashes and you should be fine. That music is usually a big indicator that one of the characters is about to do something.

You might notice sometimes that your flashlight won't shine down the hallways when you hold down the button. This is another warning that something's about to happen, so prepare yourself for the worst. Stay calm, your flashlight isn't broken for the rest of the night, and even if it turns out to be Foxy in the hallway again, your flashlight will be working in time to send him away.

The original Freddy Fazbear is back too, and just like Toy Freddy, he'll come at you directly from right down the hallway in front of the security office, so apply the same tactics to him as you did Toy Freddy. Wait until he's really close, then throw on the empty Freddy Fazbear Head and you should be fine.

So now your focus should be on three things—the music box, checking in front of you down the hall, and checking the vents to either side both on the security cameras and actually in your office. If you can check all of these things and respond well enough by continuing to wind up the music box when you can, and using both the flashlight and the empty Fazbear head when you need to, you should be able to make it through the night.

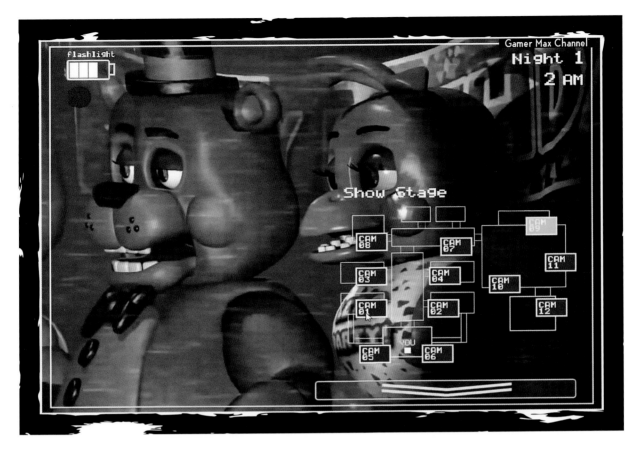

By the end of the night you should be spending most of your time either underneath the mask or winding up the music box, with only occasional breaks to check down the hallway when you hear that creepy music letting you know that Foxy is on his way.

If you can keep up with all of this then you've made it to the fourth night and you're rewarded with yet another spooky video from inside one of the animatronics!

Night Four: Night four is basically about how skilled you are at this point. A couple of things have changed that make everything you've been doing to stay alive up until this point way harder.

The animatronics are going to start moving around a lot faster, getting up to mischief in the vents and coming right for you directly down the hallway.

Now even the music box is going to be affected, winding down a lot faster than it did before, meaning you're going to have to check up on it a lot more often or else the Puppet is coming for you. Have strength, because there is a way to get through this night despite how hard it seems.

You're going to be using one strategy all night long. It may seem a little boring to be doing the same thing over and over until 6:00 am but if it keeps you alive then it's probably worth it, wouldn't you say?

This strategy works in just five easy, repeatable steps:

• First, check one of the vents in your office by turning on the vent light. It doesn't matter which vent you check.

• Next up is to look straight down the hallway with your flashlight to see who's there.

- Now you need to check the other vent by clicking on the other light switch. This is going to be different for everybody depending on which vent they checked first. Just know by the end of this routine you need to have checked both vent lights in your office.

- Head over to the music box on the map and wind it up as much as you can before you need to go back to your office to put on the empty Freddy Fazbear head.

- The last step obviously is to wear the empty Fazbear head for as long as you need to, if you even need to, because it's not guaranteed someone's going to be there waiting for you. Although this late in the game chances are someone will definitely be there waiting for you.

The last thing we're going to mention here is to watch out for Mangle. She's going to be all over the place and a big part of the job is reacting to her as quickly as you can by wearing the Fazbear head. If you don't manage it in time she might sneak into your office and once she's there, she won't leave. Deal with Foxy first with the flashlight but never forget Mangle.

So, that's the strategy—rinse and repeat those steps, listen for audio warnings, and watch out for Foxy and Mangle. Lastly, be as quick as you can when switching from the security cameras to wearing the Fazbear head. As soon as you see someone in your face you need to wear it. With all of that down you should be able to survive the night.

Night Five: Now that the final short and creepy video is over (along with the creepy message afterwards) we head into our fifth and final night.

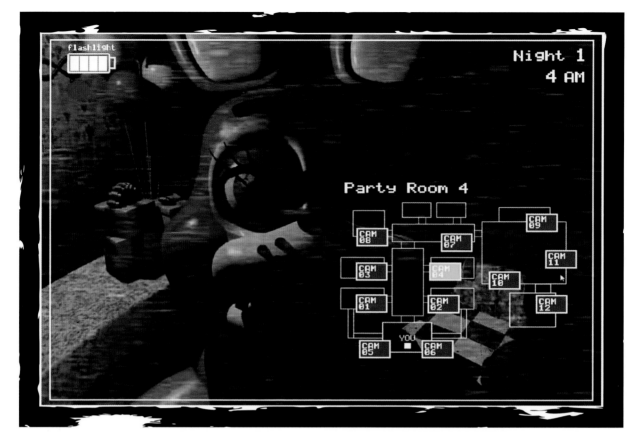

Do you remember the strategy you learned to deal with the previous night? You know, the one you read about maybe a couple of seconds ago? That's good because that's the strategy we're going to be using again to get through this night. Turns out it's a pretty good one—here's hoping you got good at it.

This is by far the craziest night. The sounds, the movements, the animatronics creeping around—it's all going to go by super fast now and the only thing standing between you and that sweet morning sunlight is how fast you can react and how well you can stick to the plan you stuck to last night.

One big change you're going to notice if you're in the middle of winding up the music box at the wrong time is that now if someone creeps into your office they're going to close the laptop on you so you're staring right into their face. If that happens, don't panic—by now you should be good enough to use that split-second of time to throw on the empty Freddy Fazbear head to protect yourself from whoever it might be. It's possible to do, so you can definitely do it.

All it takes to beat this night is the same strategy as the fourth night, just much faster, so if you've got talent or practice you should be able to hack it. With a little luck and a lot of skill, you can do it!

Take your check and maybe go find another job or some side hustles for work in the future. ●

FIVE NIGHTS AT FREDDY'S 3

Welcome back to the third installment of your favorite horror jumpscare video game franchise, Five Nights at Freddy's 3!

If you're playing this game after having gone through and beaten the previous games in the Five Nights at Freddy's series, then prepare for a shock because this game is different in a big way compared to the other two. The Freddy Fazbear's Pizza restaurant is gone and done with. No more party rooms or stages and no more confused animatronics walking around in the night trying to off the only security guard working to try and protect the place. No, things are much different this time around.

The new place you find yourself working is a sideshow attraction based off of the scary things that went down at those old locations. It's hosted in an amusement park, it's one of those "house of horrors" attractions that everybody loves but with a special twist in that all the scary things that go bump in the night are based off of all the scary things you know and love from the first two jobs as a security guard.

Sounds like a lot of fun, doesn't it? Well, the people who run the amusement park thought so, and what better way to scare people than to use bits and pieces of real events?

After playing the two previous games you're probably thinking this isn't the best idea—the animatronics they had to entertain the kids were dangerous even when you were inside a family friendly restaurant and now they've made a horror attraction? It almost screams disaster, and yet none of the old animatronic characters have followed all of the stuff from the old restaurants. During the first night it's only you and whatever small pieces and parts of the old place the theme park owners managed to dig up for their attraction.

Rest easy when you sit down in your new office. This at least will be a familiar setup to you. You've got your cameras for spying on the different rooms, or anyone going through the spook house who might be hiding in the corner. There's the clock at the top left of your screen and you'll see a big window just to the right of your seat where you can see out into the hallway beyond.

A new feature you might be surprised to use is the audio function on the security cameras. Now whenever you check on a particular room you can check to see if there's any sound in there playing at the same time. You know, just in case.

It's a walk down memory lane for any old players who've been following along in the series of the Five Nights at Freddy's games, and to anyone who's just picked up this one for the first time they're in for the scariest treat. There's going to be so much different about this game compared to the others you could almost believe that it isn't related to Five Nights at Freddy's games that came before.

We said almost—it won't be long before you start to see things that are probably a little bit too familiar. But before we go into what those things might be let's have a look at what tools you're going to be working with as you once again try to make it through Five Nights at Freddy's.

DYK? UNLIKE PREVIOUS GAMES IN THE SERIES, YOU CAN ACTUALLY EARN A FOURTH STAR BY COMPLETING NIGHTMARE MODE WITH THE AGGRESSIVE CHEAT TURNED ON!

THE NEW TOOLS AT YOUR DISPOSAL

Your New Office: The first thing you're probably going to notice is just how much bigger this office is compared to your old ones. Because of this increase in size it's now going to take just a little bit longer to scroll from one side to the other. Just like Five Nights at Freddy's 2, there won't be any doors for you to close but there still is one open doorway on the left.

Scroll around the office and you'll notice some new things, like the big window that shows you the hallway outside and some fancy ceiling lights. You're also going to see a lot of old stuff that will be really familiar, like the metal desk fan, some bits and bobs here and there from the old animatronics, maybe even an old drawing or two that used to be on the walls in the old restaurants way back when.

A crowd favorite are the small stuffed-animal versions of the animatronics that made their debut in the second game.

To the left of your office just before the door you can see there's a nice creepy box full of masks of Freddy Fazbear and friends and what seems to be Toy Bonnie's guitar from a long time ago. Peek just outside your door and you can find what appears to be a hollowed-out shell of some nameless animatronic you might have been scared by before.

All in all, other than what you might sometimes see through that window, there's not much here in the beginning that actually does anything. Heads up, though—just like in the last two games you might be able to find a little Easter egg picture of Freddy Fazbear whose nose squeaks when you click it.

After you've had your fun looking around at all the new stuff, scroll to the far right end of your office and we'll take a look at our new upgraded security camera system.

The New 3-in-1 Security Cameras: On the far right of the office, you'll see near the top of the screen a blue see-through rectangle with two triangles inside it. Click this to bring up your new and improved system for spying in on different rooms throughout the attraction.

There might be a little bit more static than there used to be in the old cameras but these things weren't built brand-new just for this amusement park. Just like everything else in this horror attraction they tried to make things as real as they could, and that means going out to get the real security cameras and the real parts and masks from the old restaurants.

Even though the view isn't always the clearest, there's a lot more you can do with this new security camera system than you're probably used to, so let's have a look.

The layout is pretty similar to what you've seen before—click on the different "Cam" buttons to look through the lens of each security camera in each room. It won't be obvious right away but there are some things you're going to actually be looking for.

If you remember Five Nights at Freddy's 2, then you remember there was a ventilation system that some of the animatronics could crawl around in and use to sneak up on you. Well, the air vents are back and there's a lot more of them this time, so naturally there are a lot more cameras to keep an eye on them all.

Over to the left of the actual map you will see one or two buttons out on their own. We say "one or two" because sometimes you might see one and sometimes you might see them both, but there's always going to be one of them there and that particular button is the one we're looking at right now. The button on the bottom labeled "Map Toggle" changes the map screen just a little bit. It changes from showing you the locations in all the different rooms you can find security cameras in to just showing you the highlighted area where all of the vents are located and where you can find the different cameras hidden in these vents.

You use this "Map Toggle" button to switch between the vent cameras and the cameras in each room.

It's kind of a big change because now you're got two sets of cameras to look through and be aware of as the night goes on.

When you actually click this "Map Toggle" button and you change the map screen, there are a couple of other things you may have noticed. First of all, what are all of those green horizontal lines you can see where each camera is located?

There's some white text at the top of the map that explains exactly what you can use these green glowing things for. These lines are the different vents throughout the place, and because a vent can either be open or closed, the power is now given to you, the security guard, to decide which ones will be open and which will stay shut. It doesn't seem too important but later on this might be a very useful feature so keep it in mind. These buttons are green when the vents are open but will turn red once you've closed them.

The second of the two buttons out to the left of the map is only sometimes there. It's the "Play Audio" button and it does exactly what you'd think it does. It plays the cutesy little "Hello" sound or the child's laughter that Balloon Boy used to make in the old games. You can choose to make this sound play in every room where there is a security camera but not in any of the ventilation ducts.

What these sounds do is keep SpringTrap in check. (What's SpringTrap, you ask? Don't worry, we'll get to that.) If you play them in an empty room they'll draw him towards it, so if you want him to stay in one place or in a particular room, play the noise and he'll be stuck in that room for just a little longer. It is the basis for a lot of the strategies to actually beat this game.

The Maintenance Panel: It doesn't need to be said that the new functions of the security camera system are important—you're going to need to use at least some of those functions to survive as a security guard for this new horror attraction. That being said, however, they did bring in all this stuff from the old Freddy Fazbear's Pizza restaurant that are a couple decades old at this point. So the technology used to put all of this stuff together isn't exactly the most reliable stuff in the world.

Introducing the "Maintenance Panel." Close out of the security camera system on the right of your office and scroll all the way over to the left side. At the bottom of the screen you'll see the small red button you can click to open up this little panel. This thing is going to be incredibly important for keeping all of your advanced security technology working the whole night long.

At some point during the night, probably multiple times, a couple of your systems are going to screw up. That might be the cameras messing up and going all fuzzy or the audio device not working and you end up not being able to draw SpringTrap anywhere. Your vents might even stop working and the fresh air stops flowing into your office. Any one of these things failing means a lot of trouble for you, so if that ever happens—or maybe even if you think it might be about to happen—you can come over to this panel and reboot any one of the systems individually. Or if they're all broken at the same time then you can choose the "reboot all" option and completely reset all of the systems at once.

The "Maintenance Panel" will play a pivotal role during your stay here so be sure to get comfortable using it.

As a side note, watch out for flashing red lights back in your office—if that's happening then one or more of your systems need to be reset and you've waited for too long. It happens to the ventilation system the most.

Your Ears: We've said this before, and chances are we're going to say it for every one of the Five Nights at Freddy's games—you need to listen for specific noises and voices as the night goes on to be prepared for something that's about to happen.

It could be a change in music or you might even start to hear some footsteps like in the earlier games. We can say for a fact that you'll hear some crawling around in the vents again so when you hear anything like that, you need to be ready and react appropriately to the sounds or it could be game over without you even knowing why.

THE CHARACTERS

The characters in this game are another big part of what sets it apart from the other Five Nights at Freddy's games. Actually it's more so the lack of characters that makes this game different.

Would you like to know how many animatronic characters there are going to be running around in the middle of the night coming for you in your slightly larger office? Take a moment to guess—chances are most of you reading this aren't going to get it right.

One. That's right, there's only one animatronic Freddy Fazbear's Pizza character in this game who can actually run through the door to your office and get you. No one's even completely sure who it is anymore— the suit is so old and beat up it's hardly recognizable.

SpringTrap: Its name is SpringTrap, and it's the most decayed looking animatronic you've seen yet. This guy will be wandering through the different rooms each night as he makes his way towards your office. Most of the things the old animatronic characters did, SpringTrap will also do. This means that not only will you be listening for his footsteps and watching for him through security cameras but he'll also be crawling through the ventilation system as he sneaks around unseen. That vent closing function is starting to make more sense now, isn't it?

He looks a little bit like Bonnie because of his long albeit broken ears, but really SpringTrap is so busted up it's really hard to tell.

His behavior is a little bit trickier to deal with than how the animatronics from the old games acted. You might be able to follow him from room to room but it's going to be really difficult as SpringTrap loves to hide and is particularly good at it.

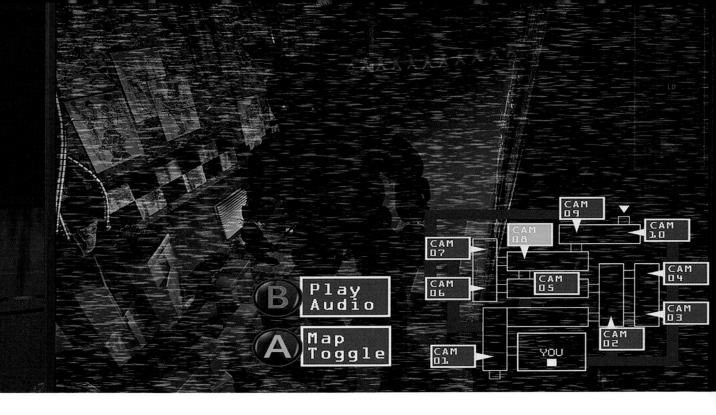

The Rest of the Characters: We did say that the only character who's really going to come and get you in this game is SpringTrap, and that wasn't a lie. If you ever get a game over it will be because SpringTrap made his way to your office. But there's a weird little thing that happens if the ventilation system stays broken for too long.

When the fresh air stops blowing you're going to start having weird hallucinations. It might be because you're hanging around all this old restaurant stuff or that in reality this haunted house just isn't your cup of tea. Somehow though, all these hallucinations remind you of all of the Freddy Fazbear's Pizza characters of the past that you've been so fond of.

You'll see them on different monitors (don't stare!), and you may even see Freddy himself walking around just outside the window to your new and improved office. Don't get too scared though, because at the end of the day (or night, in this case), they're just hallucinations and there's nothing really there that can hurt you.

What they can do, however, is make you go crazy. If you manage to see one of these hallucinations on one of the security cameras look away as fast as you can by clicking another camera or just backing out of the system, all the way. Staring at these creepy visions of animatronics from the past start to affect how well these old machines work.

Depending on which character you stare at too long through a security camera, different parts of the security system will be affected negatively. For example, if you see a hallucination of Mangle from Five Nights at Freddy's 2, then your audio system might fail and suddenly you won't be able to hear anything going on in whichever room you're looking into.

We'll go over exactly what each hallucination affects when we start talking strategy, but just know for now that no matter which vision you see, you'll need to look away from it as fast as you can because it will always mean bad news.

FIVE NIGHTS AT FREDDY'S HOUSE OF HORRORS

It might not seem like it but because you really only have to watch out for one animatronic character this time around, for the first time you are going to have the advantage. Because of that, and how many different places SpringTrap might go and the different ways you can stop him, there's going to be a bunch of different strategies out there you can use to beat this game.

We don't just mean a bunch of different strategies for each night either. In this game you can basically just pick one and use it the whole way through to the fifth night. That doesn't mean it's going to be easy. In fact, it's going to start being a challenge from the second night onwards but for the most part Five Nights at Freddy's 3 is about deciding on your strategy and then getting good enough at it to be able to keep using it as things get harder and faster the further you get.

With all that said, we know there are multiple strategies we could talk about that you could use to beat this game and win. It's just that we really only have so much space in this book to write it all down so what we're going to do is just cover one sure-fire way that will get you through until the end.

Even though we're only going to be covering this one method of beating the game and surviving five nights with SpringTrap prowling around, we will still go over all of the different things you need to be aware of as the night actually progresses. This means that even if you wanted to go off and use another strategy you might have heard of or maybe even one you made up yourself, you can do that and still be confident in your skills because you know what to watch out for.

Now let's get down to the strategy.

Before we start we need go over a few things pertaining to the behavior of SpringTrap. One of the biggest things to remember is that he loves to hide. He can hide in every room there is but when you're looking for him you have to be extra careful because he's very good at being unseen.

The security cameras also do weird things when they're looking at SpringTrap—he has some sort of effect over them. If you catch him in a room and watch him for too long, the video feed will go all fuzzy. During the time where the screen is all full of static is when SpringTrap actually moves around to another location.

It's also possible to tell when SpringTrap is entering a room you're already looking at. If he's currently not in the room you're seeing through the security camera sometimes the screen will go all fuzzy anyway. It's actually kind of hard to tell because the screen can go fuzzy in this case for two reasons.

1. The screen you're looking at will fill with static when the security camera system needs to be rebooted because of a random hallucination.

2. The screen you're looking at will fill with static for a slightly longer period of time when SpringTrap is moving into it. The challenge will be figuring out what kind of "static" means he just walked in, and what kind of static means you need to reboot the system.

It's learning this behavior and being able to guess where he's going to go that makes getting through Five Nights at Freddy's 3 possible.

Night One: Your first night will be a breeze because at this point they haven't brought SpringTrap in so really there's no way for you to lose. The best thing you can do on this night is to get familiar with where all of the cameras are at and figure out how to use the different security systems in place for when you actually will need to use them. We don't really have to worry about using the strategy this night because at this point in the game there's really no one to use it on.

Night Two: This is where the fun begins. If you've been following along you'll know you need to keep all of your systems up and running well, so you know what to look at and when to reset what system.

If your camera feed is down you reset the camera system. If you can't control the vents you reset the ventilation system. Last but not least, if your audio device system fails you reset it as well. You do this same thing for each of them over at the maintenance panel. If you can get a good handle on all of this, you're really doing good.

The next thing is to try and figure out where SpringTrap hides in every room. The second night is the best for this because he's actually there and he's not as fast or as vicious yet as he could be.

The best way to find him in each room is to look for the whites of his eyes in dark places. There are a few places where you can see his full body but most of the time he'll be in some dark corner where you cannot see him at all except for his eyes. So get good at spotting them.

Once you've gotten locating him down pat, the next step is to start using the audio device to lure him where you want him to go.

Our strategy this time is to lure him to where you can see him on "Cam 10." If you spot him in that room or in another room that's pretty close to it, use your audio device to play the little kid voice and lure him in there.

Now keep in mind, in almost every room there's a vent connected to the rest of the ventilation system. That is also true for the room we're going to use, so if we don't want him to escape and get to us (which we don't) then the next step (or maybe even the first step—it's up to you) will be to click the "Map Toggle" button and close the appropriate vent. In this case you check on the vent cameras and double click "Cam 14" to make sure SpringTrap can't get through it.

Once you have all this done, the trick for the rest of the night is to get him to stay where you can see him on "Cam 10." It's fine if he moves away—usually he either tries to go through the vent (which you sealed, so it's fine) or he'll move to another room close by. If that's the case just keep using the audio device to lure him back to "Cam 10."

This seems simple enough, and for the first couple of nights it is. But remember that as each night passes it gets more difficult to keep up with system errors and hallucinations that will prevent you from keeping SpringTrap where you want him to be. The strategy is simpler in this game but it still takes skill to keep everything working well enough to get done what you need to.

In the later nights it starts to get really bad. Now even if the ventilation system is working fine you're going to get random hallucinations that will mess your game up.

Some of the old characters pop up out of nowhere right in your face and can mess any of your other systems up. Don't worry too much though, like we said before, they can't kill you.

Just keep a cool head, reboot what needs rebooting, and make sure you keep luring SpringTrap to where you can see him on "Cam 10" while making sure the vent for "Cam 14" is closed. Do that and you should be able to manage the entirety of Five Nights at Freddy's 3 with relative ease.

FIVE NIGHTS AT FREDDY'S 4

Welcome to the scariest Five Nights at Freddy's game so far!

When we last talked about the third installment there was a lot to say how different it was from the first two games. You had a lot more equipment and there was a big difference in how the game worked.

Prepare to have your mind blown once again as we head into the fourth installment in the Five Nights at Freddy's game series. In each of the past games you had your office, you had security cameras, and you had pizza restaurant scenery all around you.

In this game, all of that is gone. You're no longer a security guard watching over a restaurant at night or an amusement park attraction meant to entertain adults and children alike. In fact, in this particular game you are the kid, and all those scary animatronics from the Freddy Fazbear's themed places in the past have followed you home to haunt you once again.

The biggest difference? They're all about a thousand percent more terrifying than they were before and there's only a couple of different ways for you to protect yourself from them. Instead of your fancy office setup with security cameras and monitors to spy on different parts of the building, you've got your two eyes and two ears in a small bedroom.

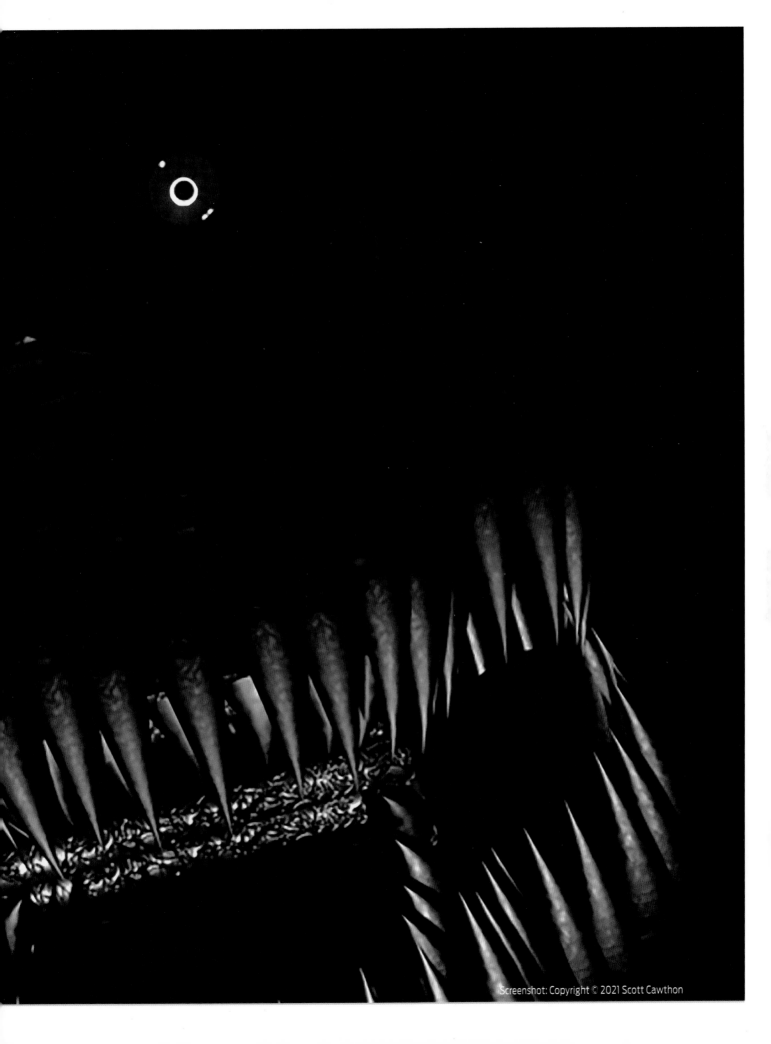

In terms of what you need to keep track of, there are only two doors to the room you're in, not unlike the office in the original Five Nights at Freddy's. There are doors to your bedroom so you don't have to worry about giving anyone free reign to just walk on in or out whenever they please. But the walls and doors must have been poorly built because unless you're standing at them to hold the doors closed, they're always going to stay open. As each night starts the terrifying new monsters are hiding throughout your house trying to get to you, so the doors are the last line of defense, despite the fact they really don't work like doors should.

There's more to how this game works but we'll go over the rest in just a bit. But first let's go over exactly how you're going to use your flashlight and the different parts in your bedroom that will keep you alive throughout the night.

YOUR BEDROOMM AND WHAT TO USE TO SURVIVE

We'll be honest with you here—there's really not that much you have at your disposal to help keep you alive. There are no more security cameras and no noise makers to lure anyone to another room. There aren't even any light switches on the walls for you to turn on or off.

Thankfully, the light source you do have, your flashlight, is one of those newer models that has battery power to last for days so you really don't have to worry about conserving power in this game. So while it is a short list overall, for the sake of covering all that we need to, we're still going to go over what there is.

FYI
FNAF 4 MARKS A DEPARTURE FROM MANY FAMOUS AND FAMILIAR FRANCHISE FEATURES, INCLUDING BEING THE FIRST GAME IN THE SERIES TO: NOT HAVE A PHONE GUY; LACK ANY SORT OF MONITOR; ALLOWS YOU TO GET UP AND MOVE AROUND!

Your Feet: Instead of just turning your head slightly to look at one screen or another like in the previous versions of Five Nights at Freddy's, now you're going to turn your character's point of view from looking at the door on one side of the room all the way to the door at the opposite side. There's also a small pit stop you can make to have a look at the closet right in the middle of the room. When you're looking at any of these three doors with your flashlight you can click to have your character run over to them and do one of two things for each: you have the choice to hold the door shut, or peek through the door depending on certain factors which we will go into later.

When you're standing in the middle of the room normally, however, please note that directly behind you will be your bed, and you're going to need to turn around to look at it more often than not. To do this all you need to do is drag your mouse to the bottom of the screen and click the button to turn around and have a gander at who or what might be chilling out on top of your sheets.

The Doors: Your doors are really your first and last line of defense against any of the nightmares that have followed you home. You have the hallway doors on either side of your room and the closet door in the very middle, and all of them at some point or another can have a horrible monster on the other side of it that you have to keep yourself safe from.

Unfortunately, these doors were all built wrong so they don't work like they should. If no one is there to hold them closed, they'll just hang slightly open. It's not very convenient but for the most part you're only going to have to worry about one at a time. That is, if you're lucky. This rule also applies to the closet door, even though there's not a long hallway on the opposite side of it. This is a decently sized closet and we all know that's where the scariest monsters like to hide.

The other thing you can do—and in some cases, need to do—is to open them wider than they were already and peek through them. If it's the hallway door and you do it right, chances are you're going to see a set of glowing eyes backing down the hallway.

If you get it wrong, well, it's game over, and at this point you probably know enough about Five Nights at Freddy's to know what game over means.

It works the same for the closet door, and although at the beginning of every night there will be no one inside the closet, that doesn't necessarily remain true for the rest of the night. There might be a couple different monsters who can sneak in and hide there, and part of dealing with them will be either holding the door shut or peeking in occasionally. It might even be a healthy combination of the two.

Your Flashlight: Just like in the previous games, you've got a flashlight to shine in certain areas and even to sometimes stun some monsters to keep them from attacking you. Unlike the other games, however, there's no limit to how long you can use your flashlight. This is probably because it's absolutely impossible to get through even the first night without it. It's nighttime in this kid's house and there are no other lights on so the flashlight is all you have. If you couldn't use it to see, it would be pitch black all night long and impossible to see anything.

Your Ears: This is the last tool on the list and we're wondering if you could hear it coming. Using your ears is a critical part of playing the Five Nights at Freddy's games and in this game using your hearing is more important than it's ever been before. To make it through the night, you really need to pay more attention to the sounds, voices, and sometimes even the music that plays, announcing the arrival of different nightmares.

There are a bunch of different things that can happen in Five Nights at Freddy's 4 that you'll never know about unless you hear them. Nightmare Chica could be messing around in the kitchen. Nightmare Freddy could sneak right up to your door and unless you're listening carefully for him laughing, you would never know it. So while it's been important in the past games to listen for audio cues and even luring animatronics where you want, it's actually pretty much impossible to win this game without waiting and listening for the right sounds to react to.

77

CHARACTERS

We're not going to devote a very large section to the characters in this game because if you've been following along in this book and have played all of the previous versions of Five Nights at Freddy's then you've met all of the characters in this game. This is the end of the story for the Five Nights at Freddy's series— you'll most likely see how everything plays out by participating in the minigames that pop up between each night. But because this is the end to the tale, all the stops are pulled and every single character in the series makes an appearance, but they're not looking the same way you remember them.

This is a game all about some kid fending off all of the Five Nights at Freddy's characters from his bedroom in the middle of the night with just some doors and a flashlight, so even to start things off it can pretty much be considered a nightmare. What makes things worse, however, is that each and every character from the old games appear in this one as nightmarish versions of themselves. They have glowing and terrifying red eyes, sharp and scary teeth, and all of their faces are warped. There's even nightmare versions of some things you didn't think would count as "characters," like a nightmare cupcake.

We'll list them out here with some quick facts about each.

Double-Tap here to run to the door!

DYK? ALTHOUGH THE PREVIOUS INSTALLMENTS COULD GET PRETTY HECTIC AS YOU CLICKED BETWEEN YOUR MONITORS AND DEFENSES, PATIENCE IS KEY FOR WINNING AT THIS ONE. HAVING AN ITCHY TRIGGER FINGER OR MAKING SUDDEN MOVES WITHOUT WAITING FOR CUES CAN EASILY RESULT IN A JUMPSCARE.

Nightmare Freddy: Still the same Freddy Fazbear with his hat and bowtie, but stretched out taller with glowing red eyes and a bunch of chunks ripped out of him all over the place. He shows up to the scene with three little mini versions of himself. These three mini versions hang out on your bed and even though it's really easy to check up on them by shining the flashlight, if you don't check up on them enough Nightmare Freddy shows up and gets you.

Nightmare Bonnie: Bonnie's back with sharp teeth, sharp claws, and a big chunk missing out of his chest so you can see inside. His eyes glow a kind of purple color, unlike Nightmare Freddy, and he comes for you through the left door.

Nightmare Chica: Just every bit as scary as you'd expect from seeing the nightmare versions of the other animatronics. Nightmare Chica is torn and decayed but she's still wearing her bib with "Let's eat!" printed on the front. Nightmare Chica will try to enter through the right door and if you let her sneak inside your room to get behind you, it'll be her cupcake that jumps up to get you seemingly out of nowhere, so watch out.

Nightmare Foxy: Foxy's back for the last time as Nightmare Foxy. He's tall, probably more red than the older version, and just like all the other walking nightmares he's torn up and tattered. He's still got his hook and his teeth are sharper and longer than they ever were before. He doesn't have an eye-patch anymore but he's developed this scary orange glowing eye to make up for it.

Nightmare Foxy only starts doing things on the second night and it's possible to see him coming down either hallway alongside Nightmare Bonnie or Nightmare Chica. If you let him sneak inside your room he's going to go right for your closet and stay there. If you leave him alone in the closet too long he'll eventually come up and get you, so every once in a while you need to check up on him by opening and closing the closet doors until he turns back into a stuffed toy.

PlushTrap: You might guess who this guy's based on if you've played Five Nights at Freddy's 3. PlushTrap is essentially just a stuffed toy version of SpringTrap and you're only going to see him during the minigame between nights. If you manage to win and beat PlushTrap at this game, it pushes the clock forward by a couple of hours the following night so there's less time you have to wait before the sun comes up at 6:00 am.

Nightmare Fredbear: Ten times scarier than Nightmare Freddy. This guy first shows up on the last night and is there the whole night long instead of Nightmare Freddy. He's bigger, meaner, and both his teeth and claws are sharper and longer. For some reason his hat and bowtie are now pink. When Nightmare Fredbear hits the scene, all of the other animatronic nightmares stay silent because dealing with him is a hassle all in itself.

However, since he's just one guy instead of four or five, you might actually have an easier time with him. He'll come at you through the left or right doors, but if you blink a flashlight on and off at him he'll run back down the hall around the corner. Sometimes you might hear him laugh and that could mean a couple different things. It means he's either going to now be in the closet or you'll just see his head sitting by itself on the bed. Shine the light on him if he's on the bed, and just close the door to the closet for a bit if he shows up there.

Nightmare: The final version of Nightmare Fredbear and the most difficult and harsh animatronic nightmare in the game. He really just looks like Nightmare Fredbear but instead of fabric flesh it's just a shadowy mass that separates his insides from the outside. Other than that, his pink tie and top hat are colored yellow now, possibly even scarier than they were before. If you've played the last night in the last couple of games, then you have experience with this sort of thing. We mention this because Nightmare is only going to show up on night seven and in 20/20/20/20 mode in this game.

HOW TO PLAY, SURVIVE, AND WIN

We're going to tell you one strategy that will work for every night for this whole entire game. It's just a simple matter of getting good at it and being able to click from one thing to the next like a pro.

For this strategy to work, and really for playing this game to win at all, we recommend some sort of stereo sound system. It could be a set of speakers on a laptop, or even some of the cheaper pairs of headphones you can find will do. But you're going to have a really hard time beating this game if you can't hear well. It might even be impossible, really.

You start every night off standing in the middle of the bedroom. The first night you're going to get all the information you need—what you listen for outside the doors and what you need to do based on what you hear. It'll all appear on screen as little instruction text but we'll go over it again here.

You need to get into the habit early on of checking different things all in order and once you've done it, run through and check them all again. It's really up to you what order you check things in but soon enough you won't be deciding anymore. You will just be reacting to the sounds you hear from outside or even inside the bedroom.

To start out, we'll give you an example of what you should be checking out and doing the first couple of nights.

Start by clicking to run over to either door and listening at it. If you hear breathing then you shut the door. If you hear footsteps then you can open the door and shine the flashlight in whoever's face it happens to be and scare them off. Keep in mind, the left door is Nightmare Bonnie and the right door is Nightmare Chica.

After you're done at the first door to the bedroom, run back and check on the bed. Slowly but surely you will start to see mini Nightmare Freddys pile up on the bed the longer you go without looking at it but shining the flashlight on them makes them go away. You need to keep checking the bed and shining the flashlight on them because if you leave it for too long then Nightmare Freddy himself pops up behind you and it's game over.

This rule for checking on the bed will eventually apply to Nightmare Fredbear and Nightmare as well. Instead of seeing the mini Nightmare Freddys you will see just the head of either Nightmare Fredbear or Nightmare and you get rid of them the same way with the flashlight.

After you've checked the bed you can go to the door at the opposite end of the room from where you checked first, and do the same thing. Listen for breathing or footsteps, then do what you need to depending on which one you hear. Either hold the door closed if you hear breathing (when you hear breathing they are right outside the door ready to come in) or open the door and shine the flashlight at them to make them turn and go the other way. (Turn up the volume so you can hear if the footsteps are getting closer or farther away.)

This is the pattern that needs to repeat for pretty much the entire game. The only difference during each new night is that new characters will be added and you're going to start hearing new and unfamiliar sounds. It could get a little confusing and hard to keep up with after a while.

Sometimes, you might mess up. That's cool, we understand, it's a very scary and nerve-wracking game so these things will happen occasionally. What we're going to do though is to give some examples of what might happen when you actually do mess up and how you can keep playing even though you might have missed something.

Normally when you mess up in a Five Nights at Freddy's game, it means game over. Normally. In this game, however, it's possible to screw up and still last until 6:00 am.

Sometimes you might hear footsteps coming towards a door and you're at the wrong place at the wrong time. If you're at the door on the right and someone's about to come in on the left, chances are you won't make it across the room in time. Usually this spells disaster unless the one who happened to be at the door is Foxy. Which it usually is.

If Nightmare Foxy or Nightmare Freddy manage to sneak in the room while you're distracted by something else, they usually make a run for the closet and hide in it. They won't be the only ones that do this either but we're just going to talk about them because they do the same thing everyone else does in the closet.

Once they're in there, they won't come up until morning so you're stuck with them. The thing is, that doesn't mean you're going to lose. What actually changes is that you now have to add an extra step to the strategy of checking the doors and the bed. If you leave Nightmare Foxy or Nightmare Freddy in the closet for too long, eventually they jump out at you and that's game over. To avoid this, you need to start checking up on them every so often and closing the closet door on their faces a couple times.

After the closet door has been closed on them a few times they will revert back to just a normal stuffed toy version of themselves and they won't cause harm to you for a bit. Keep in mind it's not permanent—eventually they're going to be big scary nightmares again and you have to do the closet thing all over again. But if you can, you can win out through the night and they'll be out of your closet when the next night starts.

We don't have the space to go over the behavior of every nightmare character but this strategy will work for all the characters and each new night.

To sum up it looks like this:

• Check for breathing or footsteps at the first bedroom door and respond appropriately (flashlight if footsteps, close door if breathing).

• Go to opposite bedroom door and repeat the steps for the first door.

• Check on the bed for mini Freddys (or Nightmare Fredbear head) and shine light on them so they go away.

• Always listen for footsteps or other signal noises in case something happens when you're not at a door. Depending on what noise you hear, respond appropriately.

• If you make a mistake and someone gets in, just hope that it's Nightmare Foxy or Nightmare Freddy and start to regularly check the closet door as well (shut the closet door on whoever is inside and they will eventually turn into a small stuffed toy).

If you practice this strategy enough, it will eventually get to a point where you could even consider this game to be easy. The steps you take over and over again will carry you all the way to the final night without any problems if you get good enough at clicking back and forth.

Definitely make sure you can hear everything you need to hear right from the start. There's no security cameras in this game, so the only real way to tell where anyone is or what they're doing is by listening to the noises they make.

Power through with this strategy until even the eighth night to finally unravel the mystery behind the first four Five Nights at Freddy's games! ●

SIST

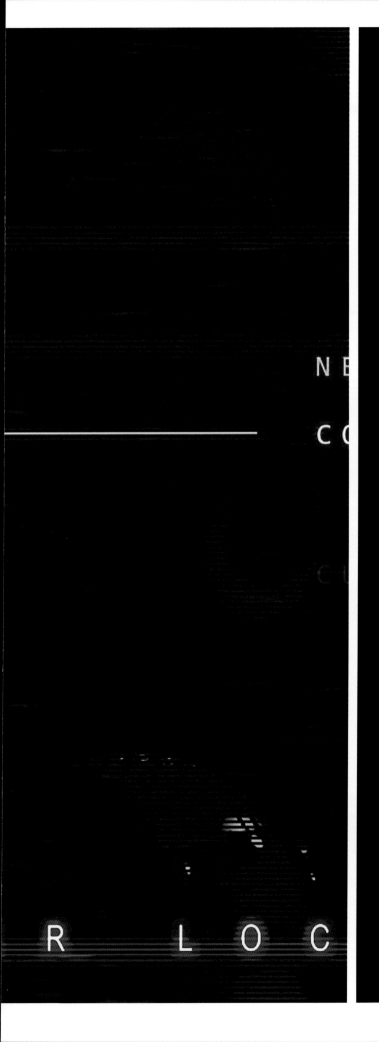

SISTER LOCATION

Sister Location marks a departure for the series in many ways. Chief among them being you can, and must, get up out of your office chair and roam the hallways--amongst the animatronics. Many new animatronics are introduced as well. Circus Baby, who you will come to fear, and maybe even come to pity, headlines the list.

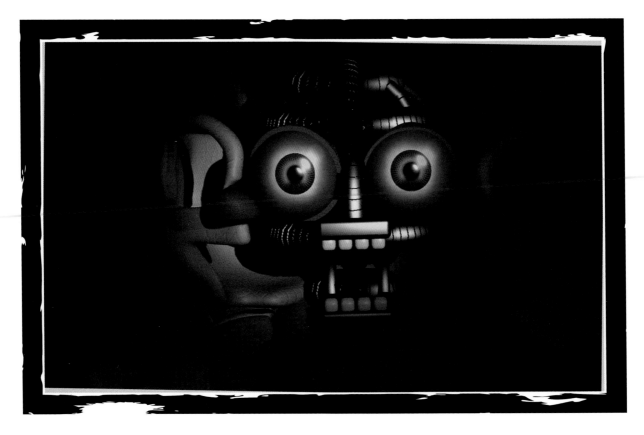

So, you survived the first game and three sequels with unimaginative names, and you and the restaurant are still standing. Are you ready to branch out into a new location as the Freddy franchise expands?

Five Nights at Freddy's: Sister Location is the fifth game in the Freddy series, and features some new twists in the gameplay. While you're still watching and dodging Freddy and friends for the most part, the elements that have been introduced into the equation require some special preparation.

NIGHT 1

As with the other titles, the first night is mostly chill. With no danger to deal with, just do what Hand Unit tells you to do and breeze through the night.

NIGHT 2

Keep doing what you're told and soon you will encounter Circus Baby's Auditorium, which is when things finally start to get scary.

Reach under the desk. There's a box there that you must keep your finger inside to close the door. Take care to keep your finger in the right place as the door moves on its own. Is the door closed?

Try not to make eye contact. Watch the right side of the door. As soon as it starts to open, keep the screen in the same spot as where you had it to close the door. Stay calm and stay there until the door stops moving.

After two attempts to pull the door open, things will calm down. Once you get the all clear, you are able to proceed deeper into the night.

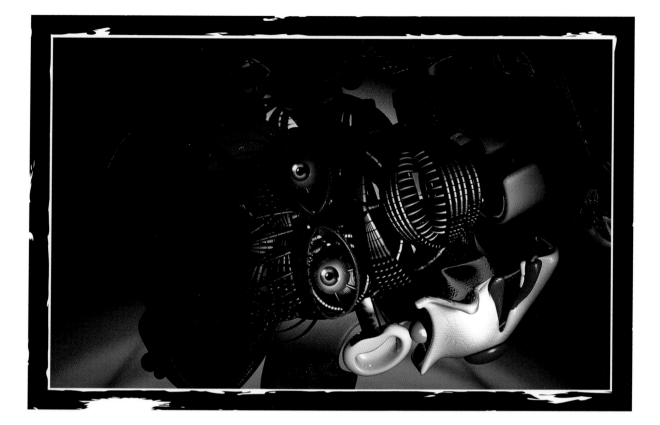

FYI EXTRA FEATURES AWAIT THOSE WHO MAKE IT THROUGH ALL FIVE NIGHTS, INCLUDING COOL BLUEPRINTS OF THE GAME'S ANIMATRONICS, INFO ON HOW THEY WERE MADE, A MAP OF THE FACILITY, AND MENU ACCESS TO CIRCUS BABY'S CUPCAKE MINIGAME!

BALLORA GALLERY

The main thing to remember here is to tap and hold to move forward, and release the screen to stop when you hear Ballora getting close.

In fact, you don't actually have to listen for Ballora. Just watch the flashing red warning sign in the top-left corner of the screen and stop as soon as you see it.

Stay still for two full seconds (which is harder than it seems). Once the warning sign stops flashing you can move again, but if you do too soon the sign will start flashing again.

Keep repeating these steps and you should be able to eventually scoot to the door. Patience, persistence, and pacing is key.

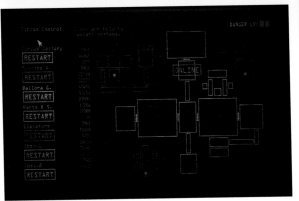

BREAKER ROOM

The game takes on a more intense pace at this point. Here, you have to bounce back and forth between restoring power on the premises, and foiling Funtime Freddy.

First thing to keep in mind here is that when you begin tapping to restore power, make sure you remain patient enough to let it top-off at 100%. If you don't, the levels will slowly begin depleting again, and if you leave uncharged breakers dormant for too long, they'll eventually drain back down to zero.

PRO TIP: Before the screen even comes into focus, you can begin the recharging process.

Find the breaker and tap and hold that spot on the screen immediately to start charging. Don't keep the screen up for too long or Freddy will sense you're not paying attention and end your night early.

Whenever you're recharging, stay aware of where Freddy is in the room. Keep an eye out for random sparks and reflections and you should be able to tell how far, or close, he is to you. You want to stay as far away from him as possible.

Is he getting too close? Play audio clips to get him to back off.

Take your time and slowly recharge all the breakers in 15-25% increments. If you get greedy and try to do more, Freddy will take you down. As you get more breakers back on line, Freddy will definitely get more frantic, so it's important to do those last few recharges in extra brief bursts at the end of the night.

DYK? PRIOR TO THE RELEASE OF THE GAME, THE NAMES OF THE ANIMATRONICS WHO APPEARED IN THE GAME WERE UNINTENTIONALLY LEAKED.

While the journey back through Ballora Gallery is scary, we found the return trip not too dangerous.

NIGHT 3

This is when things really get scary fun, and what better place for that than Funtime Foxy's Funtime Auditorium?

FUNTIME AUDITORIUM

Funtime Foxy is almost the mirror opposite of our friend Ballora, as she hunts by motion detection instead of sound. Because you're completely in the dark, this part of the game can be extra challenging, so steel your nerves and be ready with your flash beacon!

Akin to Ballora, the best advice to get you through this night is to chip away in small doses. The greedier you are with trying to do a little too much at once, the more likely the game is going to punish you for it.

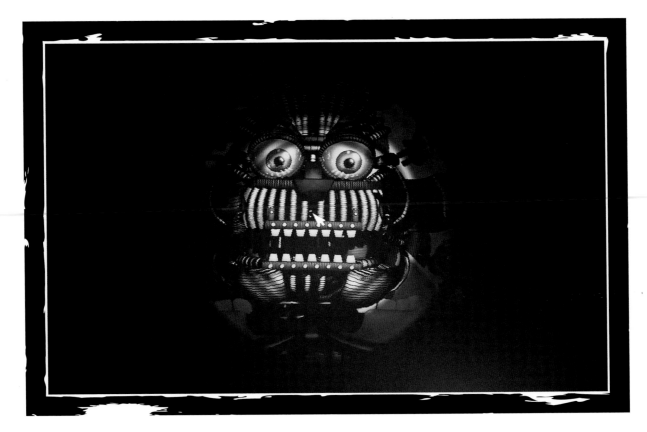

To avoid Foxy's attention, move just a little bit at once. If you try and move too far, she'll most definitely come for you.

Every time you pause, bust out your flash beacon and see if you can spot Foxy. If you see her, stay still! Don't move; give it a few seconds. Use the flash again and if you don't spot her inch a few steps more. Rinse and repeat this sequence to shuffle your way through.

PARTS AND SERVICE

This room is extra creepy, as it's where the animatronics go for repair. Funtime Freddy needs fixin', and you're the lucky one that gets to perform the duties

When it's time to assemble the puzzle, don't assume you know where everything goes. Just take your time and don't press anything until Hand Unit tells you to.

When it's time to pull the power whatever it is from the Bonnie hand puppet, the puppet will have disappeared. Don't worry, it'll come back.

Keep looking around Funtime Freddy until you spot the puppet peeking out. The bright blue should make it easy.

FYI A TOTAL OF EIGHT STARS CAN BE UNLOCKED IN THE GAME'S TWO MODES — FOUR STARS IN THE GENERAL PLOT, AND FOUR IN CUSTOM NIGHT MODE.

Don't look directly at the puppet or it will hide and find another spot to peek from. Wait until the black button underneath the bowtie is visible and then tap it to complete maintenance.

FUNTIME AUDITORIUM: PART 2

Here you basically just have to backtrack through the auditorium. Similar to the end of Night 2, it's pretty uneventful for the most part. Retrace your steps and be prepared for when Foxy pops out on you. It's part of the game, she's gonna do it, so accept your fate and brace for the attack.

93

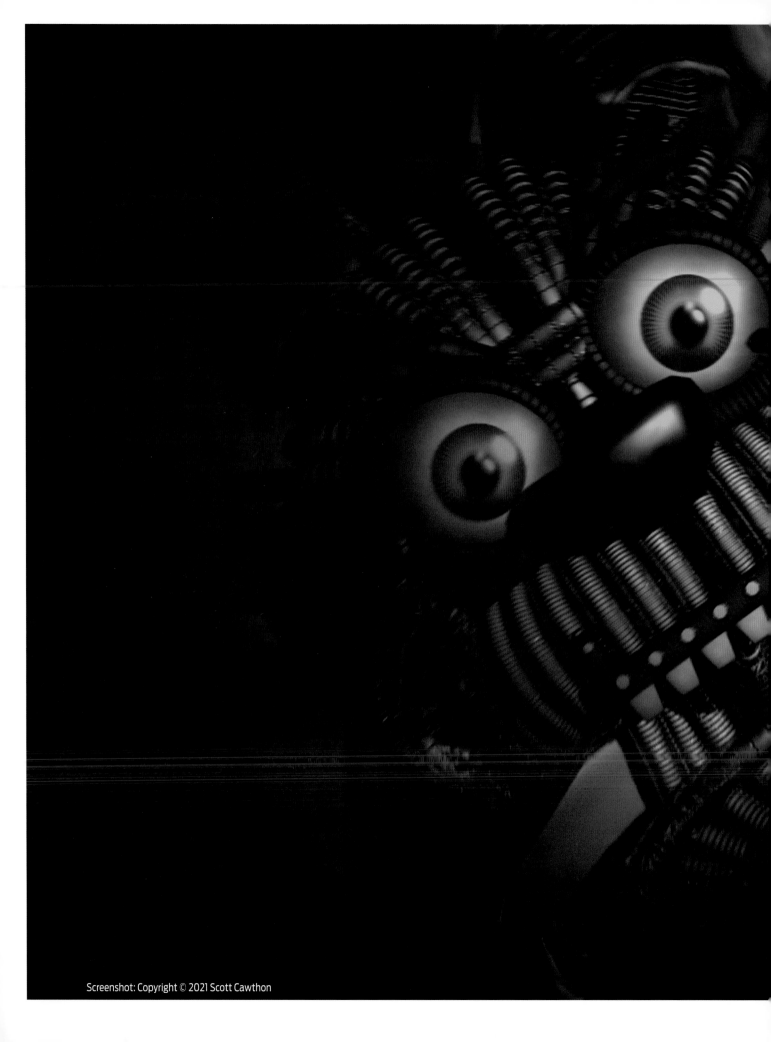

PRO TIP

If you keep mashing the flash button, it will lose its effectiveness and do the opposite of what you need it to do — Foxy will eventually hover near you and you may never make it through the night!

NIGHT 4
THE SCOOPING ROOM

What's in the Scooping Room? The Scooper, of course. But what is it? Definitely not of the ice cream variety, the Scooper is a machine used to dismember the costume for repair, and remove the endoskeleton from an animatronic.

Before it is used, it emits a loud, distinctive beeping noise so learn that pattern and timing.

After the faceplates are open, the spring locks along the sides of the suits get slightly brighter, so you can spot them more easily in the low-light conditions. Begin tapping and holding on the spring locks one at a time in order to wind them. Keep tapping until there's no more clicking, ensuring a snug fit.

Keep in mind spring locks are springs, which means they will inevitably unwind over time. The more you move the more they unwind, so try to stay still (not easy), monitor both sides of the suit, and wind away for every second you can.

It's not easy to stay still because you're going to see shadows creep up on both sides of the suit. You have to wiggle a little bit to shake them off, but like the flash beacon in Night 3, don't overuse it or it will backfire.

Once the shadows recede, get on with your winding.

DYK? ALWAYS HAVING FUN WITH HIS FANS, CAWTHON POSTED ON OCTOBER 4, 2016 THAT SISTER LOCATION HAD TOO DARK OF A STORYLINE AND HE'D NEED TO REWORK IT FOR SEVERAL MORE MONTHS. THIS TURNED OUT TO BE A DELIGHTFUL HOAX, AS THE GAME DROPPED TWO DAYS LATER.

PRO TIP: Blinking red spring locks indicate they're ready to blow. Address these first, keep your cool, and you should be able to survive the night.

NIGHT 5

When you begin Night 5, you don't know how it's going to end, because...there's two endings!

Your goal here is to fix Circus Baby. You learn in the elevator from Hand Unit that technicians may be on site, but you should ignore them. It turns out that's not too hard as the animatronics that appear to be on stage are actually technicians that are seemingly hanging from nooses, so at least you don't have to worry about getting any jumpscares.

Back to Circus Baby. Follow instructions in order to pull up Circus Baby's hidden keypad. She will give you a code to open her suit. If you enter the wrong numbers or take too long, you'll get jumpscared out of the game.

"THE SCOOPER IS A MACHINE USED TO DISMEMBER THE COSTUME FOR REPAIR, AND REMOVE THE ENDOSKELETON FROM AN ANIMATRONIC..."

However, if you enter the correct code promptly, a hatch will pop open on Circus Baby's left arm. Remove the glowing green card by tapping, then press the green button on the nearby conveyor to proceed.

Be careful to take your time and follow the directions precisely to scurry back to the Scooping Room.

To move forward, tap and hold the top middle of the screen, tap the top-left corner to go left, and tap the top right corner to go right.

Along the way, you can't use the flash. Just go into hokey pokey mode: listen carefully to your instructions and move precisely where and when you're told.

Once you reach the Scooping Room, your night's over, right?

Nope. Welcome to some old-school video gaming...

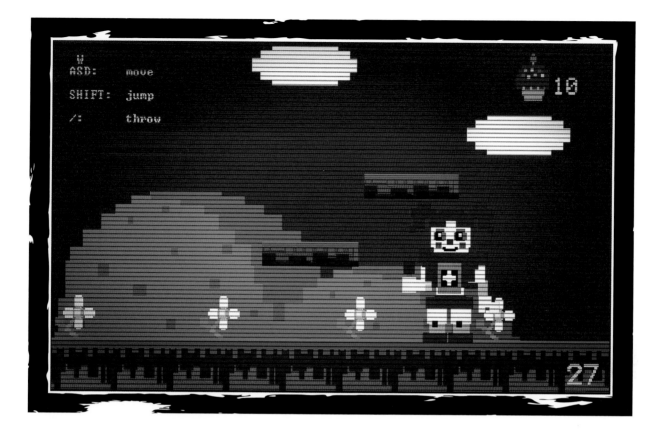

CIRCUS BABY'S MINIGAME

This minigame is a recreation of the story Circus Baby tells on Night 3.

In the game, there are three types of cupcakes: red, blue, and green. Each one has different characteristics so choose and use your cupcakes wisely.

Red cupcakes are single-shot and are used for picking off kids one-by-one.

Blue cupcakes fire three shots at a time that spread outward, and are best used on kids stacked vertically.

Green cupcakes are single-shot but they pass through every kid in a horizontal line, making them great for when the kiddos bunch-up horizontally.

You have to "feed" cupcakes to all of the kids and then return to the start of the level within a set time limit.

Best way to do that? Familiarize yourself with the layout of the game. Locate where the clusters of kids are forming, and make note of how they're aligned, to make the most of your cupcake "ammo." ●

FREDDY FAZBEAR'S PIZZERIA SIMULATOR

Pizzeria Simulator introduces fans to a whole new punch list of experiences, including challenging players with the responsibility of running a successful pizzeria. The biz sim part of this game is no joke, as you have to look for ways to improve your atmosphere, maintain a healthy and safe environment, and even manage your liability risk.

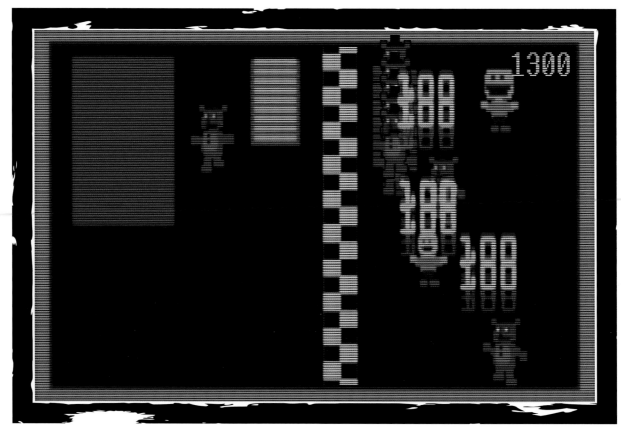

There are three main parts to this game including surviving the night, salvaging animatronics, and perhaps unexpectedly, running a pizzeria in a fairly detailed business simulation.

In an ode to first generation video games, Freddy Fazbear's Pizzeria Simulator starts out as a blocky 8-bit game in which you shoot pizzas (blocky things) at people (larger blocky things).

The nostalgia quickly wears off though, as suddenly you're cast into running a pizzeria and thrust into a whole new experience for this franchise. Considering this game's heritage, of course you're not just making pizzas—you know there are some creepy animatronics lurking nearby, just waiting to jumpscare you.

The main goal in Freddy Fazbear's Pizzeria Simulator is to complete tasks on your computer as you work in the cramped back office. You actually engage in typical restaurant management such as advertising, managing food stocks, and activating cleaning systems.

From your patrol in the back office, see if you can make it through some more scary nights.

Just when things are about to get mundane, you learn that some pesky animatronic monsters are creeping your way via the ventilation ductwork. It's time to get busy.

You should get familiar with optimizing the use of the following:

Audio: Play like a DJ ventriloquist and project beats to a different location to shake an animatronic off your tail.

"IN AN ODE TO FIRST GENERATION VIDEO GAMES, FREDDY FAZBEAR'S PIZZERIA SIMULATOR STARTS OUT AS A BLOCKY 8-BIT GAME IN WHICH YOU SHOOT PIZZAS (BLOCKY THINGS) AT PEOPLE (LARGER BLOCKY THINGS)..."

Fans: The fan is noisy, but you need it or the room gets too hot. Definitely use it, but do so as sparingly as possible.

Motion Detector: Since motion is implied in the word animatronic you know this little sensor, which detects movements in the surrounding vents, is gonna come in handy.

Your overnight goal is to complete tasks. There are three categories at the top of your screen, Order Supplies, Advertising, and Maintenance. The fourth tab is labeled Equipment, which allows you to upgrade your restaurant equipment to help you handle your restaurant responsibilities faster.

PRO TIP: Aim to implement as many upgrades as you can as soon as possible, as those upgrades will remain in place for the duration of your game.

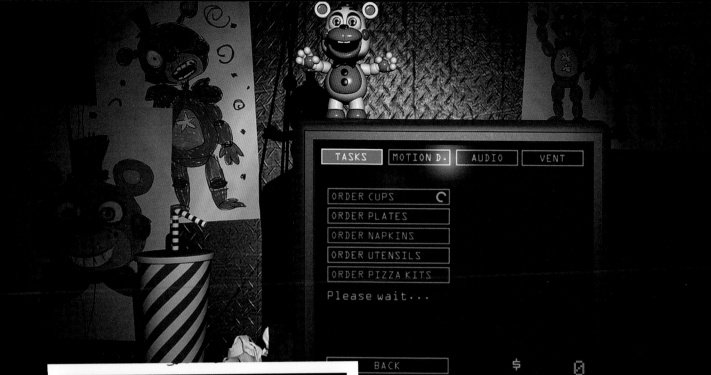

GENERAL STRATEGY

Like the prequels in the series, there is a rinse and repeat element to your survival tactics. It may seem complicated at first, but eventually you'll get down the muscle memory to overcome the nightly animatronic onslaught. Sequencing your steps and being patient is key.

PRO TIP: Once you activate a tool let it complete its cycle—if you interrupt it with another tool function while still processing it will cancel the first one, and leave you with nothing accomplished.

For a winning strategy, first you should activate the Motion Sensor and keep an eye on the animatronics' locations. Next, go to the Audio tool and click in the room above the animatronic to distract it, whilst you jump to the next task on your to-do list.

If/when you hear an animatronic close by, shut off your screen and fan immediately. Take some deep breaths and wait until you hear the animatronic wander away. This is how you can survive most nights—by being patient and methodical and not trying to do too much in a hurry.

PRO TIP: Animatronics will often crawl in the vent to the right or to the left of you, if you hear crawling through either vent, stop what you're doing. Listen carefully and you can hear which vent it's coming from. Shine your light in that direction and they'll scurry.

Now let's take a look at your control screen. You have four main tabs showing:

TASKS

Basically, a punch-list of what you need to accomplish during your shift to get you through the night and prepared for business the next day. Most folks don't realize how much goes on behind the scenes of a restaurant, and Pizza Simulator gives you a legit little taste!

MOTION D.

Your second tab is labeled Motion D. (for Motion Detector). Clicking on this enables you to monitor animatronic movements and current positions—but only if they're moving! Remember this is a motion detector, which means if they remain still when you activate the search beam, they won't appear on your scope.

AUDIO

The Audio tab lets you steer animatronics into other rooms and/or farther away from you. It's not as simple or convenient as it sounds though, and it's not exactly 100% reliable.

VENT

The last tab is labeled Vent, the use of which is underrated. Activating the vent allows you to still draw in air to keep the temperatures down, albeit at a lower and quieter rate. Learning to master this is actually a hidden hack hiding in plain sight that can help you defeat the game.

PRO TIP: If you sense (but aren't sure) if there's an animatronic lurking nearby, sit back, relax, take a deep breath, shut everything down, and wait for the coast to clear.

SALVAGING ANIMATRONICS

At the end of each night, you have the option to examine an animatronic and complete a survey. You should definitely take the time to do that for two reasons—the hefty payout you'll earn that you can use to enhance your joint, and the fact that you won't have to face that animatronic when you're trying to wrap-up your punch-list.

The salvageable animatronics from the back alley are Molten Freddy, William Afton, Scrap Baby, and Lefty. After Henry explains what options are available, you can either proceed with the salvage or toss it back into the alley.

If you throw the animatronic away, you skip this entire phase and the animatronic will not appear as a threat during the management portion, though you will miss out on lucrative salvage income. Also, discarding an animatronic will lead to your certain firing at the end of the game, for skipping over one of your key duties.

When you salvage, the process is simple and starts straight away. Henry will play one of five audio prompts through the tape, and the player must match the responses on the form to whatever animatronic responded to the unique sound.

When the player sets down the salvage report, and notes whether there were any responses to audio prompts, the animatronic may have moved. There are three states: Neutral, Attentive, and Hostile.

Animatronics begin in the Neutral state, but may change when the checklist is raised. If an animatronic is in its Hostile state, it has a chance to jumpscare you at any time and end your game.

You can protect yourself with a taser, which will reset the animatronic to Neutral. You can use the taser safely a maximum of three times, any more will deplete the value of the creature you're trying to salvage.

DYK? FREDDY FAZBEAR'S PIZZERIA SIMULATOR IS ONE OF THREE FIVE NIGHTS AT FREDDY'S GAMES WITHOUT THE WORDS FIVE NIGHTS AT FREDDY'S OR FNAF IN ITS TITLE. THE OTHER TWO ARE ULTIMATE CUSTOM NIGHT AND FREDDY IN SPACE 2.

Your salvage is a success if the survey form is completed and all five prompts are played. Your payout will be added to your income for the next day. If you are jumpscared by a Hostile animatronic, you fail. Whether your salvage is successful or not, you can expect to see the animatronic again in the management section of gameplay.

If you salvage all of the animatronics, the game will continue to the "true" ending. The tradeoff is that you'll now have a lot more animatronics to reckon with during the management phase, especially on that last night. Failing a salvage doesn't hurt you immediately, but it does mean those extra animatronics will remain active and stalking you during the management phase of your night.

FYI THIS WAS THE FIRST GAME IN THE SERIES TO HAVE MORE THAN FIVE NIGHTS IN THE STORY, BY FEATURING SIX MAIN NIGHTS.

CATALOG CAUTION

In the catalog segment, some items may be marked down as "Poor" or "Terrible." Beware that buying one of these items has a chance (based on condition; worse condition raises the risk) that the item will contain one of the unsalvaged animatronics. If it does, the animatronic reactivates during your management phase.

During salvage, the animatronic is replaced with a cardboard cutout of a winking smiley and a sign reading "There's No One Here (I'm Already Inside)". No salvage income can be earned when you see this.

PRO TIP: Items that may contain animatronics include the Discount Ball Pit (Molten Freddy), Nedd Bear and Pigpatch (William Afton), and the stage (Scrap Baby). Lefty can be purchased for cheap in the "Rare Finds" catalog, but you'll miss the chance to earn a tidy sum by salvaging him.

RUNNING THE PIZZERIA

Once you learn how to balance restaurant operations with monitoring the monsters, you can get into the finer details of making your pizzeria as popular as possible. There's a whole other side to this game, as running the pizzeria is no joke in this refreshingly original twist.

You have a few key things you must handle to make your parlor profitable:

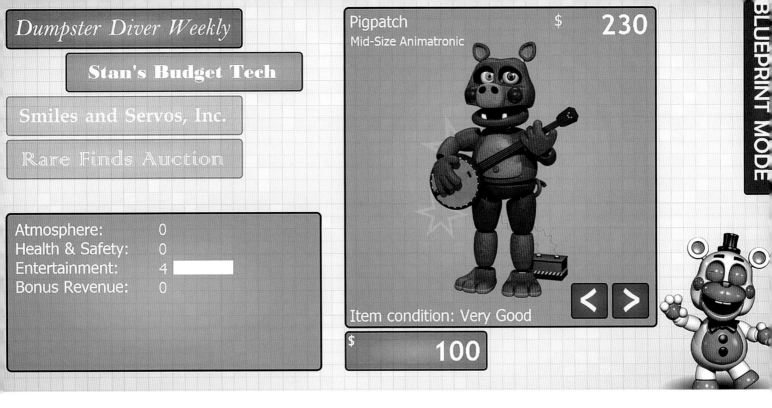

Dumpster Diver Weekly

Stan's Budget Tech

Smiles and Servos, Inc.

Rare Finds Auction

Atmosphere:	0
Health & Safety:	0
Entertainment:	4
Bonus Revenue:	0

Pigpatch $ 230
Mid-Size Animatronic

Item condition: Very Good

$ 100

DYK? ALTHOUGH FREDDY, BONNIE, CHICA, AND FOXY AREN'T ANTAGONISTS IN THIS TITLE, THEY SHOW UP IN VARIATIONS OF THEMSELVES AS ROCKSTAR ANIMATRONICS.

ATMOSPHERE

The more fun the atmosphere, the more customers you can attract to buy pizza—and also hang out and spend money at your joint. Start by focusing on creating quality pizzas, and then slowly purchase entertainment upgrades that will help keep customers around.

BONUS REVENUE

When planning and building your pizza empire, it doesn't hurt to have a plan first, and then lay out your attractions in a way that can maximize customer participation. If everything is spread out, they may not spend as much time and money as they might have if things were arranged in clusters.

ENTERTAINMENT

Customers come for the pizza but stay for the entertainment, so do your best to keep them entertained. The catch is, the biggest and best attractions cost big bucks, so you have to grind your way up with the more simple, timeless, and cheaper attractions stuff first.

Monday

Dumpster Diver Weekly

Stan's Budget Tech

Smiles and Servos, Inc.

Rare Finds Auction

Atmosphere:	0
Health & Safety:	0
Entertainment:	3
Bonus Revenue:	0
Liability Risk:	1

Mr. Hugs
Light Animatronic

$ 15

BLUEPRINT MODE

Item condition: Very Good

$ 0

< >

HEALTH AND SAFETY

Bet you never expected to be discussing restaurant Health and Safety guidelines in this franchise, but here we are. The higher your value here, the more customers will wander into your store.

LIABILITY RISK

While it's understandable that you'd want to stock up on cheap attractions, they usually carry a much higher liability risk. That said, let's dive into the dumpster in our next section, start picking items, and set up our restaurant.

DUMPSTER DIVER WEEKLY

After paying for the rights to use the company's brand name and images, you have some cash left over to begin building out your pizzeria. Start shopping in the "Dumpster Diver Weekly" catalog, and buy as many items as you can from it. Be careful though, as you can't resell old stuff when you eventually have enough money to buy newer and shiner stuff so whatever you spend is gone for good.

STAN'S BUDGET TECH

Stan's Budget Tech should be the next stop for your upgrade shopping. By now you should be making enough money to pay for better goods, and it would also be a good time to consider expanding your location. With more floor space, you can fit more customers, and attractions and products for them to spend money on.

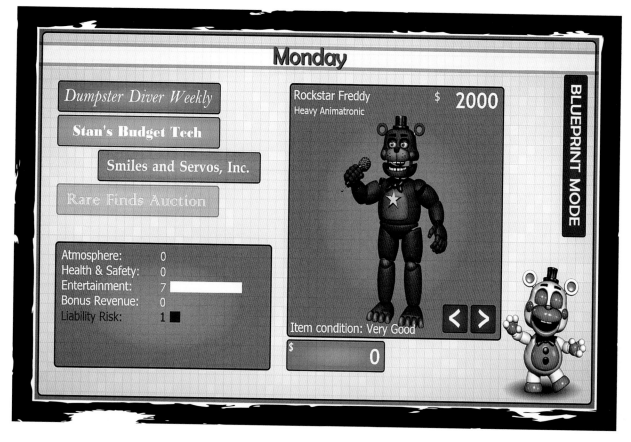

"WE'RE SUCKERS FOR NOSTALGIA, SO TO LIVEN-UP OUR JOINT SOME OF OUR FAVORITE ITEMS FROM STAN'S BUDGET TECH CATALOG INCLUDE THE FRUITY MAZE AND MIDNIGHT MOTORIST ARCADE GAMES, AND THE COLORFUL CANDY CADET."

Candy Cadet can pay out up to 6,000 points, the highest bonus available from this catalog, but the Midnight Motorist Arcade, which delivers a minimum of 2,500 points towards bonus revenue every time it's played, may be a a better buy and steadier earner.

SMILES AND SERVOS, INC.

When you're ready to stay up to Disney caliber animatronics and attractions, you need to shop in the "Smiles and Servos" catalog. This is where you can find the fabled Deluxe Concert Stage, the Star Curtain Stage, and more.

Both stages allow for five animatronics on the stage at once, and can be used at the same time. If you can manage to make this happen, the crowds will swarm your establishment and you can count on booming business.

After you've spent your money, you can figure out where to put everything in Blueprint Mode!

BLUEPRINT MODE

After picking a spot on your floor, a menu of all your purchases will show up, and you can decide what item you want to put there. While you don't start with a lot of space, you increase the size by clicking the "Upgrade" button in the lower right corner. If you have the cash, your floor-plan will increase in size instantly.

To place your items, use the directional keys to move the camera and click on the spinning triangles to place your objects. The game helps guide you as you can't place objects where they don't belong. For example, animatronics can only be placed in the northern section of the building.

Each item you place will increase one of your key business values such as Atmosphere or Health and Safety. Additionally, certain items allow you to increase specific values and is not as complicated as it sounds. For example:

• Safety Straps decreases an item's RISK value.

• Clean & Polish increases an object's Atmosphere.

• Add Coin Slot increases an attraction's Bonus Revenue.

It's not a bad idea to test some of your newly acquired purchases out to be sure they're safe and working properly, and you can also earn a bonus Faz-Rating. Some games give better Faz-Rating than others, so make sure you study the game and learn how to unlock its maximum potential.

Once you like your new layout, you can click finished and get one step closer to welcoming more customers than ever.

FINISHED!

LIABILITY AND LAWSUITS

Welcome to the "real" world, where parents and guardians and just waiting for an accident at your establishment so they can sue you and take you for all you're worth.

And just as in the real world, if you have money, it will help you wiggle out of tough situations. You can choose to settle the case out of court by paying the plaintiff, or you can litigate and pay legal fees to fight the lawsuit. It takes a day for the judge to decide who wins.

Ways you can avoid lawsuits include not buying nor displaying low quality items on your floor; and ensuring you have no "Risk" at the end of each day in Blueprint Mode. If you run out of funds while trying to settle or paying fees on any case, you will go bankrupt and lose the game.

Now that you know how to run the business end of things, it's time to circle back and focus on the ever encroaching animatronics! ●

PRO TIP

IF YOU'RE STRAPPED FOR CASH, SPONSORS ARE ALWAYS LOOKING TO INVEST IN FAZBEAR ENTERTAINMENT, SO BE SURE TO ACCEPT SPONSORSHIP OFFERS OCCASIONALLY TO REPLENISH YOUR COFFERS.

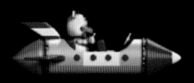

FIVE NIGHTS AT FREDDY'S: ULTIMATE CUSTOM NIGHT

Finally, time for a mashup! Ultimate Custom Night not only lets you select all your favorite animatronics from the previous versions of the games, it also allows you to customize their aggression settings.

As a compilation tribute game designed to celebrate all of your favorite animatronics from all of the games in the series so far, Ultimate Custom Night is the monster mashup Five Nights at Freddy's fans have been waiting for.

More than 50 characters make up the terrible tapestry of adversaries that have appeared in the previous games in the series, so settle into your familiar desk surroundings and be prepared to foil your furry foes. With the ability for you to choose whatever characters you want from the roster, and adjust their difficulty from easy to super hard, this game lets you customize the best part about FNaf games.

Unlike the custom nights from earlier games in this series, there are no required presets: all nights are completely malleable, and characters can be preset to a difficulty between 0-20, with 20 being the most aggressive.

The character select screen shows a record of your high score, as well as your best time in 50/20 mode, which means you took on all 50 characters at their maximum aggression setting of 20. Each level of difficulty for a character is worth 10 points, which means you can earn a maximum of 200 points per character you defeat. So, if you play with the maximum of 50 characters at their highest settings, your mythical perfect score is 10,000 points. How close can you get?

Back to your desk. As you monitor the two side doors, two vents, and two air hoses which all lead into your office, you must also handle a slew of new duties, including operating an air conditioner, heater, system-wide music box, power generator, set up snares in vents, accumulating Faz-coins to purchase items from the prize counter, and more.

Since this game is so different from the others in the series, we're going to take a different approach. While you play the game using the familiar office and desktop interface, the focus of this title is on the 50 characters you can select, and some which you can't select, so we're gonna do a deeper dive on all of 'em.

CHARACTER ROSTER

Without further ado, we present the 50 selectable characters that appeared in the prequels leading up to this title, plus all animatronics spawned by Dee-Dee, with tips and tidbits on each.

FNAF 1

Freddy Fazbear: The one, the only! Watch for his approach from the left hall. He'll try to inch his way towards your door. He gets nimbler as the building warms up, so try to keep your joint below 70 degrees.

Bonnie: If Bonnie is peeking out from behind the curtain when you view Pirate's Cove, he can flash his blinding eyes and scramble all of your cameras. You can avoid this by peeping at the figurine on your desk, as it will switch between Bonnie and Foxy depending on who's in Pirate's Cove.

Chica: If you hear Chica clanging around in the kitchen, that generally means things are ok. If she stops making noise, that means she's sick of the music you're playing to pacify her. Change the music and she'll be content, but if you change it too quickly, you can expect a visit from her.

94%

Foxy: In Pirate's Cove with Bonnie, when you see that aforementioned figurine showing his likeness, be sure to pause and view Foxy in the Cove. If you don't, he'll eventually slink out and wind up on your doorstep, and might even unleash his new attack, which is dismembering himself piece by piece, throwing his parts in your room, and then reassembling himself on the other side. Yikes!

Phone Guy: Voiced by the game's creator, Scott Cawthon, he'll call at random and you will only have a couple seconds to mute his call. If you don't act quickly you have to listen to his entire message, which is sure to annoy you and arouse any animatronics ambling about. In a maddening twist, the mute button pops up in unpredictable locations whenever he calls.

FNAF 2

Toy Freddy: He likes playing video games but is not very good at it, so it's up to you to watch over him. You'll find him in the Parts and Service room playing Five Nights with Mr. Hugs on his big screen TV. Check the cameras on Toy Freddy's monitor and be sure that the appropriate door is closed to prevent Mr. Hugs from jumpscaring him, or he will come to jumpscare you next!

Toy Bonnie: He sneaks in through a trapdoor to your right, and you can't stop him from entering your office. Your only defense is to put on your Freddy Fazbear mask to fool him. If you stare directly at him, it will compel him to leave faster, so buck up and be brave.

Toy Chica: She can enter through a trapdoor on your left, and also can't be stopped from entering your office. Like Toy Bonnie, put on your Freddy Fazbear mask to ward her off. She's faster than Toy Bonnie and will invade your office more frequently, but is also easier to repel, especially if you stare directly at her.

Mangle: Although Mangle makes her way through the vent system like other animatronics, once she reaches the vent to your office she will never leave, and will enter your office the moment the vent door opens. You can only stop her using the Vent Snare, but you have to keep checking to make sure you have the correct one active or she'll make distracting noises and eventually jumpscare you.

BB: Old Balloon Boy tries to squeak in through the side vent. Just close that vent and wait until you hear a thump, which means he left. If he sneaks in, he will disable your flashlight and annoy the heck out of you.

JJ: She'll also try to sneak in through the side vent. Close that vent and wait until you hear a whoomp indicating she left. If JJ makes it in, her housewarming gift is to disable all your door controls until she decides to leave.

The Puppet: All you need to do is make sure his music box is wound, and he's good. If you don't, he'll come calling. You can also use the global music box to deter him.

Golden Freddy: He'll appear after you lower your tablet, so raise it up immediately. Be careful not to stare at him too long or he will take matters into his own paws.

Shadow Bonnie: A sinister silhouette of Toy Bonnie with a full set of teeth visible, he will cause your office to become pitch black for about 10 seconds and there's nothing you can do to avoid him.

Withered Bonnie: He makes his entrance through the trapdoor as you view your monitor. You can detect his presence from his ominous audio and visual distortion cues, and only have a few seconds to put on the mask or he's gotcha.

Withered Chica: Unlike Ennard and the other vent-crawlers, she gives no audio cues when she is at the door, which means you need to track her position using the vent radar. The upside is, her backside is so big she'll get stuck right at your vent door. While that may block some of the animatronics, Mangle can still get through, and there's also a chance she can shake free at any time.

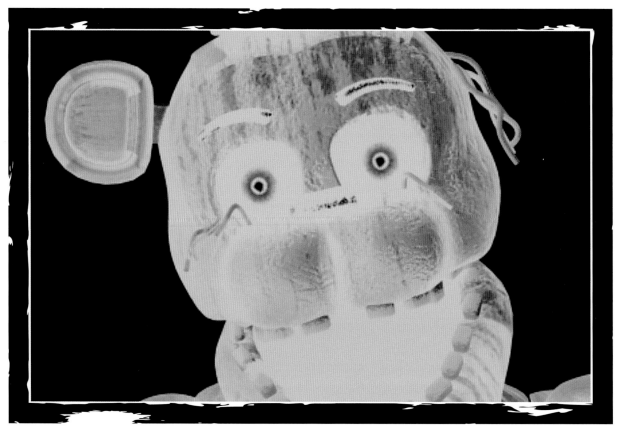

FNAF 3

Springtrap: Silently climbing around in the vent system, you have to track him with the vent monitor. When he's about to strike you will see his face looking back at you from the vent. Slam the door shut immediately!

Phantom Freddy: Being an apparition, he will slowly take shape before your eyes. The only way to dissolve him is to shine your flashlight on him. Handle him before he fully materializes or he will jumpscare you and knock you out briefly.

Phantom BB: He will pop up on your monitor randomly. Change cameras quickly or close the monitor to avoid his jumpscare. If he gets you, you'll blackout briefly.

Phantom Mangle: This Phantom also appears randomly on your monitor, so close it or switch viewing modes to dissolve it. If you leave him onscreen for too long, he will enter your office and cause all sorts of audio distraction and general mayhem.

FNAF 4

Nightmare Freddy: With your attention focused elsewhere, mini-Freddys, or Freddles, will congregate about your office. Point your flashlight at them to shoo them away. If you allow too many in the room they can summon Nightmare Freddy, and your shift will end with a jumpscare.

Nightmare Bonnie, and Nightmare Mangle, and Circus Baby: The strategy to defend and defeat this terrible trio is oddly intertwined, so we have a game plan for you to implement on them. They all approach from the right hall, but each only attacks once per night. You don't know who's going to attack first, but when they do, make a mental note of the order in which they appear. To stop this terrible trio, you can either leave the right door shut, which you can't do forever as it drains power, or buy their plush toy from the Prize Counter. Your cash is limited so make sure you buy them in the same order that they popped up on you.

Nightmare: Here's something not-so-comforting: these next two are invisible to the camera. You can only see them when they're literally at your doorways, and even then, only their eyes are visible! Nightmare comes from the right, so be ready to slam that door shut.

Nightmare Fredbear: A mirror image and perhaps scarier reflection of Nightmare, Nightmare Fredbear attacks from the left. When you see those evil eyes bearing down on you, slam that door shut before it's too late!

Jack-O-Chica: Here's a terrifying one: if it gets too hot in your office she appears in BOTH doors at the same time! You have to close both doors...although this is not effective if it's over 100 degrees in your office so if you can keep things chilled, you can be chill.

Nightmare Mangle: Our advice for this demonic animatronic? Just buy his plush toy from the Prize Counter to avoid his attack from the right. Don't think you can stop him with your office door—ya can't.

Nightmarionne: Drifting from one location to another during your game, he'll take shape if you move your cursor over him. Best thing to do is avoid the area where you see him lurking or you can count on a jumpscare in your future.

Nightmare BB: What a slouch! Let him sit—when he stands up light him up with your flashlight. He'll sit back down, and you don't have to worry about being attacked.

FNAF: SISTER LOCATION

Circus Baby: Best plan for her is to just hit the Prize Counter and buy her plush toy so when she pops up in the right hall, you're safe. Don't be foolish enough to think your flimsy office door can prevent her from entering and ending your night.

Ballora: After your cameras are disabled, she'll approach from either side of the hall. Listen carefully for her music, and then close whatever door you hear the beats coming from.

Funtime Foxy: Stroll by his stage and see what time his show starts, and then make sure you're there before the curtain drops. If you are, he'll postpone his act. If you're not, he'll postpone you winning the game with a jumpscare.

PRO TIP: Each in-game hour is 45 seconds long. Keep an eye on the timer to make sure you're watching Foxy's curtain at the appropriate time.

Ennard: This funky fella is another vent-crawler, and is harder to track than the others as he only appears when moving. Listen for squeaky metal before he attacks, and slam the vent door before he can enter.

FREDDY FAZBEAR'S PIZZERIA SIMULATOR

Helpy: Helpy is anything but handy, as he will pop-up on your desk at random and won't hesitate to blast his air-horn, which certainly doesn't help your audio sensitive equipment. Click on him quickly!

Trash and the Gang: This rickety crew take animatronics to a whole new, low-tech direction. They're funny to look at and are not a menace, but they cause a ruckus and can distract you from keeping your eyes and ears open for more serious threats.

Nedd Bear: Not the nimblest animatronic, he inhabits the overhead duct system. You can fool him half the time with the audio lure, and keep him at a safe distance with the heater.

Happy Frog: Hopping about in the overhead duct system, she'll come through the hoses that drop into your office. The audio lure is totally effective while the heater has no effect, so stick with the sounds!

Mr. Hippo: Also ambling in the overhead duct system and heading for the hoses that drop into your office, you can use the audio lure indefinitely to hold him in place, or the heater to repel him.

Pigpatch: Coming through the overhead air ducts, you can use the heater to deter him when he arrives at your office. You can use the audio lure to repel him, or the heater to send him away.

Orville Elephant: An elephant in your air ducts? Yup, he, too, climbs around in the overhead duct system on the way to your office. The heater will hold him off, or the audio lure freezes him. Believe it or not this pachyderm is slightly faster than old Nedd Bear.

Rockstar Freddy: This guy has the audacity to occasionally activate and demand a payment of five Faz-Coins. If you pay him, he will return to sleep-mode. If you're light on cash, you can dial-up the heat for a moment and he'll malfunction himself back into oblivion.

Rockstar Bonnie: When he pops up in your office, he's looking for his guitar. Scan your monitors and when you spot his guitar click on it promptly; he'll leave you alone to go get his beloved axe.

Rockstar Chica: Keep an eye on both the left and right hallways as she can approach from either side. Closing the doors will not make her leave, so you have to click on the "wet floor" sign and drop it in front of the door that she is standing at. Since she's afraid of slipping, she'll slink away.

Rockstar Foxy: One of the more interesting characters in the game, his parrot will occasionally fly by your office. If you can click on the colorful bird in time, Rockstar Foxy will drop in...and may even offer you some help in the way of power-ups! You can't count on a helping paw or claw from him though, as he can be moody...

Music Man: Always behind you, he will slowly become more active and louder with his clanging cymbals if you make a lot of noise and get him riled up. Stay chill and on the quiet side or he'll unload a jumpscare on you.

El Chip: El Chip is 100% business; he's not here to cause anyone any harm. He might annoy you with some blaring ads, but that's nothing worse than you see in the real world. Don't totally tune him out though, or his advertising efforts may mess up your monitoring duties.

FYI THIS IS THE FIRST GAME IN THE SERIES WHERE MOST CHARACTERS ARE BROUGHT TO LIFE WITH VOICE ACTORS.

Funtime Chica: Another character that isn't here to stalk you, she just wants to be in the limelight. Let her strut and tolerate the flash bulbs from cameras and learn to maneuver around her because you can't avoid her, and watch for more aggressive adversaries that might be closing in.

Molten Freddy: Another vent denizen, he is much quicker than the other animatronics and can also avoid the vent snare! Keep track of him on the vent monitor and listen for his laugh. When he's about to attack slam the vent door on him.

Scrap Baby: Once per night, she will appear on the opposite side of your desk with a shock panel sitting next to her. Every time she moves zing her with a shock, but remember that you're draining your power every time you zap her, so use it smartly and sparingly.

76%

usage

Lefty: Sitting in the closet off the left hallway, he becomes more animated and aggressive when it gets too hot or noisy. Once this builds there is no way to calm him down except by playing the global music box, which carries its own tradeoffs in terms of power consumption.

Scraptrap: Featuring perhaps the simplest mechanic in the game, it might also be the scariest. He will only attack once per night, and there is no way to know where, when, or if it'll happen. If he does, the lights will flicker beforehand, so close the right vent door to block him.

FNAF WORLD

Old Man Consequences: Use the C button to reel in a fish when his minigame appears, or he'll lock you out of your monitor for a few moments.

NON-SELECTABLE CHARACTERS

In UCN, you can also expect to encounter these non-selectable animatronic adversaries, as well as a few surprises, during your night patrol.

Nightmare Chica: For some reason the rows of fangs protruding from an elongated beak make Nightmare Chica extra scary. When you see those nightmarish jaws begin to close on your screen, flip on the AC before they do or you'll be jumpscared.

91 %

Plushtrap: One of the better-conditioned animatronics, this brownish brutal bunny appears repeatedly on the same screen and will randomly sit down. If you don't scare him out of his chair he will eventually spring forth and you're toast.

Bonnet: As with earlier installments, you can stop her by clicking on her nose when she struts across the office.

Lolbit: Not as funny as he thinks, Lolbit's face will appear on the screen with the words "PLEASE STAND BY". With your view and access to cameras and doors blocked, the only thing you can do is punch L-O-L into your keyboard to make him disappear.

Minireenas: When summoned, several Minireenas will appear and block your view. The blockage will last about an hour in game time, which is roughly 45 seconds.

Fredbear: Should a player set the night to only have Golden Freddy at 1 difficulty, then, upon using the Death Coin on Golden Freddy, Fredbear will jumpscare the player and end the night. One time this can't occur is if Dee Dee shows up during the night.

Dee Dee: A truly unique character in the game, she appears at random and can either add a new animatronic to your posse, or increase its difficulty level. In 50/20 mode a new animatronic named XOR will appear. She is black and white, with no eyes, and flitters about your office muttering the names of her roster one after another in this order: Shadow Bonnie, Plushtrap, Nightmare Chica, Bonnet, Minireenas, and Lolbit.

During your frenzied five nights, you may also catch quick cameos by other beloved characters from the franchise, so keep your eyeballs peeled and prove your Freddy fandom be seeing if you can spot them all! ●

FIVE NIGHTS AT FREDDY'S: HELP WANTED

According to the title, the Five Nights at Freddy's empire had trouble hiring staff long before the rest of the world did due to the pandemic. In this installment, originally designed as a virtual reality experience, you must complete a series of minigames that are odes to previous versions of the game.

ht**s at Freddy's**™

HELP
WANTED

ss Any Button

"The Freddy Fazbear Virtual Experience" was created by Fazbear Entertainment to help repair its public image after a series of high-profile devastating lawsuits, animatronic attacks, and other unpleasantries occurred at multiple branch locations.

In this pseudo-VR game, you play from a first-person perspective and must complete a raft of classic games and original minigames that are odes to previous games in the series, all while avoiding attacks from those always active animatronics.

FNAF 1

The game begins with the original Five Nights at Freddy's. You manage security cameras, trap doors, and lights. Be sure to keep an eye on your power and don't overuse, as your goal is to simply make it to until morning.

There are four animatronics to deal with: Bonnie, Chica, Freddy, and then Foxy appears after Night 3. Make a mental note that Bonnie and Foxy will only attack on your left, while Chica and Freddy will only attack on your right.

Bonnie and Chica are easier to handle so let's focus on them first. Listen for their footsteps as they approach. You can easily see them in the cameras and catch parts of their bodies and arms in the doorway before you have to close it. Be especially cautious with Chica because if she's in your window when you open the door, she'll attack.

Foxy can be tough, too. Keep watch on 1C which is Pirate's Cove. You'll see him peek through the curtains, approach the camera and then vanish. Soon after, you can expect him to come charging at you, which you'll hear from his frantic footsteps, and you have to be quick to close the door before he arrives.

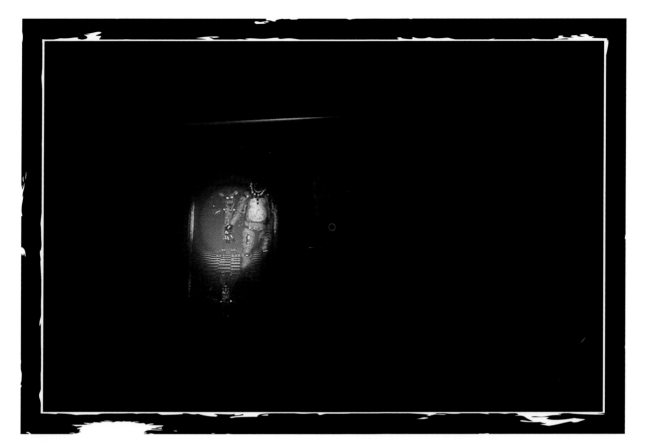

DYK?

THIS IS THE FIRST TITLE IN THE SERIES TO NOT BE DEVELOPED PERSONALLY BY CREATOR SCOTT CAWTHON, AND IS ALSO THE FIRST TO BE PUBLISHED FOR CONSOLES.

If you survive and make it to Night Five and think it's been a challenge so far, wait until this night begins. The animatronics are more aggressive, and about every 18 seconds or so, the doors are going to open and shut three or four times. Then the lights will turn on so be ready to turn them off immediately.

If there are any animatronics outside your doors and they open you're toast so be sure to turn off the light and then look at camera 1C to make Foxy descend upon you faster. If Freddy's to your right and the doors are getting ready to open, try to look at him at camera 4B long enough for him to go away.

If you know Freddy's not around you can open the door for about 4-5 seconds at a time but be vigilant as he can pop out at any moment. One last note, even if you run out of power you can still make it to 6:00 am, but the coast has to be clear.

Keep your finger on the music box to charge it on camera 11. You can basically ignore the other security cameras. When you see something pop up in the vents put on the Freddy mask immediately and wait for it to go away.

When wearing the mask, you won't be able to charge the music box so pay attention and keep it up as much as possible as this keeps the puppet from coming out of the present box, and the puppet can end your night even if you're wearing the Freddy mask.

As Freddy comes down the hallway he'll pause at the doorway. Don't panic! Keep doing your thing until he eventually starts entering the room, then put the mask on. Just repeat this process until 6:00 am and you should be fine.

PRO TIP: Conserve as much power as possible; always know where Foxy is; keep the door closed on Freddy.

FNAF2

Yikes! Now here's something different right from the get-go: you don't have doors to close and hide behind!

You just have one big lonely hallway in front of you with two vents on each side. The good news is this is one of the easier games. There are three key things to know to survive: spam the light and keep checking the vents on the side and also ward off Foxy in the hallway.

FNAF 3

While Five Nights at Freddy's 3 might be the most difficult of the first three games in this series, it might also be the most rewarding. It definitely has the most jumpscares, but on the upside, there's only one boss that can kill you: Springtrap! Additionally, there's also appearances by different Phantoms.

As instructed by the voice on the phone, you're back monitoring security cameras, covering different vents, and rebooting systems that go down.

Springtrap is lured to the sound of children. You have a button that cues the sound of a little girl's voice and can be used to steer Springtrap away from you. But the catch is, Springtrap can also go through vents to reach you.

As such, you should draw Springtrap as far away as possible while also keeping an eye on any vents that he might use to sneak attack you. Seal these off asap.

Meanwhile, it's important that although the Phantoms can't harm you, they will definitely make your life more chaotic. When they take your systems down, you'll have to look to the left and reboot, and if Springtrap gets through the vents while this is happening, you're toast.

If he makes it down the hallway path, before he attacks, he'll pause at your doorway for a moment. Immediately switch to camera one and use the girl's voice to try and lure him into that room. Phantom Foxy may also appear in the corner of your office. If he does, just keep your head down while you're handling the reboot system and he won't budge.

Keep an eye on Springtrap and keep him as far away as possible using the girl's voice, and also be sure to close any vents that are nearby. Try to avoid just randomly scanning different monitors, because there's going to be Phantoms throughout the building. If you look at them, they will most definitely jump at you and knock your system out.

Springtrap becomes a lot more aggressive on Hard Mode, and there's also Phantoms fixing to jumpscare you frequently. We recommend keeping him on cameras 5, 9, and 10 and close any vents nearby. One last thing: you're better off to just reboot all your systems every time—you're just trying to survive until 6:00 am and can forget about individual reboots.

MINIGAMES

DARK ROOMS
PLUSHTRAP

Plushtrap is your first challenge, and he's actually not too tough. The goal here is to keep your flashlight off of him long enough to let him advance towards you and when he reaches the red X in front of you, catch him with the flashlight.

Although you have just 90 seconds to defeat him, wait five or six seconds until he gets close enough to the door that's on your immediate left or right. Once he reaches one of these, count to three-one thousand. He should be right there on top of the X, so hit him with the flashlight!

NIGHTMARE BB

Also known as Balloon Boy, you can defeat him by generally the same gameplan as Plushtrap. Sit tight for a few seconds at first and let him get close, count to three-one thousand, and light him up! The main difference here is, you guessed it, there are balloons involved, so it makes everything more complicated.

Comically enough, you can make the balloons work for you—when BB's super close just look for the balloon shape to drift straight above you and as soon as that happens, hit 'em with the flashlight!

PLUSHBABY

Plushbaby is next, and they're no joke. There's actually three of them attacking you and if you shine your light right off the bat looking for them, they'll pounce instantly, so chill out. Instead, wait to hear their laughter before you begin your search for them.

FYI
IT WAS RUMORED THAT SCOTT CAWTHON PLANNED TO LAUNCH A WEBSITE DEPICTING THE FAKE COMPANY, SILVER PARASOL GAMES, THAT HELP ENGINEER THE FREDDY FAZBEAR VIRTUAL EXPERIENCE, BUT DECIDED NOT TO BECAUSE HE DIDN'T WANT TO CONFUSE FANS.

Two things to keep in mind: you should be aware of all the spots they can attack you from. Also, you have very little battery life, so just tap the button for the flashlight and flood the area with light as much as you can in a quick burst. Avoid holding the flashlight down until you need to dispatch one of the Plushbabies.

You should have a brief moment to let the flashlight charge right after you get rid of one, but be ready for another one to pop up on you shortly. If you know the spots to look you can be efficient with your illumination, and save battery life for when you hear noises that are getting closer or almost upon you.

In Hard mode, there is nothing in the room but Plushbaby dolls, but watch for their glowing green eyes and although they're more aggressive, the strategy to defeat them remains the same.

FUNTIME FOXY

While Funtime Foxy might not be as much of a handful as the Plushbabies, he creates his own form of panic. The goal is to get to the end of the room without getting caught by FF. Two things to know: first, move diagonally and two, flash your light every five seconds.

Focus on the wall to the left and move diagonally towards it, flashing the light every five seconds while you glance to the right. Do not move while you flash the light or Foxy will get you. Keep doing this until you reach the wall, and then turn and face the right wall and start moving diagonally in that direction.

Keep flashing the light every five seconds while looking to the left (and not moving when you flash the light) and keep using this pattern until you reach the exit sign. You're home free once you get behind Funtime Foxy.

One more thing: don't flash your light too close to Foxy. Back up if you have to and don't move too suddenly or he'll definitely pounce on you.

PARTS AND SERVICE

Parts and Service is the next minigame, and is fairly straightforward. In fact, if you simply follow the onscreen instructions, and try not to touch or drop anything, you should be able to get through this game without much trouble. The goal here is to return an item to one of your guests, who left it behind on one of your attractions.

MANGLE

Fortunately, beating him isn't too hard. All you need to do is shine your light on Mangle while spinning dials, pushing buttons, and cranking levers. There's a Simon Says puzzle to the left and after you complete this, you're done!

ENNARD

The vent repair level for Ennard is fairly straightforward as well. Locate the device with the red light on it by using your flashlight to follow the cable to the buttons, and then press them in order. Once you get the first three you can punch the fourth.

The next section is a secondary service elevator ventilation shaft, which is motion triggered. This final part only has two puzzles, but they can be tricky. You basically have to rotate all the connections and pipes so that the gas flows through them. The sounds and flame effects are pretty cool as you try to solve the puzzle.

NIGHT TERRORS

This final group of minigames can be a little confusing at first, but like old-school video games, are pretty easy to beat once you get your timing down.

FUNTIME FREDDY

Keep shining your light to keep the creepers away, and then move door to door and aim your light down the hallway to find Funtime Freddy. If you see him just make sure you hold the door shut until he retreats to the other side, and keep repeating this process.

NIGHTMARIONNE

Next up is Nightmarionne. Use the same strategy of running back and forth between the two doors and while you do, check down the hallway and see if you see a pair of glowing eyes. If you do, it's Nightmarionne so slam the door shut and don't flash the light down the hallway.

87

Instead, use it check under the bed, ceiling, and closet to scare away any tentacles that may be creeping out from the shadows. Continue this process as you move back and forth checking down the hallway for those glowing eyes. If you don't see anything but hear squishy noises, check again for tentacles. If you don't see any, run to the other door immediately and be prepared to slam it shut!

CIRCUS BABY

With Circus Baby, make sure you close the door before she gets too close or you're already toast. Also be sure to check the Plushbabies inside the closet with you—the longer you hold the door shut the more restless they get. Once they start vibrating, it means they're ready to attack, so let go of the door straight away.

If Circus Baby is still there, she's either got you or you have less than a second to slam the door shut. Though nerve-wracking, this is all you have to do to defeat Circus Baby.

NIGHTMARE FREDBEAR

Last but not least is Nightmare Fredbear. The strategy for him is similar to Funtime Freddy and Nightmarionne, but this time you're moving across the closet as well.

Fortunately for you, the heavy-footed Nightmare Fredbear stomps around pretty loudly, so just go in the closet and close the door, and listen to which direction he is walking in.

DYK? THE DEVELOPERS REPORTEDLY HAD TO REDUCE THE POLYGON COUNTS AND DIAL BACK SOME OF THE DARKLY RICH DETAIL OF THE ANIMATRONICS DUE TO UNREAL GAME ENGINE LIMITATIONS AT THE TIME.

Once you figure out what direction he is going, sprint to that door, slam it shut, and wait for him to walk away. Continue this process until 6:00 am and then you've safely survived another crazy night.

Once you've beaten all the levels in Hard Mode, you got one last level—the maze-like pizza party. Have fun winding your way through this final challenge, and congratulations on completing the Freddy Fazbear Virtual Experience!

FIVE NIGHTS AT FREDDY'S: SPECIAL DELIVERY

In this title, Freddy Fazbear and the gang finally break free of the shackles of their pizza and party parlor, and come visit you on your turf with the help of your phone or tablet and some pretty clever augmented reality (AR).

Whatcha gonna do when they come for you?

ETERNAL PACKAGE!

We're thrilled you chose our service!
You may now look forward to

999 years

of excitement!

OK

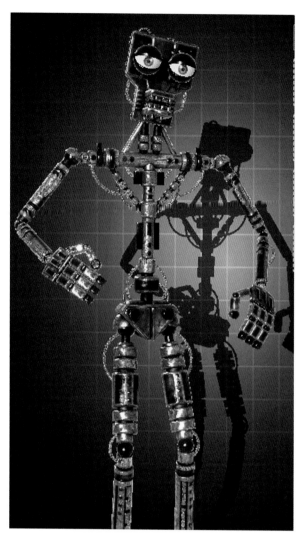

Typical with games like this, gameplay is presented from the first-person perspective. You have a flashlight and controlled shocker, and your screen is whatever you direct your phone or tablet towards.

You can move around and interact with the animatronics, and unlocking new ones by beating them. Your goal is to locate static based on where the animatronic is, and giving it a controlled shock when they charge at you.

This is pretty much the game, and it's definitely a hoot to constantly change your environments, but another cool feature is that you can send animatronics to your friends' house, and vice versa.

CHARACTERS

Picking up where Five Nights at Freddy's: Help Wanted and its DLC left off, the game features new and returning supporting characters including Freddy, Bonnie, Chica, Foxy, Golden Freddy, Toy Freddy, Toy Bonnie, Toy Chica, Mangle, Balloon Boy, Springtrap, Plushtrap, Jack-O-Bonnie, Jack-O-Chica, Baby, and Ballora.

The new cast includes:
- Holiday
- Chocolate
- Arcade
- Wasteland
- Heatwave
- Circus
- Forest
- Winter
- Aztec
- Scary Tales
- Wicked Tides
- Screampunk versions of the animatronics.

We're gonna say it right off the bat, this game is AR, which means it runs on your iPhone and Android device, and operates much like the Pokémon AR experience. It is a whole new direction for the franchise, and brings those ambling animatronics into and about your abode!

The ninth installment in the Five Nights at Freddy's series features a clever storyline that allows you to subscribe to Fazbear Entertainment's "Fazbear Funtime Service" and have your favorite animatronics visit you on-demand. But due to shoddy manufacturing, again, the visiting animatronics go haywire and begin stalking you instead of providing entertainment.

FYI UPON RELEASE, THE GAME WAS ORIGINALLY RATED E10+ (FOR EVERYONE 10+), BUT WAS LATER CHANGED TO A T-RATING IN NOVEMBER 2019.

SETTING

After the typical FNaF intro, you're thrust into the game. But this time, it's wherever you are!

Your flashlight will help you see any distortions. Closer and stronger static means the animatronic is almost on top of you, so get a feel for the size and scope of the indications and eventually you'll get a sense of space and distance to help you handle your adversaries.

GAMEPLAY BASICS

Eventually the animatronics will charge, but do not use the taser if their whole body isn't visible. It can be hard when their outline first comes into focus, but take a deep breath and hold your fire until they're fully exposed and you're sure you can take them down. If they're fully visible but not running at you hold your fire. Save it for when they are coming straight for you. When one does, shock it before it gets there.

PRO TIP: Your shocker zaps 10% of your battery instantly, so you have limited chances, while the flashlight burns battery life at a clip of 2% per use.

WORKSHOP

After gaining some combat experience, it's time to trudge off to the Workshop. To find it, look at the bottom right corner of your HUD. Tap the Freddy head with a wrench on it. You start with one Endo but as you watch ads you get more Faz tokens, which allow you to buy your favorite animatronic or other cool stuff, such as CPU chips which can give your animatronic the same AI as the one you just defeated.

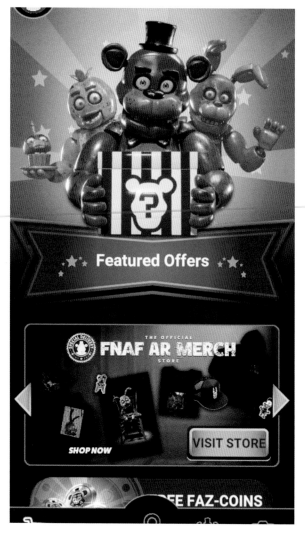

THIS IS THE FIRST GAME IN THE FRANCHISE DESIGNED SOLELY TO BE A MOBILE GAMING EXPERIENCE.

After customizing your animatronic you can send it off to a friend's house to take them on.

What if your animatronic is broken? After you fight off an animatronic or when you're salvaging, you earn parts and pieces to fix it. To fix your Endo, click repair and use the parts to patch it up. During the game you also earn mods, which can also make your animatronics faster and more aggressive.

THE STORE

To go shopping, click the grocery cart icon in the bottom left. There are a lot items to purchase but let's focus on the lures and mini packs. At the store, you'll find that Freddy, Bonnie, Chica, Foxy, and BB lures cost 300 Faz tokens. Mini packs for these guys include a plush suit and three character lures, and cost 600 per. Circus Baby lures cost 500 tokens while her mini pack is priced at 1,250 tokens. Springtrap was originally the priciest purchase before Toy Chica came along—his lures cost 1,000 tokens apiece while his mini pack cost 2,500. Finally, Toy Chica's lures cost a whopping 1,600 tokens while her mini pack cost 4,200 tokens.

EVENTS

Events for this game usually occur around holidays. The last Christmas event introduced two new characters including Toy Chica, and the mythical Freddy Frostbear. During that same time period a Toy Bonnie event that gave him a voice and cool suit occurred. The good news about this game is that because it's designed to play on mobile devices, you can still participate in events even if you're visiting family and friends for a holiday.

ROBOTIC ROSTER

Here's a roundup of some of the animatronics you might be lucky, or unlucky, enough to face in the game:

ENDO-01

This first guy is pretty easy to handle—if he doesn't have any mods or CPU chips and even then, you should be able to handle him. His pattern is to run right at you and then...move really slow. Be forewarned, even though he might be a pushover in the early going, he picks up speed and aggression as the game wears on or your winning streak becomes longer. You can easily hear his distinctive footstep pattern so listen for it closing in on you, and you should be able to shock and stop him even at the higher levels.

FREDDY

The star of the show, Freddy is a fan favorite and leader of the band. He has much heavier footsteps and you can be sure it's him if he has the CPU chip, as his voice will be different. His catch phrases include "I hope you enjoy my visit; I got a special delivery just for you" which he says when he's about to attack, and "I bet you didn't expect me to show up," even if you sorta did.

Other famous Freddy phrases include "When you wake up just remember friends are forever," which he say as he's about to turn out your lights. In the heat of battle, he might blurt out, "Round and round we go, where we're going nobody knows!"; "Now, now all that fear isn't helping either of us" or "What's that you didn't invite me...too bad!" You go, Freddy!

He like to play his music box when he's trudging around in the dark and might mutter, "Now would be the best time to hold your breath" which is a warning that he's about to attack. Freddy also has a penchant for talking smack after taking you down. Some of his go-to phrases when this happens include, "That sure was fun," "Looks like someone wasn't ready for Freddy to come to the party" or "Most people like my hugs."

BONNIE

Bonnie has undergone some revisions in this installment of the FNaF franchise. He exchanges his fur for a smooth, shiny skin, which gives him more of a purplish hue. He also looks more worn out in this go around, as he's sporting bumps, scratches, and stains on his skin.

Appearances mean nothing though; he's as able as ever. As with the other enemies in this game, you can identify him by his distinctive static, movements, and sounds. You have to wait until he is visible to shock him—but allow him to charge you first. In Haywire Mode remember to look away asap when he starts twitching, or you're toast. One final note: If you defeat him, you can acquire his CPU and slick suit.

CHICA

Battling Chica is fairly similar to Bonnie, but the main difference here is that you hear chewing noises from her, and she's a bit more aggressive. Once you recognize her static and she eventually goes Haywire, look away quickly, then be ready to blast her with your bolt when she fully materializes and charges at you. She is another character which, after defeating her, you can acquire her CPU and plush suit.

FOXY

The rarest of the main four animatronics in this game, Foxy is also the fastest and most formidable. You won't see him early in the game or streak, but once you hit a streak of five or so, you can expect your chances to run into him to rise drastically.

Speaking of running, that's his thing—he's known to circle you while hurling taunts your way, play "chicken" and act like he's charging you, and more. It can definitely be disorienting even when you're in the comfort of your own home. When he pops-up directly in front of you and begins twitching, look away asap or you'll get jumpscared. If you're still alive, get ready to shock him when he charges.

BB

While BB may appear small, he packs a serious wallop. Keep your eyes pointed downward as that's where the little guy is gonna be. To see him you have to sport his static. Since he's wee, there isn't much to see, even with your flashlight. When walking he blows a balloon up and faintly says "Hello." More dangerously, when he goes Haywire he goes into stealth mode—he is totally silent and his attacks are quick and lethal. He'll normally say "Haha" as he attacks, so be ready!

153

CIRCUS BABY

Everybody's favorite humanoid robot clown is back for Special Delivery, and Circus Baby does not disappoint. Known for her mostly reserved nature up to this point in the franchise, she is among the most aggressive animatronics in the game and generally only pops-up when you've got a long streak going.

As with the others, do not look at her eye when she goes Haywire or you're a goner. Be ready for a few fake charges before she actually materializes, and when she does, be ready to shock her before she can jumpscare the daylights out of you.

SPRINGTRAP

Arguably the most dangerous animatronic in the game, Springtrap is hopping with unpleasant surprises for you. He will go Haywire on you left and right, and will even reel off multiple Haywires back-to-back. If you see this, be ready to glare at him when his eyes are white, and look away when they turn red.

Be prepared for taunting and fake charges during his attack, as Springtrap is relentless. As soon as he materializes for a charge, brace yourself and shock him quickly. Perhaps the best part, if you can actually manage to defeat him, you can claim his CPU and plush suit, and unleash him on all your friends—and frenemies.

TOY CHICA

First, an interesting tidbit: Toy Chica did not appear in the original version of Special Delivery, but was dropped in with some DLC and is now a permanent and formidable fixture in the game.

Like some other animatronics, Toy Chica will circle, taunt, and fake-charge you, but does something decidedly different when she goes Haywire. When she does, equip the Freddy Fazbear mask right away by holding it up to her face, and stare straight at her. You have a slim chance of winning her CPU or plush suit, but don't count on seeing it too often.

DEVICES

Here's a quick list of the secret weapons and gadgets you can use to help get you through the night:

Extra Battery: Cost is 100 Faz coins. This super handy upgrade recharges your battery life more than half, more like 70% in fact, so wait until your battery is more than half empty and you can top off your battery. For 100 tokens you get three fresh batteries.

EMF meter: Cost is 1000 parts. Using one of these will increase the Remnant quality for a random but substantive number of Remnants you acquire.

155

Salvage Scanner: Cost is 500 parts. For this you get 12 scanners, which amplifies your ability to get more and better parts from each salvage you perform.

Transponder: Cost is 90 parts. When you activate this device, it will show you the identity and location of all active animatronics on the map.

REMNANTS

Remnants are an especially important part of Special Delivery. A remnant is the "soul" that possesses an inanimate object and brings it to life.

There are two kinds: Light and Shadowy. The light ones are typically orb-shaped objects with bright colors, the shadowy ones are swirling swarms of dark colors. Light Remnants can be used in the Workshop for enhancing the animatronics' attacking and salvaging abilities, come in many colors, and sport different stats. Quantity refers to how much the Remnants spawn, value refers to how much Remnant you get for collecting it, and speed refers to how quickly the Remnant moves once the flashlight is turned on.

You can usually spot a Remnant before the animatronic. Using your flashlight, you can drag both light and dark remnants types towards you, though be advised the shadowy Remnants, which you want to avoid, move much faster.

Often times the dark remnants will circle the light ones so just be patient for a moment, wait for the dark swirls to dissipate, and then grab the light ones. If you grab too many dark ones you will summons a sinister and shadowy surprise that you'd rather not have to reckon with, but we won't spoil who might pop-up, other than to say he isn't just some keyboard gibberish as his name implies.

Armed with this knowledge and using these techniques, you should be able to become the master of your domain no matter where and when the animatronics arrive. Start looking wherever you are!

FNAF WORLD
Spring Bonnie

Male? Female? It's a rabbit, who cares.

FNaF World is the first official spin-off game of the Five Nights at Freddy's series, and fifth title. Released in early 2017, it gives us a glimpse of how this fun and frightening franchise might expand.

Like the previous games, the interface and settings are pretty simple. The game has two difficulty levels to choose from, Normal and Hard, and two modes of play: Adventure and Fixed Party.

You begin by choosing two parties consisting of four characters each. Your party can be made up of more than 40 characters from the first four games. In the game, your main goal is to explore and unlock new worlds. As you do, you can jump from one to the other via teleports.

Along the way, you encounter the "home turf" of many of your favorite characters, and battle them to win Faz-coins or tokens. During your trials and tribulations, a notable new character makes his debut: Fredbear. He'll give you teasers and tips on what might be coming next.

Battles are turn-based encounters punctuated by boss battles for each of the main areas. You must choose one of three commands, which vary by character. Commands include: single-target attacks (orange), general area attacks (red), poison attacks (green), one-shot kill attempts (black), healing (pink), status buffs (white), and more.

A carefully constructed team that has a mix of offensive and defensive attributes will help you win the day—or night, haha.

FNAF 57: FREDDY IN SPACE

FNaF 57: Freddy in Space is one of the more famous minigames in the FNaF library. First introduced in a FNaF World update, the most important thing to remember here is that in space, no one can hear you get jumpscared.

Seriously, you take control of Freddy Fazbear in a side-scrolling shooter, akin to genre classics such as Contra or Metroid. You blast your way through increasingly complex outer space-themed levels with increasingly powerful weapon upgrades, so that by late in the game you have some serious interstellar pyrotechnics.

Your weapons upgrades are embedded in Chica's Cupcakes, so be sure to scoop them up to give Freddy's blaster greater range, faster fire, and more lethality.

Some of the unexpected enemies you'll encounter in the other worldly game include a robot rodent that will scurry back and forth along the floor, trying to nip you; a security camera that rains laser pulses down upon you; a flying blob that will bounce haphazardly towards you, and multiple menacing mechanical monsters.

The best way to survive these types of games is to go fast and hard: keep blasting away, grab all the power-ups you can, don't dawdle, and press onwards asap to reach the end of each level.

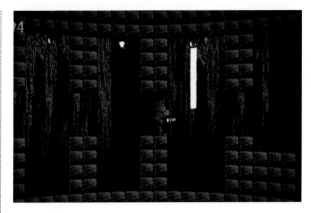

Freddy in Space 2 was a free sequel released in late 2019. The game was specially created to support the #CancelCancer charity livestream on YouTube for St. Jude Children's Research Hospital.

SECURITY BREACH: FURY'S RAGE

Security Breach: Fury's Rage dropped in spring 2021, and is another ode to classic video games, in this case side-scrolling beat 'em up titles. Early examples of this type of game include Double Dragon and Streets of Rage.

In this type of game, you can decide what type of hero you want to play—a heavy-hitting warrior or a more acrobatic assassin, and choose a corresponding character accordingly. In Security Breach, you can start out with Glamrock Freddy, Glamrock Chica, Montgomery, and Roxanne, with each one packing pros and cons in their fighting style.

You strut through five levels, fighting everyone in your path until you reach a boss at the end. You can jump, block, attack, and jump attack. Each boss has unique attacks and vulnerabilities, so be patient and learn their pattern before engaging them in a fight to the finish.

If you emerge victorious, you'll earn jewels that can be used to buff your character in various ways such as healing, strength, stamina, and more. Additionally, as you progress through the game your stamina and health bars will become more substantial. ●

SCOTT CAWTHON
A MODERN HORROR MASTER AND A TRUE ORIGINAL

Since its release in 2014, Five Nights at Freddy's has been one of the most popular independent survival games around. Within two years, the game became known for its tense gameplay, creepy ambience, and mysterious backstory, making it both a fun and exciting game, and an instant hit with YouTube gamers, racking up millions of views and becoming a huge seller on the Steam, IOS, and Android platforms. Your goal is to survive all five nights, a task that becomes harder and harder each night. Events come faster and faster, and the tension mounts, creating a one-of-a-kind gaming experience that has brought gamers back again and again.

FNaF's creator, independent game developer and animator Scott Cawthon, says the concept behind the game was equal parts accident and inspiration.

"I'd made a family friendly game about a beaver before this, but when I tried to put it online it got torn apart by a few prominent reviewers. People said that the main character looked like a scary animatronic animal. I was heartbroken and was ready to give up on game-making. Then one night something just snapped in me, and I thought to myself—I bet I can make something a lot scarier than that," Cawthorn told Indiegamemag.com in 2014.

Cawthon, a Texas native, first came on the scene in 2007 with a series of animated YouTube videos, and several independent games such as The Pilgrim's Progress, Chipper and Sons Lumber Company, and The Desolate Hope. At the time, these games found limited success.

Even though the Five Nights at Freddy's franchise has been universally praised and received huge acclaim, Cawthon is careful to still be the person he has always been. "I spend my evenings playing Megaman 3, Buster only, with my kids. And I try to (do) good with what's been given to me," he told Toucharcade.com in 2015.

By 2015, the game had received several awards, countless positive reviews, and the film rights had been sold to Warner Brothers. Once Five Nights at Freddy's took off on multiple platforms, a sequel was soon in the works. Three months later, in November of 2014, Five Nights at Freddy's 2 was released on Steam. In January of 2014, Five Nights at Freddy's 2 won two FEAR awards—Best Indie and Game of the Year.

Five Nights at Freddy's also won for Most Original game. With two solid hits under his belt, Cawthon moved ahead with the release of Five Nights at Freddy's 3 in March of 2015, expanding the backstory using hints, Easter eggs, and vague messages that had gamers playing over and over, looking for clues to the history.

Cawthon, while very in touch with and considerate of his fan base, does enjoy using mysterious messages on his website as teasers for upcoming releases, and has even gone so far as to pull a prank on the game's fans. While developing Five Nights at Freddy's 3, he released a fake message stating that he had been hacked and that the new game was cancelled, even going so far as to provide a link for a fake game that was intentionally bad.

By the summer of 2015, it was time for a new chapter in the series, and Five Nights at Freddy's 4 was released that July. The latest chapter proved to be a departure from the previous games, and added another twist to the history behind the games. In October of 2015, Cawthon released bonus content for part 4, a Halloween edition that replaced the nightmare creatures with Halloween versions.

Its popularity with fans has led to endless web pages dedicated to figuring out the mysteries that lie at the core of the game's storyline, although, according to Cawthon, nobody has gotten all of it right as of yet.

In August of 2015, he told Forbes, "You know, when I released the first game over a year ago, I was amazed at how quickly everyone found every bit of lore and story. Then the same happened with part 2, fans and YouTubers dug in and found everything. Game Theory did an incredible video on part 2; getting almost everything right. Then part 3 came out, and once again the story was uncovered by the community.

It seemed that there was nothing I could hide! But then I released part 4, and somehow.... no one, not a single person, found the pieces. The story remains completely hidden. I guess most people assumed that I filled the game with random Easter eggs this time. I didn't. What's in the box? It's the pieces put together. But the bigger question is, would the community accept it that way? The fact that the pieces have remained elusive this time strikes me as incredible, and special, a fitting conclusion in some ways, and because of that, I've decided that maybe some things are best left forgotten, forever."

In January of 2016, Cawthon took the franchise in a different direction with the release of Five Nights at Freddy's World, an RPG based on the horror hit. Responding to the fans, and wanting to improve the game's quality, he quickly pulled the game, revamped many elements of the gameplay, and re-released it on Steam a couple of months later for free.

167

Cawthon has expressed his hope that part of the future of the Freddy franchise would be crowd-sourced. He hopes that kids find inspiration in his independent games, and that they, in turn, will become the next generation of game creators. "I'm getting too old for this. And when I retire someday, I'm going to want to sit down at a computer and play YOUR games, read YOUR stories, and watch YOUR videos. Don't fall in with the people who have already given up on themselves. You are tomorrow's next big thing," he told Toucharcade.com in July 2015.

Next up was the release of Five Nights at Freddy's: Sister Location, which dropped in October, 2016 and was embraced by an enthusiastic fan base that was growing by leaps and bounds. Eight months later, Cawthon pulled a trick-or-treat with his fans by announcing that the next installment of the game, which was the sixth, would be canceled—which led to the surprise drop of the much beloved Freddy Fazbear's Pizzeria Simulator in December, 2017. The seventh game in the series, Ultimate Custom Night, followed in June 2018 and was released on Steam for free.

As the spotlight on him was growing brighter than ever, Cawthon was becoming increasingly uncomfortable with his unintended fame. He continued to focus on the franchise and his family as the FNaF brand kept expanding.

In 2019 Cawthon partnered up with video game developer Steel Wool Studios, announcing they would be making the next Five Nights at Freddy's games together. By the end of the year, Five Nights at Freddy's: Special Delivery launched, marking a first-time foray for Cawthon, Freddy, and the crew into an AR world that has been popularized by Pokémon.

In the summer of 2020, Cawthon announced his intent to help other passionate developers create games around his franchise and characters. He would help fund projects he felt were worthwhile, but would not dictate the process. The first game to launch under this arrangement was One Night at Flumpty's. Other titles incubated in the program include the Five Nights at Candy's series, The Joy of Creation trilogy, Popgoes Evergreen, and more.

One of the worst kept secrets of a pandemic-ridden 2020 was that a new game was going to drop soon with the name Five Nights at Freddy's: Security Breach, but as the year wore on, it became apparent the game would be delayed into 2021.

Meanwhile, the spotlight unexpectedly shifted on Cawthon, transforming from a warm glow to a harsh glare. His personal and private life came under scrutiny when his fan base found out he was a contributor to conservative politicians and causes.

Cawthon announced his retirement from public game development in June, 2021. He thanked his fans for their love and support of the franchise and pledged that the FNaF universe would carry on regardless of his involvement. ◖

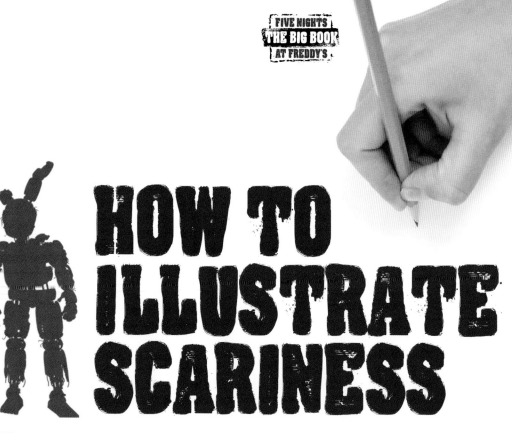

HOW TO ILLUSTRATE SCARINESS

Drawing scary creatures can sometimes be as rewarding as fighting them or running away from them in a video game. The creation of illustrations is a huge part of video games, both to create an artistic vision as well as to create what you actually see on the screen. Artwork can also be used to enhance books, and to make entire cartoons and animated movies. Some films use traditional drawings, some use stop-motion figures, and others use computer programs, but the techniques for character creation remain the same.

All of the tools and skills used to draw people and animals can also be used to make these characters scary. Recent films such as *ParaNorman* and the *Hotel Transylvania* movies have found lots of success using equal amounts of cute and creepy to tell their stories. By learning a few basic techniques, you can turn any type of drawing into a scary creation, and come up with your own creepy creatures to terrify your friends and family.

WHAT MAKES A DRAWING SCARY

There are many different ways to make an illustration scary, and it will always come back to figuring out what makes you scared. Drawing a figure in a menacing posture or giving a creature or person an angry face can be a good place to start. Slanted eyebrows can change a face dramatically. Changing parts of a person's physical structure also works really well. Making the eyeballs one solid color, stretching the face, and giving your character really long fingers are just a few examples of small changes to what we consider "normal" that can make a person or animal look scary.

Removing everyday things also works really well. A famous example would be Slender Man. The main reason he is scary is because the artist made him without a face. Another thing to consider is the size of the scary subject. A creature can be cute and fun when it's tiny, but make it the size of your bed, and all of a sudden, it's not nearly as cute anymore.

Another example would be the animatronics in Five Nights at Freddy's. Large animals that sing and move around can be lots of fun during the daytime, but if you are alone with them at night, it can be really spooky. Play around with making arms and legs longer than usual. Little changes can go a long way towards turning regular objects into things you wouldn't want to bump into at night.

Just like when writing a story, the location of your subject and the environment can have a huge effect on how scary a picture is. Imagine a drawing of a stuffed rabbit. Not so scary, right? But take that same rabbit, and put it in a graveyard at night, or make it come out of your dark closet while you are sleeping, or put it in the middle of your lawn on Halloween night... all of a sudden, it's not as cute and cuddly as it was just a moment ago.

The more you practice, the better you will get at both drawing and making your drawings spooky. Always keep pushing yourself to try drawing new things and using new materials, but remember: the most important tool in your toolbox is your imagination. Experiment and have fun!

ANIMATED BEAR

1: Start by drawing two circles and an oval. Finding the basic shape of your art subject is the first thing you should do. Circles, ovals, and cylinders work great to make bodies, heads, arms, and legs on living creatures like animals and people.

2: Draw circles for the ears, eyes, snout, and stomach. Draw shapes for the arms and legs. You can see your drawing begin to take form as you add more shapes to your basic figure. Even at this early stage, you can already tell what it's going to be. Notice how the placement of our basic shapes creates a pose that gives a sense of motion.

3: Add more circles for the ears, eyes, mouth, nose, hands, and feet. As we add more shapes, the details begin to come to life....hopefully this bear doesn't!

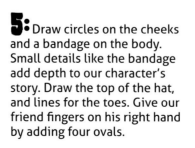

4: Add eyebrows, and draw lines connecting each part together. Draw two ovals in the left hand. What do the eyebrows tell you about the bear's mood? Right now, he looks angry, but change the angle and he can look surprised or happy. Also keep in mind that a happy face can be scary if the environment is spooky!

5: Draw circles on the cheeks and a bandage on the body. Small details like the bandage add depth to our character's story. Draw the top of the hat, and lines for the toes. Give our friend fingers on his right hand by adding four ovals.

6: Draw eyes. Add extra lines to the hat, arms, and neck. It's these final details that bring the drawing together, and make our bear seem much more real. You now have your own animatronic bear to entertain during the day and terrorize at night!

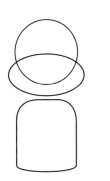

1: Start by drawing a circle, an oval, and a square body. Our cat will have a similar setup to our dog character.

2: Draw triangles for the ears, almond shapes for the eyes, a peanut shape for the snout, and four ovals for the feet. Add a half circle below the snout for the cat's mouth. You can give him a slightly different expression by rotating the eyes slightly.

3: Add triangles to the ears, lines to the eyes, a shape for the nose, and ovals for the mouth and front legs. Draw notches at the cheeks to simulate fluffy fur.

4: Draw lines connecting the ears to the head, and the head to the body. Draw half circles for the back legs and to mark the paws. Add a tail. I really hope he is an outside cat.

5: Add lines for the toes, the tip of the tail, and to mark the brow. Draw circles for the teeth. The round teeth give the impression that the mouth is open.

6: Add eyebrows, eyes, and whiskers. I sure can't wait to see him at the foot of the bed in the middle of the night! Here kitty, kitty!

GIANT SPIDER

1: Start by drawing two curved lines for the spider. Draw an oval and five curved lines for the runner. Even at this early stage, you can get a sense of action in our character.

2: Draw an oval for the runner's eye, and add lines to shape the rest of him. Draw two ovals to start the spider's mouth. Begin drawing long lines to create the spider's legs. Notice how the drawing is even scarier because the spider is so big.

3: Add two more ovals to make the runner's other eye and mouth. Draw pointed teeth for the spider's mouth and add circles for its eyes. Draw curved lines to create the spider's claws and lower body. When you draw the claws above and below the runner, it adds a feeling of danger.

4: Add hair to the runner and add lines to mark his thumb. Draw a jagged line to finish the spider's mouth. Add more curved lines to complete the spider's claws. Extra teeth tend to make a monster scarier.

5: Draw lines to mark the runner's clothes and add an oval to create his tongue. Begin to draw more lines behind the spider as you decide where to place his legs. Not only do the legs on the far side of the spider enhance the sense of movement, they also add a three-dimensional quality to the drawing.

6: Add two circles for the runner's eyes. Stripes or other patterns can be placed on the spider's back. Good job! You've made your own giant spider... now start running!

DOG

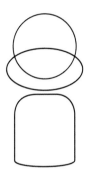

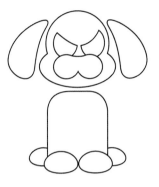

1: Start by drawing a circle, an oval, and a square body with rounded shoulders. Just like with our bear character, the basic shapes set up what the drawing is doing.

2: Draw teardrop shapes for the ears, half circles for the eyes, a peanut shape for the snout, and four ovals for the feet. Instead of using eyebrows, this time we will change the basic eye shape to look angry.

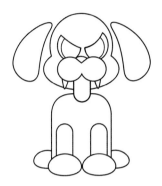

3: Add lines for the eyes and nose, triangles for the teeth, and ovals for the tongue and front legs. I don't think this dog wants to play!

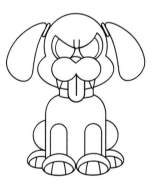

4: Draw lines connecting the ears to the head, and the head to the body. Draw half circles for the back legs and to mark the paws. Notice how you have created a collar with the neck lines. Adding spikes is optional.

5: Add lines for the toes and to mark the brow. Draw a center line for the tongue. Just a few more details, and he will be ready to bury some bones in the backyard.

6: Final details include circles for the eyes, and a small crease at the bottom of the snout. Take him for a walk and introduce him to all your friends!

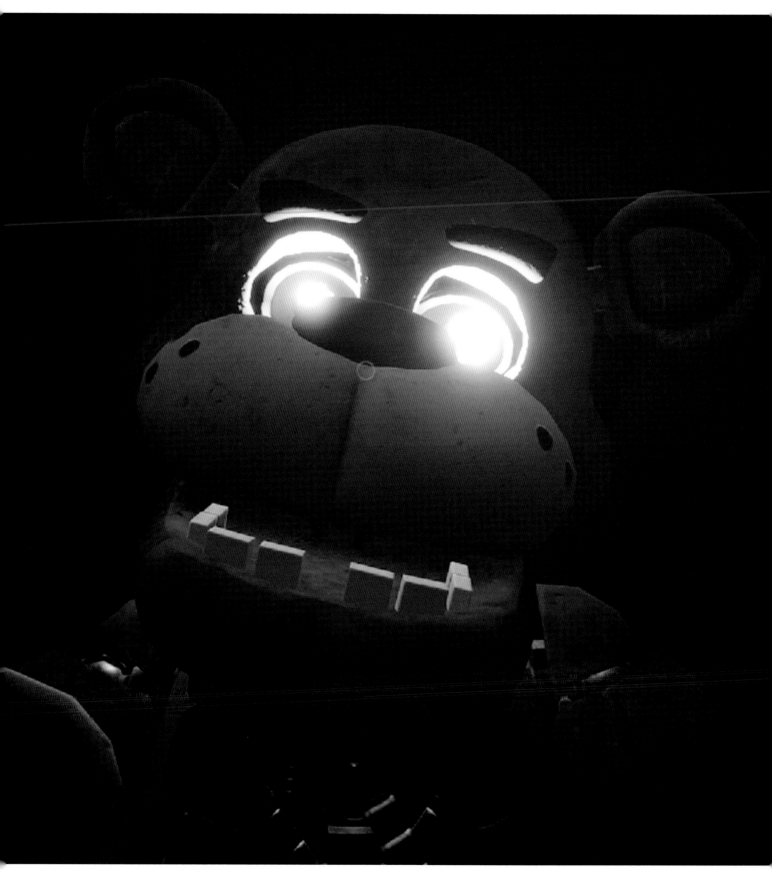

HOW TO WRITE A SCARY STORY

Everybody loves a good story, and because of that, there are many different types of fiction that appeal to the many types of people in the world. Epic adventures, fairy tales, comedy, and serious dramas are just a few of the styles used to tell different types of stories.

If you look at your favorite book, movie, or video game, the one thing they all have in common is that they present characters and situations that draw you in, take you on a journey, and make you want to know how the story ends. Writing stories of your own is a fun way to use your imagination to bring characters and places to life. But what if you wanted to write a scary story? And what is it, exactly, that makes a story scary?

WHAT SCARES YOU?

In order to make a scary story, the first thing you have to do is answer a question—what scares YOU? Some people are scared of the dark, or monsters, or clowns, or spiders. The best stories come from your own experiences, and the scariest stories will always come from the things that scare you.

Another thing to consider is if whatever it is that scares you is scary to other people as well. You might be completely terrified of

puppies, but that may not be true for other people. When something can scare you as well as others, it's called a "common fear." Using a common fear in your story will make it scary for more people, and the more people that get scared by it, the better the story is.

A smart way to begin is to make a list of all of the scary things you can think of, and then pick one to begin with. Making lists is a great way to keep track of your ideas for future stories.

SCARY PLACES, SCARY TIMES

Another way you can find your common fear is to use places that people consider scary. Old, empty houses are almost always haunted. Nobody wants to walk through a graveyard at night. What happens at the circus after the lights go out? All of these are great places to start, but if you use your imagination, you can make a scary place out of almost anywhere. Most people have been afraid of the dark at some time in their lives, so nighttime will always create a spooky mood. Everyone knows that if you're not careful, bad things can happen at midnight. Events like Halloween and other holidays can also make a nice beginning for your story.

Nature Can Be Scary, Too

What mysteries are hiding within the fog? Do thunder and lightning make you want to get under the covers? Why do forests sound spooky at night? What might live in that cave? Are those voices in the wind? Nature is a fantastic way to give your story depth and can provide plenty of creepy settings. Deep water, snowy wilderness, never-ending forest, craggy mountains, murky swamps—the natural world can be a frightening place, especially after the sun goes down.

STARTING YOUR STORY

Before you can get to any of the scary stuff, a writer needs to set up some basic story elements. Who is the main character? Where does the story take place? What situation is the character in? Once the audience has this information, you can bring in the scary part. If you pretend that you are the person in the story, you can also get a sense of what could be scary.

For example, if we take a boy named Billy, put him in his house, in his bedroom, and we make it nighttime, we have set up a quick, easy way to introduce our common fear. Is there a sound outside his window? Or in his closet? Or under his bed? Is there a stuffed animal looking at him? By setting up a scene—a boy alone in his room at night—we have everything we need to make the story scary.

But why is it that a boy named Billy in his room at night is a scary thing? It's a very simple answer, and it's the main reason that a story is able to be scary. The reason is because we have ALL been alone in our room at night, so we understand what he is going through. Since we have all shared this feeling, as an audience we start to care what happens to the boy. We share his experience, so when he gets scared, WE get scared. When Billy makes a decision, we agree or disagree. When the reader cares, they have no choice but to go on the journey you are creating, and that is the magic of storytelling.

EVERY STORY HAS THREE PARTS

Now that we have a character, a place, and a common fear picked out, what comes next? If you look at most stories, they usually have a beginning, a middle, and an end. The beginning is the introduction we already talked about. We tell the reader who the character is, where they are at, and what they are doing.

The beginning section will also be where we bring in our common fear. Once we have that in place, we can move to the middle. This is where young Billy would make a choice. Will he investigate the sound? Will he hide under his blankets? Will he run out of his room? Whatever choices Billy makes will lead to the ending.

After we have our intro and our middle, we can write our ending. Think of the ending as an answer to a question. We meet Billy, Billy is scared...is there a reason for Billy to be scared or was it Billy's imagination? That answer is the ending of our story. When you need to ask story questions, answer them as you would in real life. If you were Billy, would you investigate the sound?

NORMAL THINGS CAN BE SPOOKY, TOO

Another fun way to use your imagination while writing a story is to see if you can take a normal household object and make it scary. What if a monster lived in your TV? What if your furniture moved around at night?

Using everyday objects that everybody has in their homes is a great way to create a common fear. You can also create common fears from other things that aren't normally scary to you. The person who delivers your mail, the school

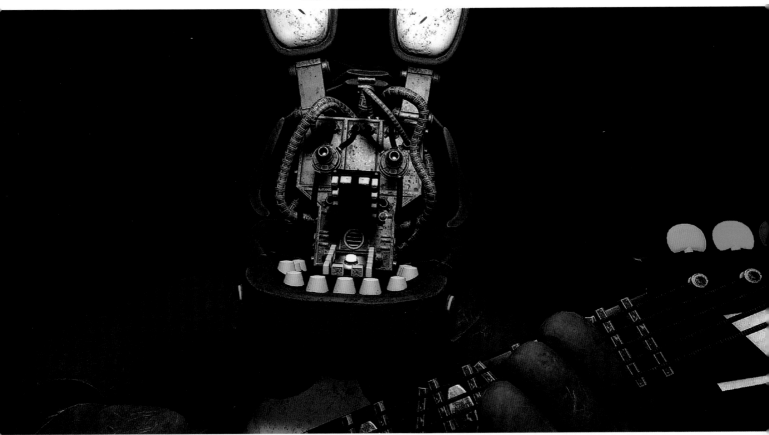

you go to, a birthday present, a favorite toy—any of those can be super scary if you put them in the right situation.

PUTTING IT ALL TOGETHER

Now we can put all of these ideas to work for us. First, you will need an outline. An outline is a type of list that contains all of your story ideas and makes it easier to remember important characters and events.

Keep your outline simple using the "Story Has Three Parts" rules. Separate the beginning, middle, and ending and put your character and location at the start. This is also where you would put weather conditions, time of day, or a holiday. Place your common fear between the beginning and the middle.

Next, write down any scary things that are going to happen to the character and the

questions that the character has to ask himself. Place the answers to the questions between the middle and end sections. Then, just write what happens to the character at the end. Once you have all of these things in your outline, writing the story will be much easier.

After you're done, read it a few times and see if it needs any changes. Letting family and friends read your story is also a great way to get ideas on how to make it better.

The fun part about writing scary fiction is that the answers to story questions help you learn about yourself. What is scary to you? What would you do in a dark forest with the wind howling on Halloween night? Would you be brave or would you run?

With a little practice, you'll find that it's easy to turn any story into a scary story, so put that imagination to work, and maybe you will be the one who writes the next great scary video game, spooky movie, or creepy book.

OTHER SCARY GAMES

LITTLE NIGHTMARES 2

Little Nightmares II is a suspense-adventure game in which you play as Mono, a young boy trapped in a world that has been distorted by the humming transmission of a distant tower.

This game animates a new kind of scary, with squishy, sickening sound effects and environments that will give you goosebumps. And sometimes the absence of sound, and the need to make use of stealth to sneak past a dangerous spot, only heightens the tension.

With a girl in a yellow raincoat named Six as his guide, Mono sets out to discover the dark secrets of The Signal Tower and save Six from her terrible fate. But their journey will not be straightforward as Mono and Six will face a gallery of new threats from the terrible residents of this world.

RESIDENT EVIL VILLAGE

With the eighth major entry in Capcom's legendary zombie video game series, the next generation of survival horror rises in the form of Resident Evil Village.

Set a few years after the horrific events in the critically acclaimed Resident Evil 7 biohazard, the storyline begins with Ethan Winters and his wife Mia living peacefully in a new location, having finally exorcised themselves of past nightmares.

But just as they are building a normal, new life together, tragedy befalls them once again. When BSAA captain Chris Redfield attacks their home, Ethan has no choice but to return to the hellscape and rescue his kidnapped daughter.

THE MEDIUM

The Medium is a third-person psychological horror game that features an innovative dual-reality gameplay, unique art style inspired by painter Zdzisław Beksiński, and original soundtrack co-composed by Arkadiusz Reikowski and Akira Yamaoka.

Discover a dark mystery only a medium can solve. Explore the real world and the spirit world at the same time. Use your psychic abilities to solve puzzles spanning both worlds, uncover deeply disturbing secrets, and survive encounters with The Maw - an entity born from an unspeakable tragedy.

UNTIL DAWN

As you contemplate and act on your options, the narrative evolves accordingly. Some of your decisions have to be made quickly, heightening your sense of panic and fear. What you decide also impacts the relationships between characters and whether or not they survive. The consequences of your choices are not always immediately clear, but let's just say it's not easy to get everyone out alive!

As you make decisions the narrative evolves in different directions. Some of these have to be made with limited time to underline the sense of fear. Your choices also impact the relationships between characters and whether they survive. The consequences of each choice are not always clear, which means that saving the whole group is difficult.

The novelty of Until Dawn is the range of possible narrative directions and outcomes, with more than 250 different endings and even more ways to reach them. The combination of suspense-horror, believable and interesting characters, and directing the protagonists makes for a unique experience.

THE EVIL WITHIN 2

From Shinji Mikami, The Evil Within 2 takes the acclaimed franchise to a new level with its unique blend of psychological thrills and true survival horror.

Sebastian Castellanos has lost everything, including his daughter, Lily. To save her, he's forced to partner with Mobius, the shadowy group responsible for the destruction of his former life. For his last chance at redemption, the only way out is in.

As Castellanos, you must return to your nightmare and win back your life and your daughter. Discover horrifying domains while proceeding deliberately with caution, face disturbing and devilish enemies, and see if you can survive the darkness. And always remember, discretion is the better part of valor.

MUNDAUN

Presented as a hand-penciled horror tale set in a dark, secluded valley of the Alps, Mundaun may very well herald a whole new way of thinking about game visuals. The artistic style infuses the game with extra doom, gloom, and time period vibe.

Explore various areas full of secrets to discover, survive hostile encounters, drive cool vehicles, fill your inventory with useful tools, and solve a variety of hand-crafted puzzles.

DEAD BY DAYLIGHT

Dead by Daylight is an asymmetrical multiplayer horror game where one player takes on the role of a brutal Killer and up to four other people can play the role of Survivors.

As Killer, your goal is to "catch" as many Survivors as possible. As a Survivor, your goal is to, you guessed it, escape and avoid being caught and killed. Go! Run!

from PS4 Pro

DAYS GONE

Days Gone is an action-adventure survival horror game. Played from a third-person perspective, it features a vast open world sandbox environment the player can explore, including many exquisitely detailed real-life locations in Oregon such as Marion Forks, Belknap Crater, and Crater Lake.

Set in a post-apocalyptic Pacific Northwest two years after a global pandemic, Days Gone follows the story of Deacon St. John, a former member of a biker gang. Hostile encounters come from both human enemies and infected beings called Freakers.

Deacon can engage in different types of combat including stealth and usage of firearms. A favorite game feature is his sweet drifter bike, which is used as your primary mode of transportation and as a mobile inventory stash.

ALIENS: FIRETEAM ELITE

Set in the iconic Alien universe, Aliens: Fireteam Elite is a cooperative third-person survival shooter that drops your fireteam of hardened marines into a desperate fight to contain the evolving Xenomorph threat.

Face off against waves of terrifying Xenomorph and Weyland-Yutani Synthetic foes alongside two players or AI teammates, as you and your fireteam desperately fight your way through four unique campaigns that introduce new storylines to the Alien universe. Create and customize your own Colonial

Marine, choosing from an extensive variety of classes, weapons, gear and perks, battling overwhelming odds in this heart-pounding survival shooter experience.

ONCE UPON A TIME IN ROSWELL

What do you get when you combine a ghost story with aliens and set it near the legendary Area 57?

Once Upon a Time in Roswell is a first-person psychological horror game that chronicles the story of a family's disappearance in 1947 in Roswell, NM.

As you embark on an investigation to find the folks, you catch a horrific glimpse of flashbacks of the world war, and beings not of this earth. As you realize the terrible truth that claimed this family, you must navigate their haunted home and the apparitions within.

VHS

A super cool, super clever tribute to the classic 1980s horror classics akin to the popular Stranger Things TV series, VHS features a quartet of small-town teens who must face-off against monsters brought to life in the aisles of a 1980s video store.

VHS combines twitch skill based-gameplay with movie set inspired maps, exaggerated weapons, and a legion of doom's worth of characters and enemies that have nothing nice in mind for you.

As the power dynamics fluctuate between the teens and their sinister stalkers, gameplay can flip-flop from climactic boss battles to skin-of-your-teeth escape and survival scenarios.

THIS ISN'T WORKING FOR ME

A PRACTICAL GUIDE FOR MAKING EVERY RELATIONSHIP IN YOUR LIFE MORE FULFILLING, AUTHENTIC, AND INTENTIONAL

ILENE S. COHEN, PHD • EDRICA D. RICHARDSON, PHD

Published by
Bridge City Books, an imprint of PESI Publishing, Inc.
3839 White Ave
Eau Claire, WI 54703

Cover and interior design by Emily Dyer
Editing by Chelsea Thompson

ISBN 9781962305037 (print)
ISBN 9781962305051 (ePDF)
ISBN 9781962305044 (ePUB)

Bridge City Books

DEDICATION

To my husband, Moises.
Thank you for always being my
biggest fan and supporter.
—*Dr. Ilene*

To all those who are learning to have a voice.
To my "framily" for their relationships.
—*Dr. E*

CONTENTS

INTRODUCTION

"Why can't you just get along?!"

Growing up, many of us heard this phrase when we were fighting with a sibling. (We may have even used it with our own children.) Wouldn't it be nice if getting along with others were that easy? There is no way around it—relationships, even the best and closest ones, are challenging.

Most of us want to prevent drama and pain in our relationships, yet somehow remain stuck in a cycle that feels too hard to stop. So hard, in fact, that it might seem easier to decide we are "done" with people (or at least with a particular person) rather than try any longer. However, relationships are an essential part of being human. Regardless of social class, gender, sexual orientation, race, or religion, we are all social and emotional beings connected to the people in our lives today and to the generations who came before us. The interconnection between ourselves and our loved ones can feel magical and rich when everyone gets along. However, when we are negatively triggered in our relationships, it can create an emotional reactivity that leads to unhealthy responses. These unhealthy responses make it almost impossible to "just get along" because they are created when our anxiety is heightened. When our anxiety is high, our logical brains get hijacked, rendering our thoughts and behavior irrational.

Anxiety is part of the survival instinct in every living thing—it's our built-in alarm system that helps keep us alive. Anxiety is a natural and appropriate response to a perceived threat. Even though the human brain has evolved to a higher level of thinking, our survival instinct is the same as it's always been. If anything, it's become even more alert to dangers other than immediate threats to our physical safety. After all, since most of us do not need to constantly worry about dangers like being attacked by a wild animal in our modern era, we're more aware of our higher-level human needs, such as our sense of purpose, value, and meaning, as well as our need for love and emotional security. Given that our relationships play an essential role in fulfilling these needs, a threat to our relationships can bring up just as much anxiety as a threat to our very existence.

Instinctive ways of managing relationship anxiety can include yelling or using harmful language, physically or emotionally cutting off communication with certain people, ignoring our own needs in order to maintain a relationship, drinking or using drugs to deal with the problems in our relationships, or brushing conflict under the rug to avoid facing the issues. These behaviors derive from our instinctive fight, flight, freeze, and fawn responses, which are activated when we perceive a threat to our survival.

One reason we can't "just get along" is that our relationship difficulties are often exaggerated by how we respond to situations when we're anxious, leading to even greater stress and difficulty in our relationships. This book will teach you how you can respond less from anxiety and more from logic when you feel threatened in your relationships. One way of working on this is understanding how interconnected you are to the people in your life—such as your family, friends, coworkers, and community—and how this interconnectedness has both benefits and downfalls.

Who We Are

Dr. Ilene S. Cohen (Dr. Ilene) has studied, written about, and worked with individuals, couples, and families for over 15 years. She believes that no matter the presenting problem, people can benefit by working on themselves in relation to their family of origin. Dr. Ilene knows the importance of this work through her personal life and professional career. She does not see her clients as having internal psychological problems but as humans struggling to live independently while remaining connected with others.

Dr. Edrica D. Richardson (Dr. E) has studied, written about, and worked with individuals, couples, and families for over 17 years. She identifies herself as a relationship therapist because she sees the client's presenting problem relationally and contextually. She believes that as you better understand your interactions with the people and things in your life, you get to know yourself better. Dr. E knows that change starts with understanding how vital it is to show up to therapy with every part of ourselves, including our family history and our personal experiences.

The Complex Dilemma of Navigating Human Relationships

Humans, like all other mammals, need each other to survive. We are social beings at our core; our brains are hardwired for connection, community, and loving relationships. From infancy onward, we rely on each other to fulfill our needs for care, tenderness, emotional support, and emotional and spiritual growth. We thrive the most when we are connected to and supported by each other, and we suffer when these connections and support are not available to us. However, many of us are never adequately taught how to create or maintain these connections throughout life.

Relationships are complex because each one is different. Each of us brings our own biology, perspective, feelings, and behaviors into each relationship, along with rational and irrational ideas of what the relationship should look like. As we grow, the perspectives we gain alter our relationships, requiring us to constantly relearn how to navigate our relationships and ourselves within them.

One of the main messages of this book is that our relationships, especially the ones we find most challenging, play a crucial role in our growth and self-improvement. Whatever emotionally triggers us or makes us anxious around someone else is telling us something about ourselves. If we can reframe relationship "problems" as opportunities to grow, change, and mature, we have a chance to solve our biggest challenges with calm minds rather than preprogrammed emotional reactions. Building fulfilling relationships ultimately comes down to making changes within yourself that change your connections to others.

Your Relationship Itinerary

It's hard to overstate the value of therapy when working to improve your most difficult relationships. There are so many benefits to speaking with a neutral person who understands human behavior and relationships. However, books like this one are helpful as a supplement to therapy or as an alternative for people who cannot commit to treatment due to time or financial constraints. To help you better understand the thought behind the guidance provided in this book, we've outlined some of the different therapeutic treatment modalities that influence our clinical approach.

BOWEN FAMILY SYSTEMS THEORY

Bowen family systems theory considers an individual's behavior through the context of their family and relationships. The theory posits that emotional behaviors within a family unit are connected, meaning that one person's emotions, thoughts, and behaviors can affect everyone else within that unit. When we understand our family and the interactional patterns within it, we can see our part of the problem in a current relationship and decide what we would like to do differently.

One of the critical concepts of Bowen family systems theory is an understanding of the importance of *differentiation of self*—that is, the ability to function as an individual while being a part of a group (Kerr & Bowen, 1988). Differentiation is key to balancing individuality and togetherness within a relationship. It permits a person to operate independently while also being emotionally involved with others. Bowen therapists coach their clients in being more of an autonomous self in all their relationships.

ATTACHMENT THEORY

Attachment is a deep and lasting emotional bond between people. Attachment theory explains how the parent-child relationship develops and how it influences a child's growth as an individual. John Bowlby (1973) developed this theory to describe how our early relationships with primary caregivers create our ideas of what love looks like. Our view of ourselves and other people is formed by how well our caregivers provided safety and security for us as infants and how available and responsive they were to meet our needs.

The four attachment patterns identified by this theory are *secure, avoidant, ambivalent,* and *disorganized* (Ainsworth et al., 1978; Main & Solomon, 1990). Secure attachment to caregivers provides protection and comfort while allowing for autonomy and the exploration of one's environment. It is marked later in life by an ability to be *interdependent*—that balance of intimacy and independence (Johnson & Greenberg, 1992). Securely attached children adapt the best to life changes and transitions.

THE GOTTMAN METHOD

The Gottman method is an empirically researched method of couples therapy that focuses on increasing closeness and friendship in intimate relationships, resolving conflict, and creating shared meaning in life. A Gottman therapist typically applies the principles from Gottman's research to each couple's unique patterns and problems. Even though these principles are usually utilized in couples work, they can help any close relationship flourish.

Latest Research on Relationships

In addition to the treatment modalities we've just listed, we draw from the latest research on relationships, including findings from neuroscience on what happens to our brains when we are emotionally triggered in our relationships and how to calm our reactive brains so that we can be more responsive. We also include information from social science on the value of vulnerability and connection.

How to Use This Book

This Isn't Working for Me is an interactive guide that offers step-by-step strategies for improving the relationships in your life. Each chapter explains the stages of growth in a healthy, fulfilling relationship and offers exercises, reflective questions, and eye-opening secrets to help you implement and integrate what you have learned.

Our goal is to give you tools for seeing yourself and your relationships in a new way so you can feel empowered and have more flexibility in your relationships. This frees you to be yourself and to respond to others in more effective ways. We encourage you to approach this book and its activities with an open mind and to bring your personal truth to the surface as you work through it. The better you can understand yourself, the more authentically you can respond to the people you're in relationship with. We wish you clarity on this new journey—we are right here with you along the way!

PART 1

UNDERSTANDING RELATIONSHIPS

When engaging in any change process, it is essential to hold on to the reasons for your effort and the goals you have in mind. In this first section of the book, we will explore why relationships are important, what healthy relationships look like, and why they are worth the effort even when they are not easy. Once you fully understand the importance of fulfilling relationships and why they can be hard to achieve, you will feel motivated to continue this life-enriching work.

CHAPTER 1

The Truth About Fulfilling Relationships

The fact that you picked up this book tells us that you already get how important relationships are, though you may not know precisely why. Forming relationships is an automatic behavior for human beings. Something within us knows that relationships foster happiness and lifelong fulfillment . . . at least, we believe that they are supposed to.

It's true that relationships are crucial for the quality of our lives. In fact, relationships have been essential to our very survival as a species. Over time, the "safety in numbers" principle that allowed families and communities to protect their members evolved into an emotional interdependence that can promote happiness and serve as a resource for us in tough times. Our connections with the people we love can delay or prevent the onset of mental and physical health concerns and are better predictors of life satisfaction than social class, IQ, or genetics. A 75-year longitudinal Harvard study supported this by showing that happiness and lifelong fulfillment were connected to the quality of the participants' closest relationships; the study also demonstrated that the participants who were most satisfied in their relationships at age 50 were the healthiest at age 80 (Curtin, 2017).

Our relationships are a primary influence on our life experiences, shaping who we become and how we see the world. In particular, our earliest relationships influence how we interact with the people that become our friends, coworkers, employees, lovers, or neighbors. If you think about it, we cannot fully know who we are (or be known for who we are) until we are in relationship with others.

Despite all these benefits, the pain that relationships have caused you may be overshadowing their benefits and worth. While many people understand that our past, specifically our childhood, impacts who we become, few understand that our struggles today are caused not by our past experiences in and of themselves, but by our tendency to recreate the past in our present relationships.

What Is the Meaning of Relationships?

A relationship is an ongoing series of interactions between people. (We usually think of them as being between two people, but they can be interactions among more than two people.) Two people who are significant to each other may go through many interactions in a day; for example, a married couple may have hundreds of different interactions in the same day. Over time, people develop interactional patterns in relationships that create their expectations, feelings, and emotional reactivity to each other.

Bowen's family systems theory teaches that relationships are a developing process of interaction open to continuous modification (Bowen, 1978). In this book you will learn more about this development process, what it means for your relationships with others, and how you can modify your interactions with others.

Have you ever noticed that you can think more clearly and be more "yourself" when you're alone or with people who don't trigger you? Bowen's theory explains that our relationships impact our inner world more than our inner world affects our relationships. While we are our own individuals, our relationships serve as a context that influences how we feel inside and how we behave in connection to another person. The more intimate or emotionally significant the relationship, the more it affects and impacts our internal selves.

This impact begins with our very first relationships—that is, the ones we form as infants with our caregivers. The information we gather in our earliest relationships is at the heart of a rich and complex brain-building process. In early brain development, experience creates expectation, which changes perception. As a baby experiences responses from their caregivers, their brain starts to form expectations for how they will be treated and how they should respond. For example, if the caregivers consistently respond to the baby's cries by holding them close, speaking in a soothing tone, and meeting their needs for milk, a diaper change, and so on, the child feels comforted and learns to expect similar responses in the future.

As repeated similar experiences strengthen these expectations, the child's brain forms perceptions of their social and emotional world. These perceptions influence how they understand their environment, relate to others, and engage in learning. While a child's relationship with their mother is typically the most important in this process, many relationships shape a child's developing perceptions—parents, stepparents, grandparents, siblings, cousins, aunts, uncles, close family friends, teachers, and others who are significantly present in the child's life. Ultimately, the interactional patterns created in these initial relationships construct certain expectations, feelings, and emotional reactivity that the child carries forward as they grow, including how that child is attracted to future relationships. With each new relationship, patterns are reinforced and the child's perceptions are deepened.

For example, if your role in your family growing up was to be the "fixer"—the person who broke up fights between your parents—you would likely automatically continue that behavior when you were triggered by instability or difficulty in a relationship later in life. Your part in the interactional cycle of your family led you to see yourself as the person who must take on the responsibilities, emotions, well-being, and needs of those around you, whether they want you to or not, in order to "calm things down." That pattern of giving up your autonomy in the hope of creating stability in your relationships may repeat in some or all of the close relationships you experience throughout your life.

As you read this book, you will come to better understand the part you play in your relationships, whether it is the "fixer" or another role you have inherited. Along with seeing clearly the interactional patterns you find yourself repeating, you'll learn the benefits of making changes to the role you're used to playing in your close relationships.

What Is the Goal of Relationships?

When you think about it, this is a very complex question to ask. As we've already established, relationships are essential to human life. While the most obvious "goal" of having relationships may be our survival (as individuals and as a species through reproduction), various scientists have said that humans' advanced brains have developed mainly as a result of the relationship process and the complexities of our interactions with others. In other words, the goal of relationships is to develop how we think, feel, and behave. This means that ultimately, your goals for your relationships are yours to define from one season of your life to the next.

In the therapy setting, we often encounter people who believe that relationships cannot change, particularly relationships that are not going the way they hoped. What they mean is that they are stuck in a pattern that they can't break out of. We agree that some patterns are deeply complicated and difficult to change. But even a "stuck" relationship can improve if one or both people in it find a way to make a small change in the part they play in the interactional pattern and learn to sustain that change across time.

As you work through this book, you will look closely at the interactional patterns you have with significant people in your life. When an interaction gets tense, our tendency is to focus on the other person: "Our relationship is in trouble because *they* do this or are that way." This is where the internal change comes in. If you can change your part in the interaction and sustain that change, the other person has no choice but to respond in a different way from before. Two people cannot stay in the same dance if one person changes their moves. If you do something outside the established pattern, both of you now have a different pattern . . . and a changed relationship! (Of course, this is easier said than done.)

Before moving on, it's important to explain a distinction that many of our clients get confused about: We are not making changes within ourselves *so that* we can change the other person. Instead, we are making changes to the interactional pattern in ways that benefit ourselves and the relationship. Doing this work on yourself does not guarantee the other person will change their behaviors. And if they don't, it does not mean that you are to blame. You only have control over yourself and the changes you are willing to make—in particular, the change from automatically reacting to relationship distress to managing your emotional reactivity with the understanding you've gained about yourself and your patterns within relationships.

IMPORTANT NOTE

This book will challenge you to take an honest look at how your actions may be contributing to patterns in your relationships with others. However, we want to make it clear that you are not responsible for the other person's actions or causing them to behave as they do. This is especially important to remember if the other person is experiencing addiction or is being abusive toward you in any way—physically, sexually, verbally, emotionally, financially, spiritually, or otherwise.

If this is the case for you (or if you're questioning whether it might be), we encourage you to seek further counsel from a trusted therapist, support group, hotline, or shelter. Ultimately, you will still need to change your own behavior—as this is the only thing truly within your control—but you may decide that your goal is to set new boundaries, reduce contact, or end the relationship, rather than attempting to repair or deepen that connection. Your safety, health, and well-being are of the utmost importance.

Diving into Your Ideas About Relationships

How you think about relationships is shaped by many variables, starting with your overall upbringing: your family's ideas and beliefs about relationships, how your parents or caregivers interacted, the TV shows and movies you watched, the books you read, and the community you lived in.

Taking all those variables into account, think about what relationships mean to you.

- What were your most prominent relationships growing up?
- From whom did you learn the most about relationships?
- How do your family of origin's ideas about relationships influence you now?

Write some of your reflections below.

_____

_____

_____

_____

_____

_____

_____

_____

_____

_____

What Are Healthy Relationships?

While all relationships are different, there are key characteristics that distinguish relationships that are healthy from those that are unhealthy. Healthy relationships of any kind—whether romantic, friend, or familial relationships—involve trust, authenticity, respect, open communication, effort, and collaboration.

- **Trust** is critical to any healthy relationship because trust is the basis for lasting psychological connectedness. Research suggests that your early attachment style (how you form solid emotional bonds) influences your ability to trust others. As we have stated, relationship experiences from early in life help shape your expectations for future relationships. If your past connections have been secure, stable, and trusting, you are more likely to have trust in future relationships. If your past relationships were unstable, unpredictable, and undependable, you might have to work on some trust injuries while reading this book.

- **Authenticity** goes hand in hand with trust. After all, it is tough to trust a partner or friend who is not fully honest about who they are or what they've done. While relationships have varying levels of openness and self-disclosure, you should never feel like you have to hide or change who you are to be in a relationship. A healthy relationship supports you in feeling that you can be your true and authentic self. Being open and honest with each other not only helps people feel more connected in any relationship, but also helps sustain relational trust.

- **Respect** in relationships requires each person to offer support and security to the others. Showing respect for one another includes active listening, not procrastinating when asked to do something important, being understanding and honest, building each other up, showing appreciation, and having empathy for one another.

- **Open communication** is the heart of all healthy relationships. Remaining respectful and empathetic as the other person discusses their thoughts and feelings, even when these are not what you expected or wanted to hear, is a sign of healthy communication and resolution. Since even the best relationships involve conflict, knowing how to argue and resolve differences respectfully is much better than simply avoiding arguments to keep the peace.

- **Effort**—dedicating energy, time, and thoughtfulness to benefit another person—is an essential component of any healthy relationship. Warm feelings alone cannot sustain a relationship; these feelings must be outwardly demonstrated through affirming words, time spent together, and support for each other's triumphs and challenges. In some relationships, efforts like these seem to flow easily between people. Other relationships require more thought, care, and willingness to go outside our comfort zone. Requiring more effort does not mean that the relationship is less worthwhile. Some of our most important relationships are the ones that ask more of us, whether it be reaching out more often, scheduling regular quality time, or being open to ideas that differ from our own.

- **Collaboration** refers to doing things with or for one another to produce an outcome more significant than one person would achieve on their own. Healthy relationships are naturally reciprocal in their collaboration; no one keeps score or feels that one person is in debt to the other. Some relationships may not always be 100 percent equal in terms of what each person offers, but imbalances are okay if each person is satisfied with the support available to them from the other.

It probably seems obvious that any relationship would benefit from implementing these behaviors. If we lived in an ideal world with ideal people, healthy relationship characteristics like these would be the norm. The problem comes in when we look to others to display all these characteristics all the time as a condition for having a relationship with them.

Have you ever found yourself wishing for more trust in your marriage, but telling yourself it's just not possible because your partner has lied to you in the past?

Have you pushed your parents for better communication, only to get defensive when they come to you with a criticism?

Have you yearned for honesty from your friends while not being honest yourself?

What if, instead of focusing on what other people can do to make your relationships healthier, you shifted the focus to yourself?

As we mentioned in the introduction, when just one person in the relationship changes their part in the pattern, it generates change in the relationship as a whole. The journey to more fulfilling and healthier relationships begins when you let people be who they are for now and instead ask yourself questions like *How am I implementing these vital characteristics in my own life?* and *How can I work on changing my steps in the dance?*

The Benefits of Fulfilling Relationships

Many studies have documented the benefits of being in a relationship with others. Healthy social connections reduce rates of anxiety and depression, increase self-esteem, teach empathy, and even strengthen the immune system. Relationships give us a sense of community, belongingness, and support; they also give us a place to grow, learn, and evolve as individuals.

Write down five benefits you think you get out of your relationships.

1. _____
2. _____
3. _____
4. _____
5. _____

Write down five benefits you think others gain from being in a relationship with you.

1. _____
2. _____
3. _____
4. _____
5. _____

Why Are Some Relationships So Difficult?

Just because relationships are essential in our lives (well, maybe *because* they are essential) does not mean they are always great experiences. The interdependent nature of being human has its downside. We all struggle to balance our innate desire for individuality with the magnetic pull of being with others. We see this struggle at many stages in human development. The urge to be our own person starts early in life, and when our efforts to find or express our autonomous self are met with pushback from our family members, friends, culture, or society at large, we might rebel, create conflict, or distance ourselves. At other times along our journey, we may connect so deeply with others or become so dependent on the comfort they provide that we lose our sense of self. Believing their acceptance will make us complete and whole, we might go overboard in accommodating, giving in, and looking to others for answers.

Whether we lean toward or away from relationships to manage the fear of standing in our own autonomy while remaining connected to others, the outcome is the same: We become more reactive and sensitive. The very things we do to manage our sensitivity to the relationships in our lives can be the things that create even more chaos in our relationships.

Relationships are best sustained by people communicating through their vulnerabilities. However, many of us carry complicated feelings from past relationships, like fear of failure, abandonment, and family trauma. This pain can make our emotions more easily triggered by those we love and who love us, especially when we feel our autonomy is being infringed upon. When we ignore our pain and emotions, we become prisoners of the past, susceptible to repeating old negative patterns in our current relationships. When we fear vulnerability, we look for reasons to run from, numb, or ignore any sign of distress in our current relationships. A significant relationship is an open abyss filled with possibilities, misunderstandings, love, hope, hurt, and growth all at once. Too often, this leads us to give up on relationships before giving ourselves a chance to see past our triggered responses and make changes to them.

The Challenge of Change

Have you ever tried changing a behavior or habit that no longer serves you? If you have, you know how difficult it can be. Change is hard because many of our behaviors are automatic, especially in long-term relationships where the interactional patterns are deeply ingrained. It's much more comfortable to automatically do what feels good (or at least familiar) in the moment instead of managing the discomfort of change while keeping in mind our future goals. Our brains register any modification, even a positive one, as a threat to our survival. As a result, your anxiety naturally increases when you change certain behaviors, even those that do not serve you.

For example, Dr. Ilene often works with people-pleasers—those who tend to give in to others' requests in an automatic way as a survival trait. They do this as a way of managing their fear of others disapproving of them or reacting to them in a negative way. When a people-pleaser begins making the changes necessary to stop their people-pleasing behaviors, their anxiety about disapproval actually intensifies for some time. They are changing their part in their relationship pattern, and with that comes an increase in fear and anxiety.

Our automatic behaviors serve to soothe us in the moment of distress, but they prevent us from living out our values and principles. Still, even though we might know that a particular behavior is harmful in the long run, it is hard to change because living in the tension is challenging. It's no wonder that we push others to change rather than make the effort to change ourselves. It's also no wonder that this tactic does not work very well. If it's hard to change even when you have the motivation, it is almost impossible to change when you feel forced.

Shifting your focus to what *you* can do to make your relationship better will push you to confront the difficulty of change. This is humbling in a good way—it helps you create room for other people to change if they choose to. After all, when a person feels criticized, disliked, or unappreciated, they tend to go into self-protection mode. They are more likely to change if they first feel accepted for who they are.

But again, we must always keep in mind that we can only influence change; we can't force it. Many people stay in unfulfilling relationships with a desire to change or improve the other person. However, change comes from the inside first, and it begins with being a better partner to yourself through genuine self-love, kinder self-talk, and grace when you make mistakes. If you focus your efforts on being your own friend and doing the best you can to improve the way you show up in your relationship, this will help you repair hurts, navigate challenging moments, and hold steady amid the tension that positive change can bring.

Your Willingness to Change

The following checklist will help you see how willing you are to make changes in yourself that can lead to change in your relationships. Think about how you might respond when in conflict with someone in your life and check off whatever applies to you from the list that follows. Please answer honestly; remember, there is no judgment here. The more self-aware you are about your usual responses to an intense relationship, the more options you have when deciding to make changes in relation to others.

- ❏ When there is conflict in my relationships, I usually blame the other person.
- ❏ I will change when the other person does what I need them to do.

❏ When the other person is misbehaving, I don't see why I should be the one to make changes.

❏ I do not want anything to do with the other person if they don't get help or change.

❏ I would rather not be around people with different opinions than mine on essential topics.

❏ If someone makes me uncomfortable, I avoid them.

❏ If I am in a fight with someone, people who care about me shouldn't talk to that person.

❏ I am relieved when I cut people out of my life.

❏ I am more focused on what other people do with their time than on myself and my own life.

❏ I often try to fix others' behaviors, views, feelings, or circumstances rather than look at what I can work on within myself.

❏ I refuse to be kind to someone who upsets me.

To assess your willingness to change, add up your points by counting the number of checked boxes:

- **Between 6 and 11:** If you fall within this range, you will likely find it difficult to make changes. You are more concerned with the other person and what they can do to improve the relationship than with the part you play. It would be best to address this by becoming an observer of your own life and reactions. In addition to working through this book, you might want to reach out to a therapist or good friend who can help you see how you may contribute to the issues in your life.

- **Between 1 and 5:** If your score falls here, you are open to taking a look at yourself, though you may still have a hard time keeping your focus on yourself when you are facing relationship difficulties. You are so close to being willing to make changes! Working on the activities in this book will help you get there.

Making Your Relationships a Priority

When we work on building solid connections, the less reactive and overwhelmed we will get when an inevitable disagreement occurs. However, all relationships, even healthy ones, can sometimes feel disconnected, especially when distractions get in the way. A common complaint we hear from couples is that one partner feels underappreciated or that the relationship itself is not treated like it is essential, but instead is pushed aside by the challenges of work, family, and housekeeping responsibilities. (We hear the same complaint from adolescents who feel their parents do not remember that they exist beyond their academic success.) However, it's more likely that the disconnection is a pattern that both partners have fallen into. While people in disconnected relationships may not argue a lot, they also do not talk beyond superficial conversations. The connections have fallen between the cracks of daily routine—each person is doing their own thing without taking the time to invest in a meaningful relationship with the other.

When other activities, interests, or preoccupations demand our availability and attention, we can end up short-changing our relationships. Even in the relationships we consider most important, we might be perceived as distant and absent. Taking an inventory of how we spend our time helps correct this problem. It shows us what we've prioritized over our relationships, allowing us to make adjustments that treat these relationships as necessary as they are.

One of the first adjustments you can make is spending more quality time with your loved one to maintain your connection. Spending quality time together is vital in any relationship. We understand that life is busy and it is hard to have consistent one-on-one time with the people we love. One way to spend quality time together is to remain present with that person in any interaction you have, no matter how far removed or brief it might be. When you are on the phone, on video, or in person, make an effort to stay curious about how the person is doing and ask what you are interested to know about, whether it be something from the past week, their childhood, or anything in between. There are conversation card games designed for families or couples that you can play together or simply use for ideas. Additionally, not all conversations have to be deep to be meaningful. Making small gestures, like sending a "thinking of you" text message or picking up the phone to say hi, helps build a connection with others by showing them that you are interested in their lives.

◇◇◇

This is especially true for children and teenagers; it is of so much value for them to see that the adults in their life are present and interested in them.

◇◇◇

Sometimes we take people for granted when we believe that they will always be there for us. When you find yourself making excuses for not fostering those connections, remember that you can always find time for what you want to be available for. Knowing that the quality of your relationships determines the quality of your life, it stands to reason that by making your relationships a priority, you are making yourself a priority.

Setting Your Relationship Aspirations

Working on your relationships is not a task but a journey. As you set out on this journey, it's helpful to keep your "why" in mind. What are the specific reasons that make your relationships worth improving? In moments of overwhelm or frustration, keeping your reasons in the front of your mind will help you stay the course. Take a moment to consider the following questions.

Why is working on my relationships vital to me?

_____

_____

_____

_____

_____

What would I like to get from taking the time to work on myself in relation to others?

_____

_____

_____

_____

_____

How do my most intense relationships affect me, both physically and mentally?

_____

_____

_____

_____

_____

If my personal relationships were more fulfilling, what difference would that make in my life?

_____

_____

_____

_____

_____

Starting Your Journey to Better Relationships

In general, people come to therapy or books like this one looking for help in creating a more fulfilling, authentic life. For most people, relationships play a major role in how they envision such a life.

You may be looking to soften an intense and challenging relationship, rejuvenate a relationship that feels flat and unfulfilling, or perhaps attract a compatible life partner. No matter what your motivation is for embarking on this work, bear in mind that this is a process, not a project. Human beings exist in a constant state of evolution, subject to ever-changing conditions. Rigid end goals and deadlines don't apply to our individual growth, so why should we apply them to our relationships?

As the saying goes, "Rome wasn't built in a day." This work can be delicate and difficult at times. Please take it slowly, one day at a time. When you feel overwhelmed, take a break and remind yourself that even though you are responsible for your part, it still is not all on you to "fix" your relationships. No one is perfect, but the fact that you are taking the time to work on yourself so your relationships can thrive speaks volumes about your character and what is important to you. Giving yourself and your relationships space and grace to grow is a gesture of true love.

That said, none of us will get it right all the time. Believe it or not, mistakes can be a valuable part of the relationship building process—admitting to them and talking about them with your partner, family, or friends will help you not only understand what went wrong, but also forgive and let go of mistakes that you make and that others make. In so doing, you will give yourself and your relationships more space and time for joy.

Positive Relationship Affirmations

Positive affirmations are phrases you say to overcome negative thoughts and build yourself up, especially amid challenging situations. Relationship affirmations work the same way, reminding you that you are worthy to love others and of being loved. Write down some affirmations that capture specifically what you want to create in your relationships to motivate you toward change. Here are a few examples to get you started:

- I am capable of creating fulfilling relationships.

- I will have open and honest relationships.

- I am strong enough to change my relationships in a more positive direction.

- I am worthy of mutual, respectful, strong relationships.

_____

_____

_____

_____

_____

_____

_____

_____

_____

_____

◇◇

Chapter Takeaways

In this chapter, you received a detailed description of relationships through a systemic lens, along with some other important information on significant relationships. We hope that you have:

✓ Explored what relationships mean to you

✓ Learned what healthy relationships look like

✓ Understood why change is so difficult

✓ Recognized that you play a part in your relationship patterns

✓ Gained motivation to make your relationships a priority

✓ Identified some personal aspirations you want to achieve in your relationships

In the next chapter, we will offer practical tips for how you can prepare yourself for your unique journey toward stronger, more fulfilling relationships. We'll also break down and summarize the six secrets and stages of healthy relationships.

◇◇

CHAPTER 2

Your Personal Journey

Life is not only about achieving one specific end goal. It's about finding out who you are and being more of that person with every experience you face. Living with the company of fulfilling relationships is an incredibly important part of that journey of discovery, offering a variety of growth opportunities to help you evolve the person you are. As you evolve, you will realize that one-size-fits-all relationships and lifestyles do not exist. Everyone is different in what they look for in their relationships, whom they want to spend their time with, and how they want to live. Something might work for you that does not work for someone else, and that is okay. When you live as an autonomous self, you are free and flexible in relationships and aren't worried about how others say you should live or what your relationships should look like. The more you live as an independent self, not basing your life and decisions on others' expectations of you, the more your relationships will feel like a breath of fresh air rather than a burden. When we are solid in who we are, the inevitable ups and downs of relationships don't rock us as much as they used to, and we can ride the waves of life, being clear about who we are while remaining connected to the ones we love.

Unfortunately, instead of living as our autonomous selves, many of us live on autopilot, spending most of our time focused on everything other than ourselves—from spouses, family members, or coworkers to politics, social media, entertainment, and even the weather. Looking outside ourselves feels instinctual, not to mention a lot more comfortable than turning our focus inward. However, inward is where you start learning about who you are.

It can be hard to look at ourselves in moments of relationship distress because we think of it as taking the blame. However, this isn't the case. We look inward instead of outward to make real and meaningful changes for ourselves and our relationships. For example, if your coworker is being cold and demanding, instead of trying to figure out the meaning behind his actions, you can consider what they mean to *you*:

- What feelings and thoughts did his coldness and demandingness bring up for me?

- What was my immediate reaction to those feelings?

- Why did I respond to him the way I did?

- How would I like to respond to him in the future?

- Who else in my life brings up a similar reaction from me?

When you see shifting the focus to yourself as a way to get to know yourself better, not as a way to take the blame, it helps with the transition. Learning about who you are is a pretty big undertaking. The best way to go about it is to take yourself on as a research project, examining yourself with curiosity rather than judgment. We know this may sound a little self-centered, but the more we learn about our instinctive ways of managing relationship tension and our automatic reactions to stress (both of which contribute to our interactional patterns), the better chance we have at changing these responses if they aren't working for us.

Since improving your relationships starts with improving yourself, let's use this chapter to help you get to know *you* better.

Mindful Journal Practice

Mindfulness is a valuable way to get to know yourself better. Mindfulness helps us to calm down and relax, giving us access to the more logical parts of our brain. When we have more access to the rational parts of our brain, the more we get to know our genuine responses to people and situations that occur around us.

One of the easiest ways to apply mindfulness is through meditative journaling. To start, find a quiet and comfortable space where you won't be distracted. Sit down, relax, and draw your focus to your breathing, inhaling through your nose and exhaling out of your mouth.

When your breathing becomes regular and even, begin to visualize yourself in a moment of feeling triggered or emotionally hurt in a relationship. Think about your "go-to" moves when someone upsets you. Do you try to please them? Do you freeze up? Do you distance yourself? Do you snap or yell at them?

Now think about the impact other people have on you when your relationship is in trouble. Think about how much space others take up in your life. When you are triggered, how much do you focus on the other person or the problem they create? Picture yourself accepting the other person for who they are in those moments. Imagine how much lighter you would feel if you decided not to take on their emotions as your own.

Afterward, reflect on your meditation by jotting down your thoughts in response to the following questions.

What are your natural responses to relationship anxiety? Do you distance yourself, try to please the other person, avoid them, escalate the conflict, or do something else?

_____

_____

_____

_____

What are the seeming benefits of your current response pattern? Does it help you in any way, even momentarily?

_____

_____

_____

_____

What is your ideal goal for moments of relationship anxiety? For example, would you like to resolve the conflict calmly? Would you like to focus on meeting your own needs rather than on pleasing the other person?

_____

_____

_____

_____

What could you do differently next time? What type of response do you think would lead you closer to your goal?

_____

_____

_____

_____

Are You Open to Starting This Journey?

In the previous chapter, we outlined how many aspects of your life are positively impacted by having fulfilling relationships. You may feel ready to have stronger relationships but not be sure what to do about it. Digging deep into our unique personal feelings and experiences can be challenging. It is hard to change what feels comfortable, familiar, and protective. We are going against what we do to relieve tension and anxiety when we work on ourselves; therefore, we will feel uncomfortable. Before diving into the work, prepare by thinking through some fundamental questions about where you are right now.

ARE YOU PREPARED TO LOOK AT YOUR FAMILY HISTORY?

In our private practices, we usually begin by evaluating a client's past, including their family history and upbringing. Without understanding who they are and where they come from, it's more challenging to dig into the unresolved emotional attachments and habitual ways of managing emotions that influence their current relationship dynamics. We all carry our family history with us into the decisions we make, the connections we form, and the ways we manage conflict. To make better choices in your relationships now, you must look closely at the choices that shaped you in the past.

ARE YOU PREPARED TO BE HONEST WITH YOURSELF?

Hiding or ignoring pain doesn't make it go away. It comes to the surface whenever we face a conflict or have a big decision to make. You must face the truth about your past and family patterns to heal your relationships and resolve what isn't working. No amount of optimism and positive self-talk will take away hurt, disappointment, or being let down; you must validate the experiences that made you feel like relationships and love aren't safe before you can move past them. The truth is that some of our experiences in relationships can feel horrible, confusing, and unfair. It is essential to be honest with yourself about the impact others have had on you and how you feel in order to manage your emotions when you're hurt, disappointed, or let down. Once we know how we feel and think about our relationships, we can be truly free in them.

ARE YOU PREPARED TO HAVE HEALTHY RELATIONSHIPS?

We all want healthy and happy relationships, but we don't always want to put in the hard work to achieve and maintain them. Building healthy relationships is far from being a stress-free process. In complex and painful relationships, simply moving in the right direction brings growing pains. However, anything worth having in life takes motivation and persistence. Ask yourself without judgment: *Am I ready to have healthy relationships? Am I clear about what that means?* If your answer is yes, then let's get to work!

How to Get Ready for This Journey

So, you have decided to work on your relationships. It takes awareness, motivation, and strength to make such a big decision and to sustain the deep work required for change. As you prepare for this new venture, keep the following ideas in mind.

BE OPEN TO SELF-AWARENESS

The beginning of any change starts with self-awareness. Shifting our focus from others to ourselves is the initial development of self-awareness. Beginning to change our interactional patterns lets us see, for the first time, how our relationships affect our lives, what the actions of others bring up for us, and what we naturally do when we are anxious, hurt, or uncomfortable. Self-awareness isn't about judgment; it's about understanding who you are and who you want to be, both as an individual and as a friend, family member, partner, or parent. A crucial part of self-awareness is acknowledging that you are ever-changing. Even your values and principles may change over time as you evolve. Being self-aware can feel odd at first, but you'll find it allows you to be more flexible in your relationships instead of rigid in your interactional patterns.

BREAK DOWN YOUR EMOTIONAL WALLS

We build walls to protect ourselves from the difficult emotions that relationships bring up for us. Our fear of painful emotions makes it difficult to break the walls down, even when we know that we're avoiding connecting with others out of our fear of being hurt. Healthier relationships require openness and vulnerability, as well as acknowledgment of how deeply other people's behavior can impact you. By looking at yourself and your most hurtful relationships with honesty, you can foster resilience (as opposed to self-protection) to the vulnerabilities of being human.

LET GO OF DEFENSIVENESS

Being defensive means closing ourselves off from looking at our flaws or mistakes. It's okay not to be perfect—being part of the problem doesn't make you less of a person or less worthy of love. Admitting to your mistakes doesn't mean taking all the blame for your relationship troubles; it means that you are open to evaluating what you can do differently. Letting go of defensiveness allows others to feel safe to come to you and express their thoughts and feelings. It also allows you to make changes instead of holding on to what may be pushing others away.

RESOLVE EMOTIONAL ATTACHMENTS

We all have unresolved emotional attachments from the past. Unresolved emotional attachments aren't easy to define, but you know them when you feel them. For example:

- Feeling like a child again when you visit your childhood home and finding yourself looking to your parents to make decisions you usually make for yourself

- Feeling guilty when you are emotionally drained by your parents and believing you must solve their conflicts and problems for them

- Becoming very angry when your parents do not understand or approve of your choices

An unresolved emotional attachment relates to the immaturity of both the parents and the adult child, but people often put the blame entirely on the other person or entirely on themselves: "My parents are too critical of me, so I shut down," "My son behaves like a child; that's why I treat him like one," or "I have to do everything for my parents so they don't get upset with me." Being confronted by our immaturities and seeing our role in the unresolved attachment can make us feel emotionally vulnerable and raw in our closest relationships. However, instead of running away, shutting down, picking a fight, or becoming passive, we can learn the skills that help us grow up, manage ourselves better, and communicate clearly. It's important to remember that there is no such thing as a perfect relationship. Most relationships have both healthy and unhealthy characteristics, but can become more fulfilling when someone recognizes that strengthening their connection requires working on themselves.

Evaluating Your Emotional Walls

While it's hard to confront and manage difficult emotions, an essential step in this journey to better relationships is evaluating the "walls" you've built. We create emotional walls for a reason: They keep us safe when dealing with trauma, stress, and pain in our relationships. However, the emotional walls that used to protect you in an unsafe relationship are likely doing your current relationships more harm than good. Healthy relationships ask us to acknowledge that those walls have served their purpose and that dismantling them will help us authentically show up for ourselves and others today.

Let's explore some emotions that you might be keeping out with walls. Check off any of the following statements that apply to you and feel free to add some of your own in the blank spaces.

- ❏ I feel very uncomfortable around others' intense emotions and discomfort.
- ❏ I don't like to think about past hurtful situations; I would rather avoid them.
- ❏ I don't think I can let people in when I am sad or tell them how I feel.
- ❏ I don't like it when people do nice things for me when I do not think I deserve it.
- ❏ I am not comfortable with feeling my negative emotions; I keep myself busy to distract myself.
- ❏ I am scared to let people see the real me because I am afraid of rejection.
- ❏ _____
- ❏ _____
- ❏ _____

If you'd like to evaluate your emotional walls more deeply, reflect on them in the following space. Keep these walls in mind as you go through this book, and as you complete each exercise, picture yourself breaking your walls down with a hammer or dismantling them brick by brick.

_____

_____

_____

_____

_____

Contemplating Your Relationship Journey

Take some time to contemplate your relationship journey so far. Use the following questions to open up your understanding of why making changes in your relationships is important to you.

List two people with whom you value having a relationship.

_____

_____

How do you show them how much you value your relationship with them?

_____

_____

_____

_____

In what ways would you like to improve these relationships?

_____

_____

_____

_____

What does it say about you that you are willing to put in the work to have healthier, more meaningful relationships?

_____

_____

_____

_____

What You Can Expect in the Next Chapters

Each of the next six chapters in this book addresses a distinct stage in building strong and fulfilling relationships. The following paragraphs summarize these stages—you can think of it as a map for your journey. As you read each summary, begin considering how you might apply that stage in your unique situation.

STAGE 1: FAMILY WORK

We use the term *family of origin* throughout this book to refer to the parents or caregivers and other family members (whether biological or adoptive) that a person grows up with; this might include siblings, grandparents, extended family, and so on. Our family history significantly influences how we see ourselves, others, and the world, as well as how we cope and function daily. In this stage of your journey, you will explore your early experiences in your family of origin, the experiences of your parents and grandparents, and other variables that affect your family and yourself, including trauma, social and cultural influences, and biological factors.

The dynamics of your family and the unique life experiences you've had with them create significant and complex effects on how you function in your life. Some families offer a place of safety, belonging, support, and nurturing, while other family experiences expose the child to abuse, neglect, or other forms of harm to their physical and mental health. Most families feature a mix of some negative dynamics or traits with some positive experiences and strengths. It is helpful to consider both problems and strengths when understanding your family of origin.

Exploring your family's interactional patterns and notable traumatic events is helpful in understanding yourself and learning to manage your vulnerabilities. This stage will help you recognize that difficult experiences can lead to unique strengths and coping capacities. It will also help you better understand how your family patterns influence your current relationships.

STAGE 2: DEFINING YOURSELF

Developing fulfilling relationships requires us to first create a sense of self that remains solid in all our roles and relationships. *Differentiation* is a word that describes when a person's independent selfhood is established enough that they can separate their emotions from those of their family members. Well-differentiated people can be adaptable, self-sufficient, flexible, and autonomous in how they feel and think. Being grounded in yourself helps you to be more objective in your understanding of and actions toward others, enhancing your ability to have strong and fulfilling relationships.

An undifferentiated person is more rigid and emotionally dependent on others for their sense of well-being. This leads to difficulties in relationships, such as failure to set appropriate boundaries. When we are well-differentiated, we can better define ourselves in all our relationships. Being clear about who we are opens us up to more thoughtful responses rather than adverse reactions. This stage will offer the tools needed for the sometimes difficult task of defining yourself in your most important relationships.

STAGE 3: IDENTIFYING TRIANGLES

Triangle is a clinical term for a three-person relationship system. A typical example of a triangle is a marriage where there is tension between the partners, who, instead of resolving it, focus on their child or children. Another example is an adult who argues with their parent, then calls their sibling to vent about it.

There is nothing inherently wrong with bringing in a third party when the tension in a relationship becomes overwhelming. A triangle is made up of three different relationships and can therefore hold more tension than a single relationship can; the third person may also offer new insight, advice, or mediation. However, when we *triangulate*, we spread the relationship tension around in a way that can negatively influence other relationships.

Nothing gets resolved when we spread relationship tension and stress around. We may feel some relief in the moment, but we aren't facing the issues that are causing the tension. Furthermore, triangles contribute to the development of mental health issues like depression and anxiety. In this stage, you will identify the primary triangles in your life and explore their cost and benefits. You will also learn how to correct or prevent triangulation.

STAGE 4: EFFECTIVE COMMUNICATION AND CONFLICT RESOLUTION

If you have been in any relationship long enough, you already know that conflict is inevitable when two or more people are closely connected with each other. Healthy relationships are not characterized by having no conflict whatsoever. In fact, people who repair their fights and move gently toward compromise or a respectful, safe space of honoring each other's differences are more fulfilled in a relationship than those who never openly disagree.

Dr. John Gottman's research on couples points out how a singular focus on conflict resolution is misguided. According to his findings, 69 percent of conflict in relationships is continuous, meaning that it has no solution (Gottman & DeClaire, 2001). Some fights are grounded in lasting differences in personalities and needs. Couples can either talk about these issues and differences or feel stuck forever trying to change them. Gottman found that those in healthy relationships take a gentle approach toward conflict and its resolution. For example, when bringing up something that bothers you, you can soften how you bring up the issue, keep your level of physiological arousal low, and take breaks when you feel agitated.

These research findings emphasize that we must learn to manage conflict in our relationships rather than avoid it or attempt to eliminate it. Even if certain disputes won't ever be resolved, clear communication provides a positive opportunity for understanding the other person and growing in your relationship. This chapter will outline how you can properly and effectively communicate when conflict inevitably hits.

Dr. Gottman's research also indicates that happy couples accept influence from one another—they are open to receiving their partner for who they are and even changing their minds based on the other's views. Acceptance creates a connection between us and our loved ones by allowing things to be the way they are without compromising ourselves.

STAGE 5: VULNERABILITY

What is vulnerability? Author and researcher Brené Brown (2012) defines it as "uncertainty, risk, and emotional exposure" (p. 34). Fear of vulnerability keeps us from taking the risk of trying to improve our relationships; it demands that we maintain the status quo. However, when we listen to our fear over what we want, like love and connection in our relationships, we miss out on deeper connections and stronger relationships.

Being vulnerable requires us to let go of the idea that exposing our real feelings and thoughts is a weakness. When we are vulnerable, we act in ways that align with our autonomous selves. In this stage, you will learn the benefits of vulnerability, how to release your fear of being emotionally open, and practical steps for showing up authentically in your relationships.

STAGE 6: SELF-REFLECTION

Imagine that, while in a fight with your dad, you begin to notice a growing defensiveness within yourself, an unwillingness to be wrong. This feeling alerts you to the fact that you are in protection mode in that moment, shielding yourself from perceived danger. This awareness brings you back to your goal of listening to understand, without needing to argue or justify yourself. This is an example of self-reflection.

Self-reflection means taking a long look at yourself and your part in your relationships, understanding what you naturally do when you are anxious in a relationship, and becoming aware of what type of person you want to be in any given relationship. Without deep reflection and motivation, we are bound to repeat our past. Assessing yourself like an objective researcher allows you to move from just reacting into a deeper understanding of self, which in turn helps you identify areas for improvement. This final stage will help you evaluate and reflect on everything you will have learned in this book.

Are You Prepared for This Journey?

Now that you know what is ahead of you, let's check in. How are you feeling as you prepare for this journey? Check off the statements that apply to you right now.

- ☐ Thinking about working on my complicated relationships has me feeling anxious and helpless.

- ☐ I tend to think about how I can avoid certain relationships instead of making them work.

- ☐ I have had issues with dealing with people for most of my life.

- ☐ I tend to avoid people when they stress me out.

- ☐ I lean toward pessimism when thinking about my tough relationships.

- ☐ I think it is up to the other person to change for us to have a good relationship.

- ☐ I don't usually give people the benefit of the doubt.

- ☐ I am not sure that these stages will help me with my relationships.

- ☐ I will give this workbook to the person in my life that needs to change, instead of using it to work on myself.

If you checked off some of these statements, try to keep in mind ways that you can be more open to the material we will be presenting to you. We know that working on our relationships isn't easy, but it is worthwhile.

◇◇

Chapter Takeaways

In this chapter, we introduced the ideas that influenced the content in this book and prepared you for what is ahead on your journey to more fulfilling relationships. We hope that now you are:

- ✓ Equipped with an understanding of what it takes to move forward

- ✓ Prepared to look at your family history

- ✓ Open to being honest and vulnerable

- ✓ Excited about growing your self-awareness and self-reflection

In the next chapter, we'll work on the first stage, which involves understanding your family of origin. You will explore your family patterns and how they impact you today. You will also learn more about the concept of *differentiation of self* and how creating more of an autonomous self within your relationships will benefit you and the relationship as a whole.

◇◇

PART 2

SECRETS AND STAGES TO FULFILLING RELATIONSHIPS

In the next chapters, we will discuss the secrets and stages of fulfilling relationships: family work, defining yourself, identifying triangles, effective communication and conflict resolution, vulnerability, and self-reflection. First, we'll explain what it means to do family of origin work. Next, we'll discuss how you define yourself in your relationships. We'll identify triangles that keep you stuck, learn what honest communication and conflict resolution look like, and explore how to express vulnerability. Finally, you will learn the power of self-reflection. These stages will help you understand what it takes to have strong and fulfilling relationships. Each step sets the framework for the next stage and serves a purpose in your relationship journey.

CHAPTER 3

Stage 1: Family Work

If you've ever tried to understand the relationship issues you currently face, it's almost impossible to avoid seeing a connection between your parents' behavior during your childhood and your behavior as an adult. This might have led you to blame your current relationship struggles on your parents:

- "I'm needy for love because my parents never showed me affection."

- "I don't know how to express myself because my parents dismissed me when I expressed my feelings."

- "I fear commitment because my parents got a divorce."

It makes sense to consider how our parents contributed to our relationship issues as adults. However, before we place all blame on them, it is essential to consider the issues they faced in their own families of origin. How might their own parents have shaped their paths? What patterns of relating to their loved ones did they inherit? What challenges did they and the generations before them face? Thinking about your parents in this way invites you to see them as humans in their family context.

Exploring our families of origin is not an effort to find who is to blame for our troubles but to see the patterns that have developed over time. Once we understand that our parents' reactions to us are typically their unconscious efforts to relieve their own relationship anxiety, not malicious attempts to ruin our lives, the closer we get to peace and resolution in those relationships.

We know how hard this might be to read if you had a difficult upbringing, and we are sorry for your troubles growing up. As therapists, we have heard about many terrible childhood experiences; we want to honor that and express that we know how impactful that is. Understanding your family's generational patterns doesn't mean letting your parents (or the parents before them) off the hook. However, it will help you know what you're up against and what changes you can make to heal, grow, and have better relationships today.

At some point, we all must realize that our parents are flawed, just as we are. Once we accept that, we can move beyond cause-and-effect thinking and start to face what we can change and heal within ourselves. This chapter will take a comprehensive look at your family system, including your relationships with your parents and their relationships with their parents.

Recognizing Family Patterns

Can you identify patterns in relating to people that developed in your family and contributed to your current relationship issues? To answer this question, think through the facts of your family relationships and the stories you've heard about your family. The following examples show the influence of various patterns that may develop between parents and children:

- If you were the child your parents worried most about, you likely got comfortable with having them step in to minimize your difficulties. As an adult, you might instinctively await or invite other people to solve your problems for you.

- If your parents' anxieties were projected onto you, you probably got used to extreme criticism and constant correction. As an adult, you may have negative overreactions like screaming, being overly critical, or thinking negatively in a way similar to your parents.

- If one or both of your parents managed their tension by giving in to whatever you wanted, you likely now find it challenging to let go of feeling entitled.

- If one or both of your parents confided in you when times were hard in their marriage, you're likely to have an easy time giving advice but a hard time accepting it.

- If you were pushed to center stage by parents who got a sense of security and self-esteem from your achievements, you might have a hard time tolerating situations where you don't feel important.

Do any of these interactional patterns ring a bell for you? Mark the ones that most align with your experience. We understand that not everyone is raised by both parents or raised by their parents at all; these ideas can apply to whomever raised you (adopted or foster parents, grandparents, aunts or uncles, etc.) or whom you spent the most time with growing up.

Are there additional patterns that you've noticed in your family? Journal your thoughts about the patterns of relating to people that you observed or experienced growing up.

Multigenerational Transmission

As we grow up, our family environment helps us develop a certain level of tolerance for upset, anxiety, disharmony, and demands from others. The ability to deal with life circumstances like these can be referred to as emotional maturity or, in Bowen's words, *differentiation of self*.

Differentiation of self impacts our satisfaction in our relationships, our longevity, our educational and occupational successes, and our general ability to function. The less of a differentiated self we have, the harder it is for us to separate our own emotions from the emotions of others. When our emotions are intertwined too closely with others', we are more uncomfortable around others' discomfort and pick up more easily on others' anxieties and fears, making us want to do something right away to mitigate that tension. Usually, that "something" means jumping to the automatic reactions that feel protective and soothing. In short, the less differentiated we are, the more reactive and less thoughtful and intentional we are in our relationships.

A better-known term for the idea of poor differentiation is *enmeshment*. Enmeshment is a concept in psychology founded by Salvador Minuchin to describe families where personal boundaries are absent and family members are undifferentiated, leading to an over-concern for others and a loss of autonomous development.

Research shows that highly differentiated people have more stable families and can offer more to society (Noone & Papero, 2015). Poorly differentiated people, on the other hand, usually have messy personal lives and depend more on others. We know this does not sound fair; however, remember that the way you function as a differentiated self is not set in stone. We have seen people make miraculous changes through motivation, trust in the therapeutic process, and a desire for change.

The *multigenerational transmission process* describes how differentiation (or emotional maturity) levels are transmitted throughout successive generations of a family system. We gain our level of maturity through family relationships and genetics, both of which determine how much of an autonomous self we will have. The more of an autonomous self we have, the better able we are to access our thinking when relationship tension makes us anxious. Our family relationships, circumstances, and education create differences in transmission through the generations. The transmission happens on interconnected levels, from the conscious teachings of others to the automatic programming of emotional reactions and behaviors.

What Is Your Level of Differentiation?

Differentiation of self determines your ability to separate your feelings about something from your thoughts. Undifferentiated people have difficulty with this. When asked to think about something or someone, they can become flooded with emotions and have trouble thinking or responding logically. They also have difficulty separating their emotions from others' feelings. They often look to their family members, partners, or friends to determine how they think about issues, feel about others, and interpret their experiences.

Differentiation frees you from your family's emotional processes to define yourself, empowering you to have ideas and values that differ from those of your family members while still staying emotionally connected to them. It also enables you to reflect on conflict after it happens, understand your role in it, and choose a different response in the future.

Below are some statements that will help you assess your level of differentiation. Read each statement and check off those that are true for you.

- ❏ It is more vital for me to make my loved ones happy than for me to do what I prefer.

- ❏ I feel very uncomfortable when I have to say no to my family, partner, or friends.

- ❏ I make more decisions based on impulse than on thinking things through.

- ❏ I find myself doing more for others so that they will like me, to the point that I sometimes feel used.

- ❏ I can't feel good about myself without having others' approval.

- ❏ If someone I care about is upset or in a bad mood, I instinctively become upset or get in a bad mood too.

- ❏ It is hard for me to express myself when someone has a different opinion.

- ❏ Thinking that I will have to confront someone makes me physically ill.

- ❏ I usually do what makes others happy instead of what would make me happy.

- ❏ When in conflict, I often place all the blame on the other person.

- ❏ I often get emotional when stressed. I verbally attack others to release my emotions, spend too much time worrying about or trying to fix the problem, or use drugs and alcohol to avoid it altogether.

- ❏ I value praise from others over my own satisfaction with how I have performed.

- ❏ I will do things for others even if they don't align with my values.

- ❏ I am very emotionally reactive to the perceived negative comments of others.

- ❏ I cannot be single for very long and jump from relationship to relationship.

- ❏ I easily become addicted to substances or deeply focused on hobbies.

Scoring Your Answers

Count the number of statements you checked off:

- **Between 10 and 16:** You are in the lower range of self-differentiation, living with intense enmeshment. You likely have high anxiety within your social system, creating significant vulnerability within your relationships. You are more sensitive to others and to your environment.

- **Between 5 and 9:** You are in the middle range of differentiation. You are guided more by what feels right in the moment and are sensitive to disharmony. Your life may be fairly functional except in times of stress, and you may struggle to stay true to yourself within relationships.

- **4 or fewer:** You are in the higher range of differentiation, which is the most autonomous. Your relationships are typically mature, as you can adjust to changes in the relationship without feeling threatened. Your relaxed stance to life stressors enables you to be honest and authentic while maintaining healthy relationships, fostering connection, and honoring other people's experiences.

Let us be very clear: Being in the lower or middle range of differentiation does not make you a less valuable person, nor does it mean that you have a dysfunction or flaw that you can't change. You do not need to shame yourself into thinking something is wrong with you. It simply means that you and your relationships can benefit from building your capacity for authentic autonomous selfhood.

Family Projection Process

The *family projection process* describes how parents transmit their emotional issues to a child, creating sensitivities that reinforce certain problematic and reactive behaviors. The intensity of these sensitivities depends on the circumstances of the child's upbringing, particularly the presence of extreme stressors like trauma, divorce, or poverty. Along with impairing the child's ability to function in a variety of ways, family projection can also increase their susceptibility to physical or mental illness.

Relationship sensitivities created through the family projection process can look like:

- Higher need for approval and attention

- Hard time dealing with others' expectations

- Inordinate tendency to take the blame or to blame others

- Taking on responsibility for others' happiness

- Thinking that others are responsible for your happiness

- Acting impulsively to relieve anxiety

The family projection process often begins when parents try to fix a problem they have "diagnosed" in their child. Feeling that they have not given enough love, attention, or support to a child they perceive has problems, they invest more time, energy, and worry into this child than others in the family. The child picks up on and absorbs their parents' anxiety and eventually begins to adopt and embody their parents' fears and perceptions, which negatively impacts their behaviors and development. For example, parents who believe their child has low self-esteem may try to "fix" them by constantly offering praise and positive affirmations. As a result, the child's self-esteem develops to be dependent on praise and validation.

Interestingly, the siblings who are less intertwined in the family projection process tend to develop a more mature and objective relationship with their parents and grow up less reactive and more goal-oriented. Meanwhile, the child that was most worried about or focused on exhibits the most anxiety and has the most trouble maturing and launching into adulthood.

Both parents (if present in the child's life) participate in the family projection process equally, though often in different ways. The primary caregiver, usually the mother, is typically more inclined to have an intense emotional involvement with their child, while the father is typically positioned outside of the closeness in that relationship (though this may change during times of heightened anxiety in the mother-child relationship). Having a less or more involved part in the child's life doesn't mean that parent has a smaller or larger influence in the projection process; everyone in the family plays a role in it.

Exploring the Family Projection Process in Your Family

These ideas can be a lot to digest if you have never thought about your family in this way before. Take a moment to think about how your parents or caregivers, grandparents, siblings, aunts and uncles, and other family members responded when there was an issue or when anxiety was high. Did they jump in quickly to solve the problem? Did they ignore the issues? Did they smooth things over at the expense of their own needs and desires? Did one person take it all on, or did the family work as a team or as partners? Did the parents look to one of the children to fix things? Did they blame one child or all of the children for their troubles?

Take some time to journal about what you remember. It's okay if you don't know or remember everything—just write what comes to you. You can also ask a trusted family member about their thoughts on how anxiety was managed in your family and who took on the most responsibility for issues that arose. This will not only help you recall forgotten memories, but also possibly generate useful conversations with your family members.

Emotional Trauma

Most people understand trauma as a catastrophic event that leads to physical and mental harm. While that is certainly one form it can take, there is much more to trauma than obvious disaster or tragedy. Emotional trauma results from any event or experience that creates overwhelming stress and anxiety beyond a person's emotional ability to deal with it. In addition to events that cause physical injury, like accidents or assaults, emotional trauma can result from experiences that do not involve immediate physical harm, such as harassment, neglect, verbal abuse, manipulation, or divorce.

Emotional trauma is less about the actual event and more about the brain's ability to regulate stress and integrate emotions over time. For that reason, it is possible for someone to experience trauma after exposure to a situation that is less intense than something they had experienced before. Many factors and variables affect the brain's ability to process stress and trauma at any given moment. A family's ability to cope and handle stress is one major factor; another factor is whether the event is perceived as intentional or unintentional, expected or unexpected, controllable or inescapable.

In addition, epigenetic research shows that trauma does not have to be done directly to a person in order to affect them. Unresolved trauma is passed down through our genes, and its associated interactional patterns (thoughts, behaviors, and actions) can also be passed on from generation to generation. When trauma patterns are repeated in our family, it's only natural for us to grow up viewing others—and the world in general—as a threat.

We may repeat trauma patterns in how we relate and respond to others, not because we choose to but because it is all we know. If you have suffered trauma or have a family history of trauma, you are likely to register others' undesirable behaviors as threats to your safety. This can lead to increased or intensified conflict, of course, but it can also create a need for approval and attention or, in contrast, a tendency toward isolating yourself from relationships. You probably experience a great deal of anxiety about your relationships that drives you to be overly dependent on others and hypersensitive to any changes in your loved ones. These behaviors may sometimes drive your loved ones away, making your fear of abandonment a self-fulfilling prophecy.

After doing our research, talking with experts, and seeing the evidence in our practices over the past decade, it is clear to us that many people carry some degree of emotional trauma and that it profoundly impacts their sensitivity to others and the world around them. Emotional trauma can explain many destructive behaviors we exhibit in our relationships. While it does not excuse the behaviors, it does help us understand them.

We've seen firsthand that tackling emotional trauma can result in tremendous healing of relationship difficulties as well as mental health issues and chronic health concerns. If you find yourself stuck in patterns despite being aware of them and trying your best to break free of them, a trauma-informed approach to therapy can help you discover why you are not moving forward.

However, it's not enough to simply decide that the cycle of trauma and its associated patterns stops with you. To change this generational inheritance, you must recognize what triggers you and how you respond to those triggers in your relationships. As we've said, when we better understand ourselves and why we do what we do, we are empowered to change what is not working for us. One way to heal from trauma and not subconsciously repeat destructive behaviors is to work on ourselves in relation to our family of origin.

Here are some examples of how trauma creates negative patterns in relationships. Make note of those that apply to you.

An Emotional Trigger Turning into a Traumatic State

Stressful situations can make us all more vulnerable to being triggered, especially when we encounter problems that remind us of a past trauma. Our ancient ancestors' dependence on their tribe for safety and sustenance influences our brains even today, causing us to react to potential abandonment or rejection as if they were threats to our immediate physical survival. When your brain senses a relationship conflict as a threat, the amygdala, the most primitive part of our brain, generates a survival reaction. When the amygdala takes over, you might resort to one of the following responses:

- **Fight:** Attacking others verbally or physically; raging at them; blaming them for all your issues; trying to control them or the situation; making demands; holding on to things that happened in the past

- **Flight:** Avoiding problems; acting impulsively; avoiding communication or intimacy; not engaging in any difficult conversation

- **Freeze:** Feeling helpless and unable to act; shutting down; disconnecting from others

- **Fawn:** Trying to avoid conflict and establish a sense of safety through people-pleasing behaviors (taking care of the other person's needs and suppressing or hiding your own)

If one (or more) of these responses helped you survive childhood trauma, your brain will automatically generate that same response when the amygdala senses a relationship threat. This response can cause others to feel attacked, rejected, or abandoned, which triggers *their* threat response, and so the cycle continues.

SHAME RESPONSES

Interpersonal traumas or rejection from essential people in your life can create shame. Even if you have truly done something wrong, shame is destructive for relationships, making you feel both self-loathing and resentful of people you perceive as having shamed or rejected you. Shame pushes you to hide important parts of yourself from your loved ones. To mask your insecurities, you might put up emotional walls, attack others, or overcompensate by doing and giving too much to others.

Shame makes it difficult to hear criticism. Even if it is well-meant, you will likely respond defensively because you cannot bear having your flaws or mistakes seen by others. You may turn to addictions or compulsive behavior (e.g., substance abuse, excessive recreation such as video games or shopping, acting out sexually, compulsively focusing on work) to avoid feeling the shame. However, these patterns only prevent you from being available to your loved one. The increased disconnection deepens the shame, validating your belief that you don't deserve love and acceptance. Ultimately, shame pushes you to give up on relationships rather than fight for them.

INHERITING NEGATIVE BELIEFS ABOUT RELATIONSHIPS

Unresolved trauma or dysfunction in your family history can shape your beliefs about relationships in negative ways. You might begin to perceive your loved ones' actions as always ill-intentioned, leading to difficulty trusting people, especially potential partners. You might become overly focused on the possibility of rejection or abandonment, resulting in a pattern of rejecting others before they can reject you. You might believe that others will never be able to understand your feelings or be motivated to meet your needs. This belief fosters a resistance to expressing what you want or need, only to end up resentful when others do not read your mind.

CHOOSING UNHEALTHY PARTNERS AND STAYING WITH THEM TOO LONG

Traumas in your family of origin can leave you with feelings of not being deserving of love. As a result, you might be more likely to tolerate disrespectful behavior or make excuses for a partner rather than setting boundaries or leaving the relationship. You may take on too much of the blame or be easily manipulated because you are scared of being alone.

Experiencing trauma can prevent you from realizing that the relationship is unhealthy. It can even make you addicted to emotional intensity, leading you to reject a friendly, honest, respectful person in favor of someone who is inconsistent, rejecting, demeaning, or manipulative. You may also be drawn to abusive or unloving partners because of "trauma bonding." *Trauma bonding* is the attachment an abused person feels toward their abuser, particularly in a relationship with a repeated pattern of abuse.

Interpersonal traumas leave their legacy through enduring beliefs and patterns of behavior that make it more difficult for you to find and maintain genuinely loving and authentic relationships. By becoming aware of these patterns, you can think and act differently, giving yourself more respect, protection, and self-love. This leads to an increase of self-worth, making you less sensitive to conflict and rejection. You can learn to make wiser decisions about relationships and whom to partner with, as well as to not have relationship discussions when you feel triggered. Over time, you will become less likely to automatically over- or underreact to relationship ups and downs; instead, you will be able to choose how you respond.

When the Past Resurfaces in Current Relationships

Life can be a bumpy ride. Some of us get dealt tricky cards while others seem to have a more advantageous hand. However, none of us get a pass from challenges. Everyone is either dealing with something difficult right now, carrying around wounds from the past, or soon to face adversity in the future. Our goal in life shouldn't be to avoid problems. Rather, life is about learning how to best manage challenges when they arise—or, at the very least, learning how to not make them worse than they have to be.

Most of us ultimately make it through challenging ordeals and relationship hurts. However, we don't always heal or resolve them afterward. Many times, we distract ourselves from the residual pain we feel or run away from anything and anyone who has hurt us. That "solution" can serve us for a while, but it becomes complicated when the past resurfaces in our current relationships. If we haven't dealt with the hurt, we end up using unhelpful coping strategies to relieve it. For example, if you coped with tension in your childhood home by trying to please others, you might do that in your current relationships as well. You might let your partner make all the decisions and never express your needs. If you expressed your childhood anxiety through fits of rage, you may lash out at the people who are currently in your life. If you hid in your room when your parents fought while growing up, you might emotionally distance yourself or use substances to avoid uncomfortable feelings in your current relationships.

These descriptions are not meant to pass judgment. When we aren't aware of our past hurts, emotional triggers, or coping mechanisms, we often end up contributing to the issues in our relationships. When past pain is not resolved, it creeps into your current life and relationships. However, if you are open to being more aware of your unresolved pain, those same triggers and stressors can help you change into the best version of yourself.

A Story of Unresolved Pain

Dr. Ilene's client Kathy is an example of how the unresolved past can creep into current relationships. Growing up with overworked parents who fought a lot about finances, Kathy learned to cope by becoming invisible, ignoring her feelings, and doing everything she could to help, especially when her little brother was born. She ensured she was the perfect little girl so she wouldn't create more stress for her parents. It was a lot to take on at such a young age.

As Kathy got older, she used the same coping skill to manage her anxiety. When she noticed others were stressed out or uncomfortable, she took on their discomfort by doing what she could to come up with solutions. Kathy told Dr. Ilene that she came to therapy because she didn't want to bother her loved ones with her emotions; she also described feeling burned out and alone in her relationships. After moving in with her long-term boyfriend, Tom, she quickly began to have feelings of frustration and resentment like those she had growing up. She did everything for Tom as she did for her parents, but it never seemed like enough. She felt like there was no room for her in her relationships but couldn't understand why, since her focus had always been on the other person and what she could do for them.

In therapy, Kathy began learning about the patterns she had inherited from her family of origin and the automatic response she had developed to ease her anxiety. This helped her understand the part she played in feeling invisible and burned out. Empowered by the awareness that it made her anxious to see others struggle, Kathy learned to resist jumping to fix others' problems and instead focus on herself when she felt triggered.

Responding to Emotional Triggers

An emotional trigger is anything that stimulates an intense emotional reaction, regardless of your current mood. When emotionally triggered, we tend to automatically resort to our programmed responses. Learning to slow down and access your clear mind when you experience emotional triggers will give you more control over your choices, behaviors, and responses, even when you're around a situation or person that triggers you.

The following steps will help you create separation between yourself and others in a triggering situation, empowering you to choose how you want to respond instead of reacting to it in preprogrammed ways.

Choose a situation, person, or type of interaction that triggered you to respond in a way you aren't proud of.

_____

_____

_____

Describe your judgment and thought process about the situation or person at the time.

_____

_____

_____

Describe your immediate feelings about the situation or person at the time.

_____

_____

_____

Describe your thoughts now about the situation or person, keeping in mind everything you've learned in this chapter.

_____

_____

_____

Imagine the situation from the other person's viewpoint at the time and try to consider their actions without judgment. Can you guess what they may have been up against in their own family or social system?

_____

_____

_____

Describe how you would have liked to respond at the time, given your perspective now.

_____

_____

_____

Finally, ask yourself whether that response would have increased or decreased your emotional reaction then. What effect would it have had on your functioning? In what ways did your initial response create more anxiety?

_____

_____

_____

Understanding Negative Interactional Cycles

If you have an intense or difficult relationship with someone in your life, you have experienced a negative cycle at some point. Negative cycles are repeated interactional patterns that put you and the other person in the wrong place emotionally and relationally.

Negative cycles often get people stuck in a space that can feel difficult to repair. One of the most successful ways to learn from and change the negative cycle is to look at your part. What are you doing that contributes to the negative interactions? Are you open and honest with those you care about?

Understanding your interactional patterns is incredibly beneficial to changing the negative cycles. After all, it is hard to improve something if you don't know how it currently operates.

You can use the following steps to understand your part of a negative cycle:

1. Identify what is triggering you.

2. Name your physiological response.

3. Label your emotions.

4. Notice your meaning-making.

5. Connect your internal reaction to your behavior.

6. Express your thoughts.

This process can bring you the awareness needed to break the negative cycles. Let's explore each step in more detail.

1. Identify What Is Triggering You

Think about what started your role in this instance of the negative cycle—what was the event that triggered you? Was it when your partner ignored you? When your dad got defensive about something you said? When your sister was complaining? Paying close attention to what drew you into the negative cycle is essential for understanding your part in it. What did you see or hear that led to your reaction?

2. Name Your Physiological Response

Like any external stimulus, the trigger that starts the negative cycle in your mind impacts your body. What did you notice in your body after you experienced the trigger? Maybe your heart started to race or your stomach tightened up. Your body sends the first signal that your brain perceives a threat. When you can identify your physiological response before you become reactive, it takes away its power, and you will be better able to manage yourself and evaluate whether the threat you currently perceive is an immediate danger or an automatic response to trauma that occurred in the past.

3. Label Your Emotions

When the trigger occurred, what emotions did you experience? Were you angry, embarrassed, sad, scared, lonely? You may have felt many emotions at once, even feelings that seemed to conflict with each other. Naming your emotions has the power to diffuse their intensity. It will also allow you to describe your feelings to others so they can more accurately understand how they impacted you. Remember, your feelings are valid, whether they seem to make sense or not. You do not need to explain, justify, or defend how you feel. Just identify what you felt and put a name to it.

4. NOTICE YOUR MEANING-MAKING

Not everyone responds in the same way to a given word, facial expression, or behavior. What you do in response to a specific stimulus is determined by how you uniquely feel about it—what it means to you.

Here are some examples of meaning-making:

- When you made that face, I thought you were thinking I am stupid.

- I felt like I was too much for you when you didn't call me back.

- I felt rejected when you said no to being intimate with me.

- I thought you were mad at me when you didn't ask me to come over.

Creating meaning from a trigger happens very quickly because this is part of the brain's survival mechanism. Our brain perceives the trigger and instantly reminds us, *This feels like that other time when I was hurt.* This is the moment when it's essential to slow down and become aware of the assumptions you are making about the situation. While it feels instinctual to try to interpret the words or behaviors of your loved ones, making meaning is actually making assumptions—and assumptions are sometimes based on our insecurities. Taking a step back to notice your meaning-making helps you recognize that your interpretation of the other person's behavior and their intention behind it may not be the same.

5. CONNECT YOUR INTERNAL REACTION TO YOUR BEHAVIOR

To keep ourselves "safe" from perceived threats, we adopt specific strategies to cope with our feelings. Understanding what protective actions you take when you feel uncomfortable is a crucial part of slowing down the negative cycle. For example, you might realize that you get defensive when you feel rejected, while your loved one might realize that they jump to problem-solving when they fear not being enough for you.

Connecting your actions with your inner world can help you learn to name what is happening for you in a moment of conflict, rather than simply reacting out of self-protection. It's also a great way to learn more about yourself and help your loved ones know more about you too.

6. EXPRESS YOUR THOUGHTS

As you and your loved one learn to notice the warning signs of the negative cycle, you can start conquering the negative cycle together by talking about what is happening. To start, you can tell the other person about your trigger, bodily response, emotion, meaning-making, and behavioral reaction.

To avoid getting sucked into a negative cycle in this part of the process, make sure to share this information about yourself in a nondefensive way that doesn't cast blame or shame.

- Sharing defensively sounds like, "I shut down when I get upset, but everyone does that."

- Sharing in a blaming way sounds like, "I shut down because you started yelling at me. We wouldn't have this problem if you learned to speak better."

- Sharing in a shaming way sounds like, "I am the worst because I shut down when upset. I can't deal with anything. You must think I'm a baby."

Here is an example of how to productively share your part in the negative cycle: "When I heard you yelling, my body froze. I felt scared that I had disappointed you. It reminded me of how, growing up, I used to get in trouble when I didn't live up to my dad's expectations. It made me want to shut down and hide because that's what I had to do to not get yelled at anymore."

Surprisingly, one reason why negative cycles occur is because of our desire to feel a connection. When we try to connect in ways others don't understand, it is easy to retreat into the behavior that sparks the negative cycle. Understanding and communicating why you do what you do is necessary to stop the negative cycle and build the connection you desire.

Becoming Aware of Your Negative Interactional Cycles

We all get stuck in negative cycles in our close relationships. We fall into patterns of behaviors, feelings, and thoughts that create continuous stress in our relationships. A negative interactional cycle is a reciprocal process—for example, your mother makes an insensitive comment, you react by yelling at her, she reacts to your reaction by getting defensive, and you go around in circles, emotionally reacting to each other. But when you become aware of your own contribution to the pattern, you can change your part of the cycle, which changes the interaction as a whole. The following activity will guide you through this process.

First, think about someone you often argue with or distance yourself from when you are triggered. Write their name in the diagram, then continue to fill in the blank lines to explore the cycle you experience with this person. Finally, reflect on the questions that follow the diagram.

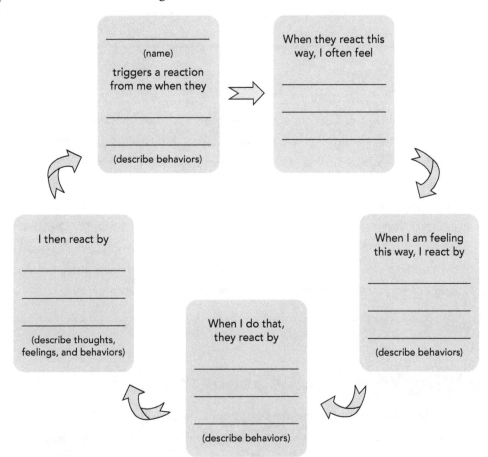

What is your part of the negative interactional cycle?

_____

_____

_____

_____

_____

In what ways can you change your part of the cycle? How can you respond differently?

_____

_____

_____

_____

_____

A Story of Breaking the Cycle

Ivy's mom believes all men cheat, and Ivy grew up hearing about her father's and grandfather's infidelity. When Ivy got married, her mom repeatedly suggested that Ivy's husband would eventually cheat on her, inevitably provoking a defensive reaction from Ivy. One day, Ivy decided to use humor to break the intensity of the interactional pattern. When her mom insinuated that Ivy's husband was cheating on her, Ivy replied, "Oh, that reminds me: Let me check the GPS tracking device I have on him." Instead of descending into their usual negative cycle, they both had a good laugh. If used appropriately, humor can be a great tool to break the cycle.

Building Your Family Genogram

We tend to be most reactive in our most important relationships. The less differentiated we are, the quicker we are to react when the amygdala senses a threat from someone we love. Remember, the brain doesn't know the difference between real, imminent danger and threats we perceive to our relationships.

The more factual and transparent you get about what leads you and your family members into a reactive state, the closer you'll get to being more thoughtful in your relationships. Building a family genogram—that is, mapping successive generations of family history—can provide surprising insights into the what, when, and how of your interactional patterns. As therapists, we often create genograms with our clients to take note of trauma, relationship patterns, and family history. Having a physical representation of their family allows our clients to see themselves, their struggles, and their relationships in their broader context.

You can build your family genogram with just yourself, with your parents and grandparents, with your partner or your children, or all of the above. As you gather information about your family, you will want to learn not only the basics, like your relatives' names and dates of birth and death, but also how each of them managed stress, what their relationships with each other were like, and how they resolved conflict.

When drawing your genogram, choose identifiers to represent each family member. Traditionally, circles are used to represent females and squares to represent males; if you or a family member has a different gender identity, you can choose another shape that resonates with you. You may also wish to indicate sexual orientation (for example, a triangle is sometimes added within the main shape to represent someone who is gay).

Indicate how the family members are related by drawing a horizontal line between two partners or parents and a vertical line down to any children they have. When there are multiple siblings, place them from left to right, starting with the oldest and ending with the youngest.

Next, modify or draw additional connecting lines between your family members to show their relationships in more detail. In the following pages, we have included a chart with various symbols that can be used when creating your genogram. These include relationship symbols to show harmony, conflict, abuse, estrangement, divorce, closeness, distance, and so forth.

Finally, next to each family member, write down or draw a symbol to indicate any traumatic events or experiences in their life. These could include the early death of a loved one, loss of a pregnancy, divorce, financial hardship, poverty, a physical accident, violence, illness, immigration, or the impacts of global conflicts such as war and genocide. Consider your family members' various identities and the forms of systemic violence and oppression they may have experienced, such as racism, ableism, homophobia, and transphobia. Think about what you and your family members have been most likely to do when under extreme stress: fight, flight, freeze, or fawn.

On the next few pages, you'll find a list of symbols that you may wish to use to represent your family members and relationships, followed by an example of a completed genogram. Finally, there is a page with blank space for you to draw your own genogram. Take your time with this exercise—you will be referencing and building upon your genogram as you continue your work throughout this book.

GENOGRAM SYMBOLS

The following are some of the symbols that are often used when creating a genogram. Note that this is not meant to be an exhaustive list of possible identities or types of relationships, simply a starting point for your reference. Feel free to modify or add symbols in your genogram to best represent yourself and your family.

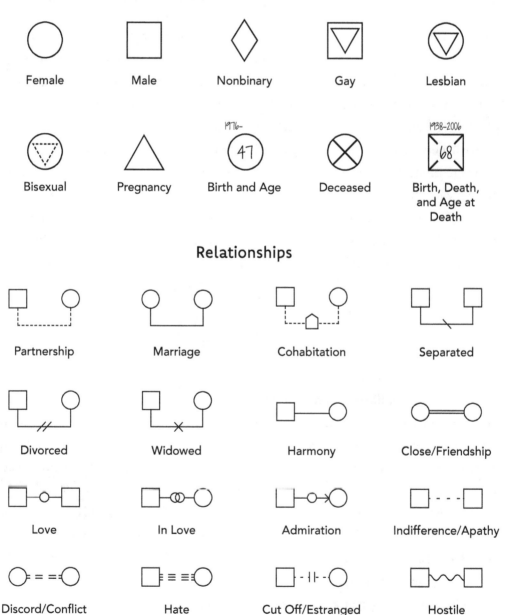

Family Members

Female   Male   Nonbinary   Gay   Lesbian

Bisexual   Pregnancy   Birth and Age   Deceased   Birth, Death, and Age at Death

Relationships

Partnership   Marriage   Cohabitation   Separated

Divorced   Widowed   Harmony   Close/Friendship

Love   In Love   Admiration   Indifference/Apathy

Discord/Conflict   Hate   Cut Off/Estranged   Hostile

Distant Hostile

Close Hostile

Fused Hostile

Abuse

Physical Abuse

Emotional Abuse

Sexual Abuse

Neglect (Abuse)

Focused On

Manipulative

Controlling

GENOGRAM EXAMPLE

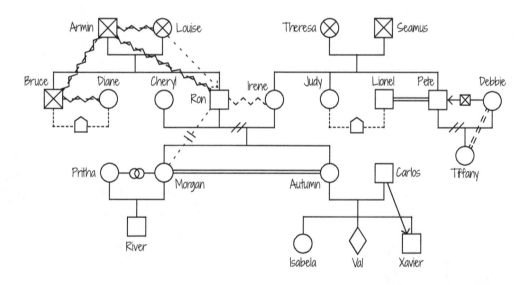

YOUR FAMILY GENOGRAM

◇◇

Chapter Takeaways

If this chapter has been particularly stressful for you, do not lose heart. Taking a deeper, more conscious look at ourselves and our family can be an anxiety-provoking experience for many of us. However, once we understand our automatic behaviors and the interactional cycles that have developed in our family, we have a much better chance at changing our relationships. With this understanding, we can break free of our reactive responses and create a life filled with less constraining, more rewarding relationships.

In this chapter, we went into detail about family work, the first stage of cultivating more fulfilling relationships. This work is invaluable for learning more about yourself and the part you play in negative interactions. When you can objectively see your patterns and where they come from, they will have less power to pull you into a negative cycle. The less emotionally reactive you become, the more opportunities you have to act thoughtfully and responsively with those you love.

In this chapter, you:

- ✓ Identified some of your family patterns

- ✓ Learned about the multigenerational transmission process and your level of differentiation

- ✓ Explored emotional trauma and what it means

- ✓ Learned how to manage and respond to emotional triggers

- ✓ Identified some of your negative interactional cycles

- ✓ Created your family genogram

The work in this stage doesn't come with a deadline for completion. You have inherited family patterns and ways of reacting to others that span many generations. This can take a long time to fully understand, and you don't have to have it all figured out before you move forward. Take your time in this stage, and be kind and gentle with yourself and your family.

◇◇

CHAPTER 4

Stage 2: Defining Yourself

How many times have you ignored someone's lousy behavior to keep the peace? Or gone along with others to avoid being criticized? Or even rebelled so that you could show that you are your own person? You might think that you're already clear about who you are and have no trouble speaking your mind to the people in your life. However, relationship issues are a sign that you may need to be more thoughtful and honest about how much of yourself you bring to your relationships.

This chapter will help you be fully yourself in the presence of people who bring up an emotional response from you. It will cover the process of defining yourself in your relationships, especially your most emotionally significant ones. Instead of just going along with (or against) others out of habit or instinct, you'll be able to define who you are and develop more solid relationships without feeling you need to be anything but yourself.

Defining a Self

You may have heard it said that you must be alone or single to really get to know yourself. That is true to some extent. However, defining yourself only happens in relationship to others. To be specific, becoming more differentiated is achieved by taking actionable steps in relationships with emotionally significant others.

When our emotions and feelings are intertwined with those of others, it can influence us to act in ways we don't like or say things we don't mean, especially when we are stressed or emotionally triggered. Not only is it counterproductive to our values and best interests, but it can also influence how we see the world and ourselves.

Defining yourself involves aligning your behaviors with your values, ideas, and goals. Needless to say, this cannot happen when you rely on automatic "go-to" moves to relieve anxiety in your relationships. Defining yourself starts with internal learning—getting to know your own thoughts, values, and ideas—then integrating what you've learned by acting in ways that align with it.

Defining yourself within your family is an essential step to defining yourself in other relationships. In this chapter, we'll use what you learned in chapter 3 about your family patterns to help you better differentiate yourself and work toward improving your part within your family and other relationship networks.

What Does It Mean to Define Yourself in Your Family?

Family relationships have a significant impact on how people develop and how they think about themselves. Perhaps that is why we all want the picture-perfect family—a family we connect with and feel on the same page with. A family in which all members agree on religion, politics, and lifestyle choices. A family that doesn't trigger us or make us question ourselves. A family that always has our back, gives us the benefit of the doubt, and allows us to be who we are without judgment.

That type of family does sound nice. However, neither of us have ever seen that kind of family in real life. Every family is a lot messier and more complex than it looks from the outside. Seldom do we get the parents we dream of, the children we planned for, or the sibling relationships we see in movies. At times, even a loving family can bring us more pain than joy.

Relationship trouble arises when our fantasy of what we think our family should look like clashes with our reality. Change happens when, instead of trying to change our family and the way it operates, we accept it and decide who we want to be in relation to it. Defining yourself in your family is a process of freeing yourself from your family's habitual emotional processes while staying connected to them. When you can hold a bond with others without losing connection to yourself, you gain the ability to reflect on a fight or argument, realize your part in it, and choose a new way to respond.

If you grew up in a family where everyone maintains tight closeness despite having different thoughts and feelings—and even brief arguments—you likely find it easy to self-differentiate. Alternately, if your family's mantra was "Being close means agreeing on everything" or "It's my way or the highway," self-differentiation is likely very difficult.

Every person possesses a division within themselves. We have our solid selves, with our own ideas and values, and we have other points of view that we've internalized from our family, our society, and so on. When we feel anxious or upset, we instinctively alter our way of thinking to better fit with our family patterns. As you work through this chapter, you will notice what triggers you to revert to old thoughts and behavior patterns. With this knowledge, you can either continue those patterns or better define yourself by making choices that allow for a more solid, emotionally mature self.

Better Understanding Yourself

We live with ourselves, but how well do we know who we are? Why we are so reluctant to attend family dinners? Why do we get so upset when we feel criticized? Meditation practices can give you a door into your innermost world, helping you become more intimate with the self inside you.

The following practice will guide you to take some time to check in with yourself and understand your inner experiences:

- Sit in a comfortable and private space.

- Take deep, slow breaths in through your nose and out through your mouth.

- When you think about your family, gently notice what feelings arise for you. Stay with these emotions; take note of them. Express to yourself how you genuinely feel about the people in your family, remembering that all feelings are allowed.

- Think about moments in the past when you had these same emotions with close family members. Was it safe for you to have those feelings? Remind yourself that whatever comes up for you is safe now.

- When you have heard and accepted your emotions, take some time to breathe deeply. Rest until you feel ready to leave your comfortable and private space.

To process what you meditated about, it is helpful to write down what comes up for you. Many of our clients discover that they're holding on to many strong emotions. At first, that realization can be very uncomfortable, even alarming. However, when we practice observing ourselves and being present with our experiences, we start to see everything we've been avoiding. Journaling is a great way to come down after the acknowledgment.

Take some time now to journal freely about everything that came up for you during this meditation practice. Use whatever words feel right to name and describe your emotions. This will help you process the experience and begin finding resolution.

_____

_____

_____

_____

_____

_____

_____

_____

_____

_____

_____

_____

_____

_____

_____

_____

What It Means to Be a Self

To be a full, authentic, differentiated self, you must have a core sense of where you are in the world and what is happening around you. To better explain how this works, let's get into a bit of neuroscience.

The core self has its roots in the midbrain, an area of the brain that serves essential functions in reflexes and motor movement, particularly eye movements, as well as in auditory and visual processing. Without the midbrain's function, we would be unable to respond to threats or even move. If you were to place your hand on a hot stove, your midbrain is what would make your hand jerk back.

As we said previously, the emotional system resides in the limbic system, the part of the brain involved in our behavioral and emotional responses, especially those needed for survival (such as feeding, reproduction, caring for our young, and the fight, flight, freeze, and fawn responses).

The midbrain and limbic system are connected and work together to alert us to what is happening around us. This is why so much of what we do as humans, including our social behaviors, is based in our emotions.

The brain's prefrontal cortex regulates our thoughts, actions, and emotions through extensive connections with other brain regions. The prefrontal cortex allows us to choose how our emotions will play out in our behaviors; it gives us the choice to override an automatic response and instead use intelligent thought to decide how to act.

These three parts working together is fundamentally what it means to be a self. A baby is born with their selfhood already available in the brain. However, the kind of family they have and their position in it affects the way that their natural self develops. The family functions as an emotional unit in which people are influenced and regulated by one another. This benefits both the family and the individual (assuming the caregivers are loving and attentive toward the child).

As we explained earlier in this book, our emotional and physical dependency on our families has allowed us to survive as a species. It also creates within us a pull to be part of something greater than ourselves and to cultivate connections that add value in our lives. However, much of being a self is the ability to self-regulate—that is, to be in a relationship with others and still be able to think and act as a self, even when others' emotions create uncomfortable feelings for us.

You act as a self when:

- You are firm in your own feelings, beliefs, needs, and values, even in intense situations or when you fear losing others.

- You are aware of your emotions and the way they push you to behave, but you separate your emotions from your thoughts and create more choices for how you will respond.

- You focus on self-regulation instead of on managing others' emotions.

- You choose to act in constructive ways, not ways that contribute to the problem.

Creating a Strong Sense of Self

Building a solid sense of self is a lifelong project. It is tough to figure out who you are and what is important to you while living in a family or culture that sends constant, insistent messages about who you should be and what you should like. Separating what we want from what others want is hard, let alone finding our voice to express our desires amid so many other dominant ideas and opinions. However, learning to do this is worth the work. To know yourself and be known by others, you must distinguish yourself by figuring out your values, beliefs, and truths apart from other people's opinions about what they should be.

Check off the statements that apply to you:

☐ You're tired of wishing you had the strength to say no.

☐ You're overwhelmed by living the life that others expect you to.

☐ You wish you didn't have to work so hard for approval.

☐ You don't dare to express your feelings, or you feel ashamed of parts of who you are.

☐ You are scared to bring up your genuine thoughts and feelings in front of certain people.

☐ You sometimes feel like you are living someone else's life.

☐ You argue with people just to have a different opinion.

☐ You prefer to keep the peace over sharing your honest thoughts, even if someone asks for them.

If you checked off any of these statements, here are some suggestions and reflection prompts to get you thinking about how you can get to know yourself better.

OBSERVE YOURSELF

Start by paying attention to yourself and your inner experience without so much focus on the world around you. When you observe yourself without judgment or impulsivity, you gain a stronger sense of who you are and can make clearer decisions about who you want to be. People who know themselves make decisions for themselves without being pulled in other directions or swayed by what they think they "should" do or what others want them to do.

How can you slow down and become more self-aware instead of other-focused? How can you check in with yourself to make sure you are making decisions that align with your values and desires? Circle any of the following ideas that you'd like to try, and write down your own ideas and other reflections at the end of the list.

- Practice meditation regularly.

- Journal about your values, needs, and goals.

- Keep a log of the thoughts you have throughout the day, then reflect on what this shows you about your thinking—for example, any patterns or thoughts that surprise you.

_____

_____

_____

_____

_____

_____

CONNECT WITH YOURSELF

How you choose to behave and think are expressions of who you want to be. Self-attunement is the ability to access the power within yourself, which allows wisdom, healing, and a more solid self to emerge. Being attuned to yourself helps you become more self-aware—to figure out what you want, decide how to spend your time, and even explore new ways to be who you want to be. When you act in ways that don't align with your values, you rob yourself of the opportunity to experience who you want to be in different situations and circumstances.

When a difficult situation occurs, instead of trying to respond immediately, take a step back and simply notice the process of your thoughts and feelings about it. The only way to know who you are is to try on specific actions for size and see how they make you feel. Over time, you may notice that acting in ways that fit with who you are feel better than acting in ways that don't align with your true nature.

How can you make sure you are connecting with yourself? How can you slow down when you feel like reacting? The following are some strategies you can use during difficult moments, before saying or doing anything in response to the person or situation. Circle any of the ideas that you'd like to try, and write down your own ideas and other reflections at the end of the list.

- Take three deep breaths to help calm your body and mind.

- Give yourself some time to think and choose what to do. You might say, "I'll have to think about that and get back to you" or "I need to take a short break now, but I'll get back to this afterward."

- Notice your body and take care of your needs. For example, a cold glass of water, a warm sweater, or a quick walk outside can help you feel more grounded and able to respond thoughtfully.

_____

_____

_____

_____

_____

SEE CHALLENGES AS A WAY TO KNOW YOURSELF

As personal development author Neale Donald Walsch (1995) says, "Each circumstance is a gift, and in each experience is hidden a treasure" (p. 33). Challenges in life can serve as opportunities to decide who you are and understand what you're capable of. Take obstacles, difficult situations, and negative interactions with people as an opportunity to express who you are and who you want to become.

How can you reframe challenges as ways to show up as the person you want to be? Below are some mantras you could use to help you face challenging situations. In the space that follows, write your own mantras or other reflections.

- I have the right to decide what is best for me.

- I will make choices that help me become the person I want to be.

- I can do hard things.

_____

_____

_____

_____

_____

Sit with and Learn from Your Discomfort

Our automatic reactions try to prevent us from feeling uncomfortable or painful emotions, but growth comes from allowing ourselves to truly acknowledge and experience our feelings. This isn't the same thing as "wallowing" in those painful emotions or ruminating on our problems; instead, it involves observing our feelings and using this self-awareness to decide how we would like to act. When you can sit with your discomfort, you will be able to:

- Line up your feelings with your logical brain by looking at the facts in the situation.

- Tolerate the discomfort that comes from your wants not being immediately satisfied.

- Think about your values without imposing them on other people.

- Uphold your ideas, values, and thoughts even if others disagree.

- Stay connected with the people in your life even when they upset you or disagree with you.

- Look beyond your initial impulsive reactions to see your real intentions and act in ways that better fit with your goals and values.

How can you practice sitting with the tension of not reacting immediately to difficult feelings? Here are some ideas; you can also write down your own ideas or other reflections below the list.

- Write down the thoughts you're having about the difficult situation or person. Then read through them and ask yourself: *What evidence supports this thought? Are there other possible explanations, and what is the evidence for those?* This will help you to notice if you've been making assumptions about the situation rather than sticking to the facts.

- Get curious about your feelings: What do your emotions and body sensations have to tell you about your deeper values and needs?

- Think about the reaction that you would usually have to the current situation. What is the goal or intention behind that reaction? How much do you think that reaction would actually help you achieve this? What are some alternative options that might get you closer to your goal?

_____

_____

_____

_____

_____

Defining a self can be a slow process, especially later in life. Take your time and remember that knowing who you are happens through slowing down, focusing on your inner experience, and making daily decisions that align with your values and goals.

Being a Self While in a Relationship

Beautiful things can happen when two separate people with their own minds and lives come together. But the outcome isn't quite so beautiful when we look to another person to make a life for us or when we take responsibility for another person's life on our shoulders. Many of us get so caught up in accommodating others or defending ourselves that we don't take the time to define ourselves.

It's understandable why we would throw ourselves so fully—too fully—into our relationships. Many of us have been taught that it's better for our relationships if we compromise, sacrifice, and give up parts of who we are for the other person. For example, in many cultures, women are expected to manage the family's housework, child care, and emotional labor, while men are expected to deliver financial support and perform physical labor around the house. These culturally prescribed functional roles influence how we learn to express our thoughts and feelings. When upset, men tend to become emotionally distant, while women typically seek solutions or someone to blame for the conflict. For many heterosexual couples, this results in a pattern where the man withdraws or shuts down during a conflict, and the woman feels like her only options are to reassure her partner at the expense of her own needs or to give up on the relationship entirely.

While these roles aren't set in stone, and many people live in defiance of them, it can be difficult to go against the pressure we're under. Sometimes it's difficult for us to even recognize how much we've internalized these beliefs from our family members, peers, religious leaders, media, and more. Societal expectations for the unique roles we play in our family relationships shape how we behave and what ideas we form about who we should be to maintain our relationships.

Many of us have learned to depend on others or allow others to rely on us, but we don't know how to value our own needs, let alone meet them ourselves. Many of us fear that if we connect more deeply with ourselves, we'll lose our most important relationships. In fact, we are more likely to lose ourselves and our relationships without even realizing it by constantly going with the flow, giving in, and acting in ways we don't necessarily prefer, much like the example of Dr. Ilene's client Kathy in chapter 3. This is where differentiation of self comes into play. The more we are autonomous in our thinking, the more we can respond to people from who we are rather than what we think is expected of us.

For example, you might feel angry, depressed, and lonely but have no idea why. These emotions would confuse anyone, especially if they've always followed the rules. When this happens, people often think that they're the problem, that something must be wrong with them. After all, they've done everything that's supposed to make them happy, but they aren't.

When we encounter clients in this crisis, we urge them to step back and observe the patterns that keep them angry, depressed, and lonely. Rather than looking for what's wrong with themselves, we encourage them to identify the broader picture before taking action. Difficult emotions aren't something to be eliminated or interpreted as confirmation of something being wrong with you. Instead, they should be seen as messengers showing up to let you know what isn't working for you in your life.

It's essential to start challenging the beliefs and ideas that contribute to you losing yourself. Taking the time to slow down and notice what you're feeling helps you to look inward and identify the authentic thoughts and ideas that come from your own experience. This enables you to share what you've been going through with others and to challenge the ideas that don't match your personal experience.

The more we look at ourselves, the better we can define who we are within the culture we were brought up in and within our intimate relationships. Ask yourself questions like *What ideas are getting in my way of being who I want to be?* and *How can I have more freedom of choice in my life?*

Relationships thrive when we're free to be who we are, when we're able to say no, and when we pursue our aspirations and goals. When we can clearly state our needs, desires, values, and opinions to the people we've usually tried to accommodate, our relationships begin to change.

As Harriet Lerner, PhD (2014), says in *The Dance of Anger*, "Defining a self or becoming one's own person is a task that one ultimately does alone. No one else can or will do it for you, although others may try, and we may invite them to do so. In the end, I define what I think, feel, and believe."

Defining Your Core Values

Once you're aware of your core values, you can assess how you'd like to better incorporate them into your life and relationships—so you can act within the truth of the person you want to be. Consider the following list of values. Circle those that best represent your core values around relationships; you can also write additional core values below the list.

- Acceptance
- Caring
- Comfort
- Compassion
- Connection
- Empathy
- Fairness

- Friendship
- Happiness
- Harmony
- Honesty
- Kindness
- Love
- Loyalty

- Patience
- Peace
- Personal growth
- Respect
- Security
- Stability
- Understanding

_____

_____

_____

_____

Focusing on Yourself

It is natural for humans to focus on others. From the moment we are born, our vulnerability and dependency make this outward focus a true survival need. Looking at ourselves is a learned skill, one that initially feels uncomfortable. As therapists, helping our clients learn this skill is one of our primary tasks.

It makes sense that some people think of therapy as a self-involved practice . . . because it should be! However, people who make this criticism would likely be surprised to see how little time clients actually spend focusing on themselves. People show up to therapy ready to vent about their partner, parents, or coworkers. They know they're angry, but they don't see how focusing their attention on things outside themselves (what we call *other-focus*) contributes to their problems.

Focusing on another person might look like:

- Always giving advice

- Trying to push others to do better

- Constantly worrying about others

- Complaining about others

- Assuming what others are thinking

- Going out of your way to avoid others

- Doing things for others that they can do themselves

Many people are stuck in a state of other-focus as a form of self-protection. When we want someone to like us or we're worried about someone we love, we try to become an expert on that person so that we feel some control over their choices. When someone disagrees with or hurts us, we try to manage our feelings by changing ourselves or making the other person change. When something makes us feel upset or helpless, we look for someone to blame: family members, coworkers, neighbors, members of the opposing political party. No wonder everything feels hard. It *is* hard because we're trying to control so many uncontrollable variables rather than focusing on ourselves.

You might be thinking, *Aren't some people just difficult? Doesn't my mom [or another family member, partner, friend, etc.] play a role in the dysfunction of this relationship?* You bet she does, simply by being a human and part of that relationship. But when you become anxious about the state of your relationship, you can only see your mom's part. You already know that your mom's behaviors are a part of the problem, so you've labeled her as the cause of the problem. This makes you see your mom as the person who must change to free you from your anxiety in the relationship.

The problem is that your mom isn't the one sitting in therapy or reading this book. Seeing only the other person's part in the relationship is an attempt to free yourself of any responsibility for issues in your own life. But you are the only variable you can alter in any of your relationships. Self-protection fails to actually protect you because it means giving up your power to make the necessary changes to help improve your relationships. Focusing on yourself might feel like letting the other person off the hook, but in fact, focusing on yourself means reclaiming your personal agency.

As humans, we can easily end up stuck in our challenges because we are programmed to ask the question "Why?" when we are anxious. Asking why conveniently gives us someone or something to blame, but it means giving up our personal agency. To shift your focus to yourself, practice changing your other-focused questions into self-focused exploration. Here are a few examples:

Other-Focused	Self-Focused
Why am I so anxious?	How do I manage my chronic anxiety, and how effective has it been?
Why doesn't my family understand me?	What part do I play in my family not understanding me?
Why do people always ask me to do things for them?	What do I do for others that they can do for themselves?
Is my partner right for me?	How can I be the person I want to be in my relationship?

Over time, as you continue to focus on *your* part in a relationship or problem, a surprising thing will happen: You'll start to calm down and be less anxious in the relationship. This is because you'll be focused on the one thing you can control—yourself.

QUESTIONS TO CONSIDER WHEN SHIFTING THE FOCUS TO YOURSELF

- In what relationships do I tend to focus on blaming others?
- When do I try to manage my relationship anxiety by getting others to change?
- What emotions and physical symptoms do I experience when I'm other-focused?
- How does my focus on others conflict with the person I want to be?

- In situations where I have tended to blame others, what might I do instead if I act from my best self?

- How can I refrain from focusing on others to manage my anxiety?

- What people and resources could help me be more focused on myself?

- What are upcoming opportunities for me to practice being self-focused?

PRACTICE AT HOME

Over the next week, make a note whenever you notice you are other-focused—when you want to manage another person's thoughts, emotions, or behaviors. It could happen when your partner doesn't put their clothes away properly or a stranger says something on social media that upsets you. Please give yourself a compassionate pat on the back for every instance you catch, and don't beat yourself up for how long your list gets. Paying attention is a crucial part of the change. The more you pay attention to your other-focus when it shows up, the more likely you are to remember to stay focused on yourself in the future.

Taking Care of Yourself

Many of us *want* to take care of ourselves, but we feel like we are being selfish when we actually do it. Given the fast pace and many demands of life today, it's normal to wonder, *How do I care for myself when there are so many other things to attend to?*

The hard work of defining yourself in your relationships makes it crucial to take time for self-care. When you take care of yourself, you can offer yourself some empathy for what you didn't know about relationships earlier, for mistakes you made in the past, and for the challenges you encounter in this learning process.

Self-care is a trendy topic these days. But while it's represented through a variety of examples (typically massages, manicures, or green juices), it's hard to find a proper definition.

We see self-care as nurturing your connection to yourself by being as good to yourself as you would be to others. In practice, it means being:

- Observant of when your energy is running low or your emotions are becoming overwhelming

- Mindful of the need to be kind to yourself and replenish your energy rather than let it drain away

- Open to replacing unhealthy habits with more beneficial ones

From a practical standpoint, self-care can be just about anything you do to be kind to yourself: making plans with good friends and family, exercising in ways that feel best for you, eating nutritious foods that fuel you, finding time to relax, or partaking in hobbies you enjoy. Sounds nice, doesn't it? However, self-care isn't exclusively about escaping, relaxing, or treating yourself. In fact, if you constantly feel like you need a break, it's a good sign that you're living a life that doesn't include the real you in it.

Self-care isn't something we should be doing just because we're so burned out that we need time away from our internal and external pressures. A world we need to escape from is a world that needs a perspective change. Rather than an indulgent annual vacation or a monthly trip to the spa, authentic self-care is choosing to create a life you don't need to check out of regularly. It means compassionately accepting yourself for who you are and doing what it takes to take care of your needs, instead of burning yourself out trying to be everything to everyone all the time. It means facing your problems head-on instead of avoiding them and trying to distract or soothe yourself later.

The way you practice self-care may change as your life circumstances change. Some people's self-care is fundamentally about taking action for their personal growth and development: making a plan to pay off debt, sticking to a healthy and mindful morning routine, or saying no when they don't want to do something. For other people, self-care looks like allowing themselves to be normal and average instead of constantly pushing themselves to be perfect or exceptional: letting the house stay messy for the night, accepting their body the way it is, letting go of an ambitious goal in order to live a more balanced life.

The better you know yourself and understand how you operate, the better you can determine what form of self-care is right for you at this time in your life. If you don't know where to start with self-care, ask yourself, *What activities make me feel alive? What motivates me and gives me energy?*

Whatever you do or don't do, the power of self-care lies in consciously choosing how you want to live your life rather than sleepwalking through it or letting others' expectations be your guide. Once you start practicing authentic self-care, you might be surprised at how simply being true and compassionate to yourself solves many of your problems.

Observing Your Life

Think about what you have noticed while observing your internal experience when reading this chapter—what it has been like identifying who you are and examining how you feel about it. With that in mind, reflect on the following questions.

How do your relationships affect you and who you want to be?

_____

_____

_____

_____

How have your reactions to your family, society, and social group affected how you see yourself?

_____

_____

_____

_____

_____

What are some of the steps you'd like to take that will help you become the person you want to be? (For example, do you want to say no more often? Do you want to change careers? Would you like to set aside more time to enjoy your hobbies?) Try to come up with three to four ideas.

_____

_____

_____

_____

_____

The Pull for Togetherness

As we've already discussed in chapter 3, your family of origin has interactional patterns and habits that you now carry on. Some of these may be wonderful traits that you find helpful, while others may create stress and anxiety in your life and relationships. Many of our negative reactions to anxiety are programmed into us by the very people who cause us anxiety.

If there are people in your family who have hurt you, you may want to get as far away from them as possible. You may also have found, as many people do, that no matter how often you think about distancing yourself from the people in your family, you still feel connected to them and obligated to support them. This is what Bowen calls *togetherness fusion*.

Togetherness fusion is the force that compels you to drive your sister to work when her car breaks down. It's what keeps you sitting in the waiting room while your mom is in surgery. It persuades you to lend your uncle money for the umpteenth time when he's gambled away all his rent money. It prompts you to feed your child when he's hungry. This pull for togetherness makes a family what it is. Our urge to be one with the group compels us to go above and beyond for the people we love.

This pull toward togetherness can also help us manage anxiety in many ways. Feeling close and connected can help us feel calm during stressful times. When we give and receive care, our tension melts away. When a crisis hits, families often come together in the most beautiful ways, with each person doing what's best for everyone.

In short, there's nothing inherently wrong with togetherness fusion. Still, it's essential to be aware of how this force can sometimes compel us to follow patterns that don't help us. Problems with togetherness fusion appear when we compromise ourselves or our needs for the sake of other people's demands or expectations. The pull of togetherness fusion can lead us to be more like our family members than we'd like to be, sometimes without even realizing it.

When we're too fused with our family, we lose ourselves, which triggers anxiety in relationships. The problem is that when this anxiety kicks in, it often amplifies our need for togetherness. This is why just one family member getting upset can cause everyone in the family to get upset. Togetherness fusion in a family softens the strain of facing a threat alone. However, the byproduct can be intensifying our negative cycles and interactional patterns.

Just as you can reprogram a website, update a phone app, or fix the broken foundation of an old home, you can make significant changes to your relational foundation. But first, you must be aware of the powers at work keeping things the same. You have to be fully aware of how strong the togetherness pull is so that you can decide for yourself whether, when, and how you will lend your support to your family members. To be consciously aware and objective about this pull is to learn more helpful ways to define yourself within your family relationships and understand how your good and bad parts were shaped by them.

A Story of Togetherness Fusion

Joseph was part of a family whose members lived very close to each other, never having left the state of Connecticut. When there was a family illness or accident, everyone would come together and take turns caring for the individual in need. They all had the same political and religious beliefs and got along well. That is, until Joseph told his parents that he was planning to move to another state to attend college.

As it turned out, everything was fine in the family as long as everyone agreed with each other and worked to meet the demands of the group. But as soon as Joseph wanted to be more of an individual and make the best decision for himself, his parents tried to reel him back in. They pleaded and cried, accused him of being a bad son, and acted like he was ripping the family apart, all to keep him from leaving.

Of course, Joseph's parents weren't consciously aware of what they were doing. They just knew that their little boy was parting from the group, doing something that they perceived threatened his—and their—safety. Underneath their outrage, they were in fact anxious.

When we don't develop enough self, we become focused on other people. To say it another way, if we don't get clear about who we are, our primary goal will be to figure out what other people (our family members, our community or culture, society in general) want us to do instead of acting from what we want. In Joseph's case, his family's habit of entirely relying on each other for emotional support was keeping them from functioning at a higher, more independent level. The family unit was thriving at the individual members' expense.

Yet it is possible to simultaneously be your own person and part of a group. The more you differentiate yourself, the more you can be your own person within the context of togetherness fusion. When we develop our sense of autonomous selfhood, we can respond in ways that allow us to grow as individuals without impairing the group.

Belief Paper

This tension between individuality and togetherness can make it very hard to define yourself. Before you start introducing your differentiated self to your family members, it can help to clarify your goals, values, and guiding principles. This clarity enables you to keep your rational brain in play when emotions threaten to sweep you away in a moment of conflict.

Writing a "belief paper" can help you determine how you want to live your life. Include in this paper what you believe, where those beliefs came from, and what they're based on. What you write might lead you to realize that some of your beliefs aren't in fact your own. If this is the case, you'll have to dig a little deeper to start living based on your values rather than on what other people tell you to value.

Some questions that you could ask yourself to help in developing your belief paper include:

- What are some principles that I strongly believe in?
- Where did these beliefs and principles come from?
- What theology or morality are my values based on?
- What do I truly value? What's important to me?
- What is nonnegotiable to me in my relationships?
- Do my actions align with what I believe is right for my life?
- What do I love unconditionally?
- What is my number one accomplishment in life?
- What do I enjoy doing when no one is watching?

_____

_____

_____

_____

_____

_____

_____

_____

_____

_____

_____

_____

Remember, we all have principles that guide our lives, but we shouldn't expect everyone to live by the same values that we do. No one but you can come up with the answers for your own life.

What Is Collaboration in Relationships?

When we first enter into a relationship with someone, we tend to concede to emotional pulls without thinking. Wanting only to satisfy the other person, we may accommodate every request and even compromise what is important to us for the sake of togetherness fusion. Over time, though, this can leave us feeling a sense of regret or loss of self.

Many of us have been taught that compromise is what creates relationship success. However, a relationship built on compromise does not always last, even with the best intentions, because compromise does not allow for each partner to be active and present. Because no two people are the same, at some point in your relationship, you will have to find a better alternative.

As we mentioned back in chapter 1, one of the key characteristics of a healthy relationship is *collaboration*. Collaboration means that all parties within the relationship get their needs met and move forward with a healthy sense of both togetherness and individuality. To do this, all relationship members must participate in acknowledging their strengths, sharing knowledge, and creating common goals. Collaboration involves:

- Assessing relationship priorities
- Talking about what each person needs
- Creating value for each other's opinions
- Fostering trust through consistent pursuit of goals
- Emotional check-ins and communication that nurtures relationship security

Collaboration assumes that both (or all) people in the relationship have similar goals in mind. These goals include interests and hobbies, shared visions for the future, and a desire to work together to keep the relationship thriving. A collaborative relationship keeps the individuals in an actively evolving state and holds each person accountable for their role in the success of the relationship as well as its growing pains.

Am I Compromising Myself Instead of Collaborating?

If you find yourself in a relationship where you suspect that you are compromising yourself instead of collaborating, asking yourself the following questions can help you understand what's happening.

In what ways is this relationship similar to the type of relationship my parents or caregivers had?

_____

_____

_____

_____

Did I vow to be different from my parents once I became an adult? In what ways?

_____

_____

_____

_____

Did I witness a lot of fights or lack of communication while growing up?

_____

_____

_____

_____

As a child, how did I see the adults in my life resolve conflict?

_____

_____

_____

_____

What messages did I receive about compromise in a relationship?

_____

_____

_____

_____

Did I see examples of collaboration in relationships? How might the relationships I saw as a child have influenced the way I collaborate now in my relationships?

_____

_____

_____

_____

When we find ourselves in similar relationships to those of previous generations, we're presented with an opportunity to explore the impact that our families of origin have had on our ways of being in a relationship.

◇◇

Chapter Takeaways

It's hard work to have fulfilling relationships, but it's worth it! (And honestly, it's a lot harder to maintain relationships that aren't working.) Even if you have skipped some activities and skimmed through some sections, we know you are focusing on the areas that are important to you. We are providing a lot of information in this book, and we know it can sometimes feel overwhelming. It's okay to take a break when you need to or slow down, as long as you come back to do the work. There is no rush in the process of building stronger relationships. After all, personal development is something that continues throughout a lifetime. With that in mind, we encourage you to keep going, and we are proud of you for how far you have come.

This chapter guided you in shifting your focus to yourself. As we have stated, you can only change yourself, not others. We are hopeful that in time and with effort, your work to define and differentiate more of a self will help strengthen your relationships. Contrary to popular belief, we don't need to give up parts of ourselves in order to make relationships work. What we need is to be more of who we truly are. In this chapter, you:

- ✓ Learned what it means to define yourself in your family

- ✓ Considered your core values

- ✓ Shifted your focus from others to yourself

- ✓ Learned how to collaborate without compromising yourself

In the next chapter, you will learn how to identify *triangles*, a three-person relationship system. You will be identifying the primary triangles in your life so that you can be clear about them and understand their cost and benefits.

◇◇

CHAPTER 5

Stage 3: Identifying Triangles

When we experience conflict in our relationships, many of us tend to recruit a third party to help us manage our anxiety. For example, if you're fighting with your partner, you might seek to ease your frustration by calling a friend to vent. This is just one of many ways that we engage in *triangulation*.

When we first learned about triangulation, we were struck by how automatic this is for people experiencing tension in relationships. Triangles are typical in families, work environments, religious organizations, and social networks. Once you look for them, you'll recognize them everywhere. The more stressors there are in a relational environment, the more triangles will occur.

There is nothing inherently wrong with bringing in a third party to ease tension in a relationship where there is conflict, distance, or complexity. A two-person relationship (also referred to as a *dyad*) can only tolerate so much anxiety and stress. If the relationship's tension increases beyond a level tolerable to the individuals in it, it's natural for them to draw on other people as allies, sounding boards, or even messengers. A third person might be helpful if they offer new insights, advice, mediation, or support. Examples of this include seeing a therapist to help with relationship issues or adding a new coworker to the team to help with an intense workload.

> There is no predetermined level of tension that a relationship can tolerate; this threshold will vary from person to person and is also context specific.

However, triangulation can also result in spreading the relationship tension around. When we triangulate without having goals for how to fix the issues, nothing gets resolved. You may feel temporary relief as you vent to your friend about your partner, but if it doesn't lead to you actually taking steps with your partner to resolve the issue, all you've done is spread your frustration to your friend.

Triangulation can be problematic in a relationship if:

- The focus is pulled away from fundamental problems in a relationship.

- The triangulated person feels pressured or forced into entering the conflict.

- An individual within the triangle feels ignored, excluded, or like an outcast.

- Someone is pulled into an inappropriate responsibility (such as when a child becomes a mediator for their parents).

In this chapter, you will learn more about triangles and identify the primary ones in your life. You will also learn how to detriangulate a relationship and the benefits of removing yourself from the primary triangles in your life.

Recognizing Triangles in Your Life

Triangulation can happen in virtually any kind of relationship. For example, a mother can be triangulated into a sibling relationship when the siblings fight. A relationship between a married couple can triangulate their daughter when the father relies on the daughter for support. Two friends may gossip to a third friend about each other.

We triangulate whenever we:

- Vent to a third party instead of addressing the person we're in conflict with

- Gossip about someone

- Ask someone to relay a message

- Focus all our attention on a third party (for example, being wholly focused on our child and ignoring our partner)

- Have an affair

- Become overly interested in other people's problems

- Bring someone to a party as a "buffer" against other people

Considering these the common triangulation practices, identify the primary triangles in which you find yourself in your family, work, or community. Write the name of each person on the lines that make up each triangle.

Deciding When to Detriangulate

According to Bowen, some triangulation is customary and even healthy during a family's interactions. Since dyads are naturally unstable, the engagement of a third person can help a two-person relationship in overcoming deadlocks, meeting each other's needs, and dealing with anxious times. When the triangulated person offers their input, it can be accepted into the two-person relationship and managed together in such a way that it moves the dyad in a better direction. Positive triangulation happens often with parents or caregivers as they join together to meet the needs of a child.

However, triangulation is unhealthy when it creates stress on the third person or when it impedes the resolution of the conflict. The following are a few example cases in which triangulation has had a negative effect on family relationships:

- Keisha and Miguel have been married for ten years and have recently started couples counseling. Miguel explains to their therapist that each time they fight, Keisha calls her best friend, Lauren, to vent about him. Miguel is now uncomfortable around Lauren, feeling she hates him because she always hears the bad. He also thinks that pulling in Lauren makes it harder for him and Keisha to work on their marriage. However, Keisha insists that she has attempted to and failed to work things out with Miguel and needs her best friend's input to process her feelings.

- Jordan is the youngest boy in a family with three siblings. As his older siblings grew up and left home before him, Jordan felt increasing tension in his parents' marriage. Lately, Jordan's father has started to talk to Jordan about the fights between him and his mom. Jordan is nervous that his parents will get a divorce once he graduates from high school, and he worries in particular that his father will be badly impacted by it. As a result of this anxiety, Jordan's grades have begun to decline, and he is procrastinating on his college applications. In fact, he is considering staying home instead of going away to a university because he is scared of leaving his parents alone.

- Bob is a single man in his forties who relies on his family of origin for support. His mother often makes critical remarks about his career, which upsets him. Bob usually vents about this to his brother, who then takes it upon himself to leave a rude message for their mother in defense of Bob. While the triangle seems to unite the brothers against their mother's critical behavior, it hasn't resulted in any change in the family members' behaviors or relationships.

In all of these scenarios, a dyad has become overtaxed by stress and sought support from a third party, and this triangulation has only served to further disrupt communication between the dyad.

In Keisha and Miguel's case, Lauren's triangulation is not welcomed by Miguel and her input to Keisha is not brought back into the marriage for both partners to process. By holding on to the advice for her individual purposes, Keisha is allowing her conversations with her friend to take the place of the emotional process that needs to happen within her marriage if it is to return to a healthier place.

In the case of Jordan, his triangulation in his parents' marriage is both active and passive. His father has actively placed Jordan as his confidant, exchanging communication with the child that should be happening between the parents. Additionally, Jordan has been passively placed by his family system into a position where he feels he must sacrifice his wants and growth to support his parents' emotional needs. Even though his parents may not verbally express this to Jordan, the message is clear: They rely on Jordan's presence to avoid confronting the issues in their marriage.

In some families, triangulation impedes the development of one-on-one relationships because everything is routed through the third party. In Bob's situation, triangulating his brother isn't helping Bob resolve his issue with his mom's criticism.

Instead of learning to effectively communicate his thoughts and feelings to his mother, he calls his brother to unload on him. This is negatively affecting both brothers' relationships with their mother and leading her to feel outside of the triangle. She may even react to feeling excluded by being even more critical of Bob—the opposite of his desired outcome.

Everyone will encounter triangulation in their relationships at some point. When you find yourself involved in a triangle, whether as one of the dyad or as the person in the middle, it is helpful to ask yourself some questions to determine whether this triangle is beneficial to those involved:

- Are both people in the dyad jointly seeking advice from the triangulated person?

- Is the advice of the triangulated person being brought back into the two-person relationship for mutual discussion and consideration?

- Is the dyad openly and directly communicating before, during, or after the triangulation?

- Is everyone, including the third person, able to speak openly and express their feelings and thoughts authentically?

If you answered yes to these questions, then the triangulation may be helpful for those involved. Additional questions to consider are:

- Does anyone involved feel forced, pressured, stressed, blamed, or anxious about the interaction?

- Does anyone involved believe they cannot speak freely, express their feelings, or ask for their needs to be met?

- Is the triangulated person being pulled into an inappropriate role (e.g., a child being triangulated by their parents)?

- Is this an ongoing pattern of interaction in which the original problems never seem to be resolved?

If you answered yes to any of these questions, then the triangulation may be unhealthy and unhelpful. In that case, it is time to pursue *detriangulation*.

Detriangulation happens when a member of the family system effectively differentiates themselves from the emotional system by gaining personal control over their emotional reactivity. This results in a feeling of responsibility *to* their family instead of a duty *for* the family.

To reach a healthy level of differentiation, you have to resolve emotional attachments from previous generations of your family and remain objective about yourself and the system you are involved in. If you're thinking that sounds like a lot of work, you aren't wrong. Differentiating yourself is a lifelong effort, requiring commitment to gradually develop throughout this journey called life.

Steps to Detriangulate

Now that you are learning about triangles, you're likely seeing them all over the place in your personal life. Maybe you often find yourself pulled into others' drama at work, or you feel like a peacekeeper in your family, or you notice that most of your conversations with your friend center around another mutual friend. If you think that unhealthy triangles are happening among the people in your life, there are steps you can take to reduce being triangulated into other people's issues. Consider the following options— which ones would you like to work on?

- You have the right to decline to speak about a conflict that involves others. You can tell the people in the dyad that you will no longer have interactions with them that make you feel like a referee, peacekeeper, or any other inappropriate role.

- Encourage the members of the dyad to speak with each other rather than telling you about it. You can say, "Have you spoken to them directly about this?" Open and honest communication between people is the most effective solution to most relationships issues.

- If a triangle is needed for the dyad to stabilize, suggest that they make an appointment with a professional counselor or family therapist. The mental health professional can step into the triangle with neutrality and objectivity, working from their triangulated position to help the dyad get to a better place.

Remember, you are not responsible for maintaining or fixing other people's relationships. It is up to you to decide whether you are willing to offer advice or whether you will simply say no to discussing their relationship issues.

Displaced Emotions

Displacement is another form of triangulation that happens when you feel unable to direct your emotions about a situation toward the person whom the emotions concern, so you instead direct your feelings someplace else, usually toward a person you consider safer. Displacing intense feelings onto a third person can relieve the tension between the two people in the prime relationship by allowing you to release emotions that feel too threatening to be open about in the prime relationship. For example, if your spouse had an affair, you may be preoccupied with anger toward the affair partner while feeling numb or flat with your spouse. If you are frustrated about an encounter with your boss but worry that expressing this would negatively affect your job, you might instead direct your frustration toward your family when you get home.

Many emotions may be involved in emotional displacement, but anger is the most common one. Redirecting your anger is a defense mechanism; it helps you mitigate the hurt you feel while getting the expression of anger out of your system. Confronting your boss could potentially affect your employment and therefore your income and financial stability. In comparison, snapping at your family has significantly less risk because you know that they will likely forgive you afterward. Another common example of displaced anger is when a parent remarries following divorce: a child might be upset with their father for getting remarried so quickly and focusing his attention on his new family, but instead of expressing their anger with him, they get upset with his new wife.

Displaced emotions are most commonly exhibited by people with impulse control issues, emotional immaturity, or a history of aggression. When they perceive a threat to themselves or their relationships, they express themselves with explosive or even violent outbursts. This is known as *aggressive projection*. A prime example of aggressive projection happens when children experiencing abuse resort to bullying for what seems to be no real reason. An abused child who cannot defend themselves and might not feel safe to report the abuse has no way to healthily process their emotions. Instead, this child might project their anger onto themselves in the form of self-harm or substance abuse, or they might take out their frustrations on another person who is not related to the situation at home, such as a friend or classmate.

With adults, aggressive projection can take the form of feeling entitled or deserving of something they are unlikely to receive. For example, this person might feel entitled to a pay raise at their job yet take no initiative in securing it; when they don't receive the raise, they might take out their aggression on their family or coworkers. Often, these adults lack reasonable emotional control or a developed sense of mature selfhood. This leads them to act out instead of communicating about what they believe they deserve.

If a lightbulb has gone off for you while reading this section, use the space that follows to journal about it. How might you have displaced your feelings onto others? Have there been times when someone else's feelings have been displaced onto you?

_____

_____

_____

_____

_____

_____

_____

Setting Boundaries

Setting boundaries is a better way to manage relationship tension than triangulating or being triangulated. Boundaries are a way to communicate what you are willing or not willing to do and what others can expect from you. We set boundaries in our relationships to feel accepted, heard, and loved, which helps us experience more fulfilling relationships. We also set them to ensure we have room for ourselves in our relationships.

Part of feeling connected to people is allowing them to see you. Expressing your boundaries is a significant aspect of showing others who you are. However, in order to set your boundaries with other people, you must first determine what your boundaries are. It's challenging at first, but it gets easier over time.

Here is some advice to help you consider the types of boundaries you may wish to set in your relationships:

- **Know your limits.** Start paying attention to how you feel about the situations in which you find yourself. What makes you feel uncomfortable, resentful, embarrassed, disrespected, or dismissed? Those feelings often point to boundaries that need to be set with the people in your life. Also consider your values: What's important to you? What do you want to keep private? Is there any behavior or trait that would never fly with you (sometimes called a "dealbreaker")?

- **Make time for yourself.** Permit yourself to prioritize caring for yourself. When you start focusing on yourself, you'll become more motivated to set the proper boundaries because you'll no longer want to accept what doesn't work for you. Making time for yourself includes understanding the importance of your feelings and valuing them just as much as you appreciate others' feelings.

- **Change your role in your relationships.** Your role in relationships keeps you engaging in routine behaviors that may consist of flimsy boundaries. For example, when you always play the caretaker role, you hyperfocus on others; it becomes normal for you to put yourself last and ignore your own needs. When you start setting boundaries, you might get some pushback from the people in your life who have come to expect certain behavior or responses from you. If this happens, remember that setting boundaries and changing your relationship role is okay. You can still be caring and loving toward others, just not at your own expense.

Take some time now to reflect on the types of boundaries you'd like to set with the people in your life. Here are some examples to get you started:

- I need time to hang out with my friends and do things I enjoy without my partner always being included.

- I am not willing to continue a conversation if I feel disrespected.

- I am raising my child in the way I feel is best, and I will not allow my mom to undermine my decisions.

_____

_____

_____

_____

_____

_____

_____

_____

_____

Maintaining Boundaries

Of course, just because you've decided in your own mind to set a boundary doesn't mean the other people in your life will automatically change their behavior. First, you'll need to communicate your boundary to them. This is an ongoing process; in most cases, you'll need to continue reminding the other person about your boundary and, importantly, be prepared to take action if they violate your boundary. This process is called *maintaining your boundaries*.

Here are some tips for effectively communicating your boundaries:

- **Be clear.** We tend to want people—especially our partners—to be mind-readers who know our desires and limits without our saying a word, but that isn't realistic. That type of thinking will only get us into trouble. Maintaining boundaries requires having direct conversations with the people in your life. In your intimate relationships in particular, you need to talk about what kinds of behaviors you accept and don't accept. This means getting specific—name the behavior so the other person isn't left to guess what they did to upset you. Also state how you will respond if they continue that behavior in the future.

- **Be firm.** It's one thing to talk about setting limits but quite another to apply them. Most people think they only have a few options for how to set limits (none of which are particularly effective): scream at the person who upsets them, stay quiet and shut down emotionally, or vent to someone else about it. But there's another, better option: speak up about it in a calm, firm, and rational way. Respectfully tell the person what bothered you and how you can work together to address the issue. This is also known as being assertive, rather than passive or aggressive. You must be firm about your boundaries, especially when they are crossed or violated.

- **Be patient with yourself.** Don't expect to become a master of boundaries overnight. This is a lifelong project, and it will never be perfected, so don't beat yourself up if you don't do it seamlessly every time. We would be lying if we told you that we have perfect boundaries in all our relationships. It takes a lot of practice to share your limits, and just when you think you have it down, something new will challenge you! If the prospect of setting boundaries feels intimidating to you, know that you don't have to set boundaries in all your relationships simultaneously. You can start small by setting boundaries with people you think will be more accepting, then work your way up to the more difficult people in your life.

Think about the boundaries you wrote down under the previous prompt. How can you start communicating these boundaries to the people in your life? Practicing what you'll say in advance can make it a lot easier to stay firm and communicate clearly in the moment. Here are some examples for you to consider:

- "It makes me so happy that you and my friends get along, but sometimes I need time with just them to focus on those relationships. I'm going out with them this weekend, but we can plan to all hang out together another time."

- "When you interrupt me while I'm speaking, I feel like you don't respect what I have to say. If you continue to interrupt me, I will end this conversation."

- "Mom, Piper told me you were making comments about her weight and her choice of after-school snack. It's important to me to help my daughter have a healthy relationship with food and with her body. If you're going to watch Piper, you cannot talk about weight or dieting."

_____

_____

_____

_____

_____

_____

_____

_____

Remember that in certain relationships, you will have to be the one to set boundaries, express yourself, and continue to speak up about what's okay and not okay with you. Some people won't make it easy for you to do this, and your relationships with those people may always seem complicated. The process of speaking up and setting boundaries is more manageable when you don't try to change anyone and only focus on managing your own internal experience and responses.

There's a saying that goes, "People who irritate us usually have something to show us about ourselves." Whenever someone irritates you, ask yourself, *What is this person bringing out in me that I don't want to see?* For example, if a family member, close friend, or intimate partner is challenging you, think about your own behavior in the relationship. Have you contributed to the situation by saying yes instead of no too often?

Have you failed to communicate that something was bothering you? If you don't look at your own actions, you make the other person out to be the sole source of the problem.

For this next activity, we would like you to speak up to someone who has crossed a boundary with you recently. Once you understand what triggered you and how you contributed to the situation, you can address the person in question. Ideally, you'll choose a close friend, partner, or family member, because those are the people it's most important to address directly. If the person is an acquaintance or distant family member whom you only see every once in a while, it may not be worth discussing the issue at this time.

Before you address this person, prepare by asking yourself these questions:

In what ways do I want this person's behavior to change?

_____

_____

_____

_____

_____

In what ways do I want my behaviors to change concerning this person?

_____

_____

_____

_____

_____

What have I experienced, over time, from this relationship?

_____

_____

_____

_____

_____

Set goals before you speak to this person, and remember that you can only control your response, not the other person's behavior. If this person responds negatively or ignores your boundary, will you walk away? Say that you'll talk later when they are less upset? Take deep breaths until you both relax? Think of some possible responses in advance, then choose whatever response works for you and your situation at that moment.

In the space below, write down your plan for approaching the boundary-crosser in your life. A few examples are included to help you get started:

- "I understand that you're disappointed, but spending time with just my friends is really important to me. Let's talk more about this later—we can make plans to all get together another time."

- "I'm not able to have a productive conversation with you when you interrupt me. I'm going to get going now. We can talk another time."

- "I'll be picking Piper up from school on Fridays now. You're welcome to come visit us those afternoons, but I won't allow any comments about weight or dieting in front of her."

_____

_____

_____

_____

_____

_____

_____

_____

Doing this work is guaranteed to make you anxious and uncomfortable at times. There's no way around it—that uncomfortable feeling is part of the change process. But with some practice, your discomfort with setting boundaries will subside. When you're able to manage your anxiety about facing issues head-on in more helpful ways than in the past, that's how you'll know you're practicing healthy boundaries.

◇◇

Chapter Takeaways

Improving your relationships means stepping out of your comfort zone. It takes courage to make changes and set boundaries. However, no one can do this work for you. You are ultimately responsible for how you communicate and manage yourself in your relationships. Remember that when you begin your transformation toward an autonomous self, the people around you will also be affected by your changes. With that in mind, take ownership of the role you play in your relationships and use your voice to contribute to those relationships being balanced and mutually satisfying.

A two-person relationship can only tolerate so much anxiety and stress before involving a third person. Triangles are a way to manage tension in dyadic relationships, but often they become unhealthy rather than helpful. In this chapter, you:

- ✓ Identified the triangles in your life
- ✓ Learned how to detriangulate
- ✓ Came to understand displaced emotions
- ✓ Learned how to determine, set, and maintain healthy boundaries

In the next chapter, you will learn about and work on effective communication and conflict resolution. The skills you discover in the next chapter will enhance your relationships by allowing you to resolve differences constructively.

◇◇

CHAPTER 6

Stage 4: Effective Communication and Conflict Resolution

Have you been taught how to communicate appropriately? Do you know that it is okay to disagree if you are fighting fairly? Differences in opinion, perceptions, ideas, and behaviors might seem insignificant to one person but can trigger deep feelings from another, depending on each person's core values or beliefs. These differences can create conflict if not properly communicated or thought out.

As you read this chapter, keep in mind that disagreeing does not mean that you must get into a fierce fight or that your relationship is not strong. This chapter will discuss how conflict happens, how to communicate through conflict, and how not to take disagreements personally. You'll understand that each relationship will have disagreements at some point and learn how to best deal with them through helpful exercises, prompts, and practices. You will also develop effective communication skills for listening, overcome your fear of conflict, and learn to manage your anxiety instead of projecting it onto others.

How Conflict Happens and How to Address It

Conflict is inevitable within relationships because no two people always think the same. Two or more individuals coming together will bring different perspectives, and those different viewpoints can create conflict. Unsurprisingly, relationship conflict can be a significant source of stress, especially if the conflict is ongoing. In addition to our personal feelings about the problem or person, many of us see different viewpoints as a threat in general. Knowing the other person has a different perspective contributes to our heightened anxiety about the situation, possibly making the conflict worse than it has to be.

Along with *interpersonal* conflicts between two or more people in a relationship, we may experience *intrapersonal* conflicts when we hold two or more differing feelings or objectives within ourselves at the same time. Having two opposing views creates internal conflict. For instance, the long and sometimes unpredictable hours you work may make you want to leave your job, but at the same time, your salary is good and helps you pay for what you need. Some intrapersonal conflicts can threaten our mental health if we ignore them and do not try to resolve them.

All of us can get frustrated when contradictory feelings and thoughts come up within and between us. Poor communication in a relationship makes it difficult to see how these conflicts can be resolved constructively. However, it's essential to work on holding on to different ideas and beliefs while remaining curious and open instead of judgmental toward ourselves and others.

◇◇

Relationships in which people say they "never fight" are not as blissful as they seem. In many cases, those relationships are built on suppressed anger and unacknowledged feelings.

◇◇

Conflict is unavoidable in any relationship, but there's a difference between constructive and destructive conflict:

- **Destructive conflict** is an upsetting and draining experience. It can happen when you bring up how you feel hurt, only to have the other person get defensive and start yelling at you. It also happens when you make a mistake and someone you care about demands to know what you were thinking or accuses you of never listening.

  Many of us have not been taught what to do with our anger in moments of conflict. As a result, we may express it in unhelpful ways, like getting defensive, withdrawing, yelling, or even using violence against ourselves or others. When we don't manage our emotions and reactions in moments of conflict, there is a negative impact on our bodies, minds, and energy levels, not to mention on the relationship itself.

If we bring up how we feel to someone who hurt us, and they meet us with anger and defensiveness, we can learn to walk away or defuse the conflict by calming ourselves down instead of getting pulled into the fight further or becoming defensive. If we learn to navigate our feelings and communicate effectively, we can better deal with destructive conflict and turn it into constructive conflict.

- **Constructive conflict** comes from learning to self-regulate and thoughtfully consider the most helpful response to the situation at hand. This helps advance mutual understanding in your relationships and may lead to fewer problems in the future.

   Expressing yourself constructively in a conflict involves concentrating on defining what you think about the situation instead of blaming or attacking the other person. This minimizes the escalation of anger and creates a safer environment for you to discuss your differing opinions.

Once a problem has been recognized, most people want to move straight to a resolution. However, jumping to find a solution without understanding the underlying concerns of each person in the conflict can result in a power struggle. Getting to the root of the conflict is crucial for a healthy resolution, especially if it's a conflict that keeps coming up.

Getting to the root involves a shift from talking about actions to exploring *intrinsic reasoning*—that is, the deeper meaning of why someone feels strongly about their position. This will require looking back at historical data of how this relates to other events or people in each person's life. Remaining curious and keeping an open mind to the experiences of others helps all parties involved share their concerns and feel heard.

You can cultivate greater understanding by enhancing connection between yourself and the other person. As hard as it can be in times of stress, being polite and respectful allows each person to participate and feel in control of the constructive conflict. The following are a few ways to demonstrate respect for the person you're working to resolve a conflict with:

- Before doing anything, help yourself feel calm and grounded. You might choose to take a walk, practice meditation, or even take a few deep breaths. This creates a space for open communication.

- Choose the right place and time to have the conversation—ideally, a somewhat private place where you can openly express your intentions.

- While you are having the discussion, remember to listen carefully and validate how the other person is feeling. This will allow you to hear the words and remain conscious of the verbal and nonverbal messages. Active listening creates curiosity about what the other person is saying and lowers their defenses. (More on this later in the chapter.)

- Limit *cross-complaining*—that is, raising an issue that is bothering you but is unrelated to the conflict at hand.

- Do not *counter-blame*—that is, blame the other person for the issue: "You moved the front door key and I couldn't find it; that's why I was late!" This language can get out of hand quickly, leading to greater frustration and stress.

- Mutually agree on solutions, with each person offering modifications while being mindful of the other's concerns.

Overcoming Your Fear of Conflict

Avoiding conflict may feel like a way to minimize whatever is bothering us. However, it doesn't make the conflict go away. Instead, it starts to eat away at us, creating more issues in the relationship and with your mental health over time. If you cannot clarify what you want and express how you feel in your relationships, those relationships will lose authenticity, honesty, and intimacy—all necessary ingredients for healthy human connection.

If you're caught up in worrying about other people's reactions, you won't be able to express your thinking and let people know when you feel angry, hurt, or violated. You'll begin to resent other people, which will keep your relationships from flourishing. You might even cut people out of your life who may have been willing to work toward repair, which can be isolating.

The best way to deal with conflict is to see it as an opportunity to grow. In most cases, conflict presents an issue that needs attention for individuals to thrive and for their relationship to deepen. Rather than carrying the issue on an unconscious level, learn to recognize conflict as a chance for you and your loved ones to resolve or accept your differences. If approached correctly and handled with maturity, conflict actually allows you to make meaningful connections, let go of whatever's been bothering you, and deepen the intimacy of your relationships.

Here are some more tips to help you overcome your fear of conflict. Highlight the sections you need to remember the most.

- **Let your feelings guide you.** Start seeing your inclination to avoid conflict as a primary indication of relationship trouble—a sign that it's time to speak up. Rather than burying your feelings (or on the other hand, letting them take over completely through reactions like shouting at the other person), reflect on the question *How are we impacting each other?* Look within to see what part you have played in the situation and what actions you can take to engage in a constructive conversation about it.

- **Remember that conflict is inevitable.** Experiencing a conflict doesn't mean that there's anything wrong with you or your relationship. A certain amount of disagreement is typical in any relationship; in fact, it's impossible to keep all your relationships conflict-free. You can learn how to face these situations constructively without allowing things to escalate. Remember that the same issues will keep arising until they're addressed.

- **Expect the expected.** Many of us overestimate how angry others will get if we express ourselves to them. We tend to imagine the absolute worst-case scenario rather than the most likely one. Your past experiences might have taught you to fear anger, conflict, and confrontation, but consider what you know about the person you are dealing with here and now: Do you feel safe around them? How have they responded to other conflicts, either with you or with other people? Have their reactions been as intense as you're worried they'll be? (Of course, if the person in question has been abusive or volatile, please put your safety first and speak with your therapist or another person you trust before approaching them.)

- **Focus on yourself.** How the other person responds is out of your control. Your only responsibility is to bring up what you think about the situation in a rational and straightforward manner. Because you can't dictate the other person's thoughts, feelings, or behavior, you may not be able to achieve the exact outcome you're hoping for—but you can always choose your own responses and maintain your boundaries.

Before you practice engaging in constructive conflict, it's important to reflect on how you've reacted to conflicts in the past. Understanding your past patterns will help you to anticipate the feelings and impulses that will likely come up for you in future conflicts, allowing you to choose healthier responses.

Exploring Your Past Conflicts

When someone triggers an intense emotional reaction in us, it is essential to manage our emotions and bring them under the supervision of the logical brain. This exercise will guide you to self-assess how you see conflict and when you tend to become triggered. This is valuable information you can use to become more self-aware so you can approach future conflicts in a more constructive way.

Describe the last conflict you had. Who was involved? What was it about?

_____

_____

_____

_____

Was this conflict resolved? If not, how is holding on to the thoughts, beliefs, or feelings affecting you?

_____

_____

_____

_____

What could you have done differently to resolve the conflict? What could you do now?

_____

_____

_____

_____

Think about the last few conflicts you had before this one. What tends to trigger a strong emotional reaction in you—what types of situations, people, behaviors, and so on?

_____

_____

_____

_____

What language do you tend to use when you are in a conflict?

_____

_____

_____

_____

What body language do you tend to use?

_____

_____

_____

_____

Counterproductive Ways to Express Your Anger

Sharing your thinking and feelings with the people you are in relationships with is vital. However, the goal of expressing any emotion, especially anger, is to let the other person know how you feel and what you think, not to try to hurt them back or also make them angry or upset. For example, "When you are not honest with me and keep secrets, I feel angry and betrayed. I feel like I can't trust you, and this makes me pull away or want to hurt you back."

Sadly, many of us were not taught healthy ways to express our anger while we were growing up; instead, we witnessed and learned counterproductive ways to show anger. These reactions usually make conflicts turn destructive instead of constructive. The following is a list of counterproductive expressions of anger, along with a few examples of each. You've likely used some of these in the past—most of us have at some point. Identifying where you have room to grow is the first step toward making that growth happen. Please check off the ones that you need to work on.

- ☐ **Blaming/"you" statements:** Unfairly putting all responsibility onto the other person, often in a harsh or accusing tone
    - ◦ "This is all your fault."
    - ◦ "What is wrong with you?"
    - ◦ "You make me so angry."

- ☐ **Sarcasm:** Saying the opposite of what you mean as a way to insult the other person or show your irritation
    - ◦ "If that's all you can offer, just don't try."
    - ◦ "Oh wow, what an effort."
    - ◦ "Yeah, I'm sure you're very sorry."

- ☐ **Exaggeration:** Overgeneralizing the situation; while there may in fact be a larger pattern involved, exaggeration falsely suggests an absolute (e.g., *always, never, everything, nothing*)
    - ◦ "You're always late."
    - ◦ "You only think of yourself."
    - ◦ "You mess everything up."

- ☐ **Abusive language:** Any use of words to demean, ridicule, manipulate, or dominate the other person; examples include but are not limited to put-downs, name-calling, and hurtful "jokes"
    - ◦ "Quit being such a baby."
    - ◦ "You are so stupid."
    - ◦ "I wish you weren't in my life!"

- ☐ **Withdrawal:** Refusing to engage with the person to work through the conflict (unless it is a temporary pause and communicated in a clear, healthy way)
    - ◦ "Everything is fine."
    - ◦ "There is no point in talking about it."
    - ◦ Giving them the silent treatment

❑ **Guilt trips:** Trying to manipulate the other person by shaming them for what you feel they've done wrong or haven't done right

- "You don't really care about me."
- "I can't count on anyone."
- "You just don't try hard enough."

❑ **Violence:** Using physical force to intimidate, injure, or damage people, animals, or objects

- Throwing things
- Threatening statements
- Hitting

When we are in the moment of anger, resorting to hurtful expressions of that anger is all too easy. Hurting someone else momentarily relieves us of the pain our anger creates. It doesn't help that we have seen many of these expressions of anger from our family members, or in movies or other media, which validates them as being okay to do when we are upset. However, these expressions are definitely *not* okay, and they are profoundly unhelpful for building stronger relationships.

◇◇◇

If you have exhibited or are experiencing physical violence or verbal abuse, we urge you to reach out to a trusted therapist, support group, or hotline for further support.

◇◇◇

Reflect on a time when you were angry and expressed your anger in one or more of the counterproductive ways we've just discussed. How did the conflict get resolved (if it did get resolved)? How were you and the other person affected by your reaction?

_____

_____

_____

_____

_____

_____

Stop Taking Others' Actions Personally

As social beings, we define who we are through our relationships. Many of us interact and get along quite well in various situations and with different people. However, you may find some people to be exceptionally hard to connect and communicate with. When the people you are connected to are critical or even aggressive toward you, or get very defensive when you bring up your concerns, it feels almost impossible not to take the things they say and do personally. Remember, we are all emotionally connected, and what one person does (especially if that person is in our family) affects how we feel.

When you allow someone else to tell you who you are instead of defining yourself for yourself, it's a natural next step to believe others are responsible for your feelings. This prevents you from responding from your most clear and defined self. Instead, you may get angry, freeze, withdraw, or become defensive. After the interaction, you may sit and obsess on those thoughts—also known as *rumination*—to the point of physical exhaustion.

It's natural to take things more personally with people who trigger you, especially those you are attached to. When someone pushes your buttons, the following steps can help you put things in perspective so you can respond in a way that's better for yourself and others:

- **Recognize your reaction.** First, acknowledge that you are taking others' actions personally or ruminating on the interaction. We can't control how we naturally feel and what affects us, but by recognizing what got triggered within you, you can come to terms with what is happening in the moment and turn your attention toward thoughts and actions that will help you feel better and improve the relationship.

- **Practice self-soothing.** Self-soothing—which refers to calming and caring for yourself—helps the body restore emotional equilibrium by decreasing adrenaline and stress hormones, empowering you to remain calm and present. A great way to start self-soothing is to breathe in and out slowly. If you need to stop talking to catch your breath, this will also allow a moment for your body and mind to attune with each other. Unplugging from the situation by using your favorite music to escape or watching your favorite movie can give you time to regroup and reconnect.

    Another important means of self-soothing is reassuring self-talk. Many of us speak to ourselves in a harsh, critical way, and we struggle to show ourselves compassion. But in order to set boundaries and constructively approach conflict with other people, we must first treat ourselves with respect and care. Reassuring self-talk might sound like, *I deserve to be treated with respect, and I have the courage to speak up about it.*

- **Explore the significance of this conflict.** Consider why this situation or person is triggering a strong emotional response in you. Are you reminded of past conflicts, perhaps with your family of origin? Is this conflict reinforcing negative beliefs you've come to hold about yourself, such as feeling like you're unwanted, not good enough, or responsible for other people's feelings? Reflecting on this will help you better understand the feelings you are experiencing.

- **Consider your relationship with this person.** Next, return your focus to the person you're currently in conflict with. If this relationship means a lot to you, try to place yourself in their shoes. People in a relationship will not always agree on everything, so it is important to honor how you see the situation but also try to understand what the other person is feeling, thinking, or trying to convey from their perspective. If this person is not skilled in healthy communication, remember that their language has more to say about them than you. Recognizing that their words and actions are not ultimately about you and are not your responsibility to control allows you to remain centered and empowers you to respond instead of react.

- **Remain curious.** Try to be open to other possibilities rather than jumping to conclusions. This allows space for a conversation rather than a confrontation. Apply that curiosity to yourself as well. Be aware of your triggers so that you can prepare yourself for interactions that try to draw you into an unhealthy pattern. This awareness will help you to avoid those knee-jerk reactions and to uphold your personal boundaries.

The practice of not taking others' actions personally will train your brain to put your initial, unhelpful reactions in the back seat and instead listen intentionally for what makes sense (and what does not) in regard to what the person is saying about you. The more you know about yourself and how you see yourself, the less you will need others to affirm who you are or that your feelings and wishes are important.

Of course, it's easy for other people (like us) to say, "Don't take it personally—it's not about you," but it's hard to remember when we fall into conflict. For a sensitive person, it can seem like only a robot could manage to be unaffected by others. We're all emotionally connected, especially to our family and friends, so we can't just not care. However, there are ways to manage our sensitivity better so that conflicts don't leave us feeling hurt for days or thinking badly about ourselves.

The following list offers tips for resisting the tendency to take things personally. You may wish to copy some of these ideas onto index cards, sticky notes, or an app on your phone so you can keep these reminders close at hand.

- **Know your inherent self worth.** Take time to get to know yourself apart from whom others may say you are. If you know yourself and your worth as a person, you won't be so quick to take the judgments of others personally. Think of five qualities about yourself that you're grateful for and call them to mind whenever you feel sensitive.

- **Know your emotional triggers.** As we have mentioned often in this book, we all have emotional triggers from the past. Hurtful experiences with people we love and trust may make us extra sensitive to particular behaviors or words. For example, suppose your father was overly critical, and you tried to be perfect to please him. In that case, someone pointing out that you made a mistake could trigger you to feel more sensitive than another person might under the same circumstances. When you get upset about a situation, ask yourself, *Am I upset about this situation in itself, or is this one of my emotional triggers?*

- **Practice authenticity.** Let go of thinking you must be someone else and embrace yourself. Authenticity—being honest with yourself and others—involves expressing your feelings, personality, and opinions through your words and choices. Self-expression ensures you make decisions that align with your values, your belief system, and what you are passionate about.

- **Make mistakes.** There's a saying that goes, "To become our best selves, we first have to be our worst selves." Accept that you aren't perfect and remember that mistakes are easier to tolerate when you learn from them. Allow yourself to make mistakes with the understanding that they're just part of the process of becoming the person you always wished you could be. Taking responsibility for your actions is essential, but don't punish yourself just because someone else disapproves of you.

- **Let it go.** We all have something that has hurt us. Don't let it define who you are. Instead, use it to grow in strength, empathy, and character. Our experiences, especially the difficult ones, help us grow into ourselves and allow us to see who we are and what we are capable of. How you handle moments of regret or shame can transform those hurt feelings into something that makes you proud. A person who can be vulnerable with how they feel is empowered to be less judgmental of others and their faults. When choosing to let go, ask yourself, *What is worth carrying with me from this experience, and what does not serve me that I can set down?*

- **Learn that kindness isn't a free pass.** We tend to expect that if we're friendly and kind to everyone, giving all of ourselves to them, we should be treated the same way back. But being kind to others doesn't always buy their acceptance and approval. We can better serve others and ourselves when we do things because we *want* to, not because we expect something in return.

- **Be logical.** When something upsets you or makes you feel uncomfortable, it's helpful to look at the situation with cold, unemotional logic. Did the problem call for your reaction or are you doing something that is counterproductive or out of proportion to the issue at hand? Is the other person doing something wrong or are you being reminded of past hurts? If someone is genuinely hurtful, can you ask for what you need or work on letting it go?

The goal is to make our emotions as sophisticated and educated as our logical brains. It's of great importance to explore where your feelings are coming from, how you can respond to them, and how you can allow the situation to challenge and inspire you simultaneously. When you educate yourself about your reactions, you can turn them into reasonable responses in the future.

It's Not Personal

When you acknowledge that what other people do and say is most likely a reaction to their own unresolved issues or hurt, you will find it easier not to take it personally when they act in ways that upset you. The following reflection prompt will help you bring this mindset into your life.

The next time someone says or does something that hurts your feelings, what steps will you take to prevent yourself from internalizing it? Here are some examples to get you started:

- If someone in my family emotionally triggers me, I will look at my family geno-gram to better understand that person and myself.

- I will check in with myself and ask, *Is it true what they said? Is this something I have to address?*

- I will evaluate whether I was doing too much for this person and expecting the same in return.

_____

_____

_____

_____

_____

Communication Myths

The art of communication can be tricky. The constantly changing ways that we communicate (face to face, telephone, texting, online, etc.) leave many attempts at communicating incomplete because the information was not clear. Our reactivity makes it even harder to listen, further hindering the information exchange needed in moments of conflict.

Let's explore five communication myths that create conflict and hinder healthy resolution in relationships.

- **Myth 1: Communication happens through words alone.** Communication is more than just what is said. It also consists of the tone of voice and pitch used, silences, body language, and more. Even in written communication, such as a text message, elements like emojis, punctuation, and the timing of replies carry meaning.

- **Myth 2: Communication just happens.** Many people believe that communication is complete once you convey your message and get a response. However, our brains need time to filter the information we receive through several biases to extract the meaning of a message. We often respond before we fully grasp what we are responding to. For genuine communication to take place, we must listen to understand, not listen to reply, and check to ensure that what we've said is apparent to the other person.

- **Myth 3: Intellect equates to good communication.** Being able to efficiently problem-solve, complete academic tasks, and use abstract reasoning doesn't necessarily mean a person also has *emotional intelligence*, a necessary ingredient for healthy communication. Popularized by psychologist Daniel Goleman (1995/2020), emotional intelligence refers to the ability to recognize, understand, use, and manage emotions positively to appreciate not only the information being shared with you but also the feelings tied to it. Like analytic intelligence, emotional intelligence can be cultivated, which means we can all learn to communicate well if we work at it.

- **Myth 4: Listening is easy.** When was the last time you just listened to someone else without replying? Even when we intend to listen, we can become distracted by someone walking in late, our stomach growling, our phone vibrating—any stimulants around us that can make it challenging to sustain our attention to the person talking to us. Listening is our access to understanding, but it must be done consciously.

- **Myth 5: Words always mean the same thing.** We use language daily yet fail to remember that even when the same words are used, their meaning can differ based on the context. Sarcasm, hyperbole, and slang are some of the more obvious examples of this; for instance, your friend may have really appreciated your joke, but did they *literally* die from laughter? A word is only a symbol, a means for understanding to travel from one person to another. Good communication involves responding to the meaning of a person's words, not simply the words themselves.

Good Communication Starts from Within

To improve our communication in relationships, we must start with how we communicate with ourselves. Whether positive or negative, our communication with ourselves affects how we hear others. This is because we filter all the information around us through ourselves first, and our emotional intelligence level plays a part in this process. If we hold negative messages about ourselves, when we communicate with others, we tend to hear the information presented in a negative way, no matter what the other person's intent might be. Most of us desire peaceful relationships and connections, but we can't attract or achieve them if we don't have a similar sense of peace within ourselves. This means we must evaluate our internal messages so that they align with the type of communication we want to receive.

Anytime we communicate, we can become anxious about being misunderstood or what will happen if someone disagrees with us. This anxiety is quite natural in relationships with others; after all, no one wants to be misunderstood or even rejected. Accepting this fear is more helpful than denying it. If you explore the emotions and triggers that accompany your communication anxiety, you can learn to work through the issues that arise in communication.

REMAINING EMOTIONALLY NEUTRAL

When we feel upset, angry, or defensive, resorting to "go-to" moves like yelling, blaming, attacking, or withdrawing is easy. However, we will have much better outcomes if we learn to calm ourselves down in our moments of distress and remain *emotionally neutral* when communicating.

Being emotionally neutral does not mean shutting down in communicating. It means intentionally choosing your words, sentences, tone, and body language to keep emotions out of your messages as much as possible. This helps you regulate your feelings and listen to the facts while working toward effective communication.

Another essential factor to consider is the timing of your attempt to communicate. If you want to make the most out of a conversation, learn to be mindful of when you're attempting to engage the other person in communication. We all need to be in the proper mental and physical space for healthy communication, especially if we are trying to resolve a conflict or find practical solutions. Therefore, it's best to avoid starting potentially difficult conversations when you or the other person is tired, stressed, or not feeling well.

It's also important to remember what is and isn't within your control when going into a difficult conversation. Even healthy communication habits can't guarantee the other person will change their behavior. We don't communicate to change others; we speak productively for ourselves, hoping it will improve our relationships.

Ineffective and Effective Communication

Healthy communication means effectively sharing your feelings, opinions, and expectations, making it an integral part of any relationship. Poor communication is one of the main reasons relationships fall apart. Despite its importance, however, many of us were never taught how to have healthy communication within relationships. The following chart shows examples of ineffective communication (including some of the counterproductive ways to express anger, which you'll recognize from earlier in this chapter), along with more effective alternatives.

Ineffective Communication	Effective Communication
You piss me off when you don't show up on time.	I feel undervalued when you don't show up at the time we discussed.
How dare you walk away from me! You are so childish.	I feel insecure and angry when you slam the door and walk away.
It's obvious you don't care about me when you don't take my side.	I get frustrated when I don't see you taking my side; it makes me feel uncared for.
I'm not insensitive. *You're* the insensitive one for accusing me of that.	I hear you saying that I am insensitive to your feelings; what is it that I did to make you feel that way? That wasn't my intention.
I can't stand you right now—get out of my face.	I need some alone time to process the emotions that are coming up for me right now.
You're angry right now, so I won't talk to you.	We both are pretty emotional right now. I think it would be best if we put this conversation on hold and get back to it when we both feel calm.
I can't deal with you right now.	I want to hear you out, but I have a lot on my mind right now. Let's catch up at dinner.
You always disappoint me.	I feel disappointed by what just happened.

As you may have noticed from these examples, effective communication involves clearly expressing your feelings and needs. It also includes expressing that you have heard and understood the other person, even if you don't agree with them, and asking for clarification if needed. With effective communication, you maintain your own boundaries without attacking the other person; your goal is not to "win" the disagreement or to hurt them, but to treat them and yourself with understanding and respect.

Speaking from "I"

Try to speak from a position of taking responsibility for how you feel while identifying how the other person's behavior has affected you. "I" statements are helpful for this—for example, "I feel frustrated because I see the trash has not been taken out today. Since I asked you about it before you left for work, it makes me feel like you were not listening to me or do not care about my needs." Providing specific examples of behaviors that the other person can recognize will help them become self-aware and enable them to explain behaviors that might have been misunderstood.

Take a moment to practice this for yourself.

Describe a recent behavior that triggered an emotional response for you in one of your relationships.

_____

_____

_____

_____

Describe your emotional response—what were (and are) you feeling about this?

_____

_____

_____

_____

What would you like to say to this person about this issue?

_____

_____

_____

_____

Considering what you've learned so far in this chapter, do you think what you just wrote down would be an effective way to communicate your feelings and needs? If not, how could you revise or reframe it to be more effective?

_____

_____

_____

_____

Turning Down the "Noise"

It's particularly important to learn the communication barriers that create "noise"—that is, anything that interferes with healthy communication, such as a negative attitude, poor timing, not listening, not showing respect, interruptions, not validating feelings, and pointing the finger of blame. Noise looks different in each relationship, and failing to identify it is often where unhealthy communication first develops. Therefore, part of your work to improve communication is to assess where the noise shows up in each of your relationships.

What are some of the factors in your life and relationships that tend to interfere with communication?

_____

_____

_____

_____

What steps can you take to turn down this "noise" so you can tune into your relationships?

_____

_____

_____

_____

Active Listening

For many of us, listening is a skill we grew up knowing we need but not necessarily knowing how to do it. As you work to improve your relationships, one essential skill to learn is *active listening*. Actively listening to others means genuinely hearing what the other person is saying, not just so that you can respond but rather with the intention to understand how the person feels and why they feel that way. Active listening demonstrates that you are trying to see things from the other person's point of view and make them feel understood.

Practicing active listening skills like the following will help ensure that you hear what the other person is saying and that the other person feels heard.

1. **Give them all your attention.** When someone engages you in conversation, set aside any distracting thoughts—including plans for your replies or rebuttals—and focus on what they are saying right now.

2. **Show them that you are listening.** Nonverbal communication is a powerful way to show that you are paying attention and acknowledge that you received the other person's message. Some reliable modes of nonverbal communication include:

   - Looking directly at the person talking to you

   - Keeping your posture open and inviting

   - Using body language, such as nodding regularly or making appropriate gestures

   - Smiling and using other facial expressions as appropriate

   You can also use verbal communication to show that you're listening, as long as you keep your interjections brief and encouraging. Comments like "Yes" and "I get it" can be very effective.

3. **Reflect back what they've said.** Our personal beliefs, assumptions, judgments, and perceptions can alter what we hear. To ensure you understand what the person is trying to say, it helps to occasionally reflect aloud on what is being said. One approach is to paraphrase: "What I'm hearing is ____" or "Sounds like you are saying ____." You can also summarize what the person has

said thus far or ask clarifying questions like "What did you mean when you said ___?"

4. **Respond based on what is being told to you.** When you think the other person has completed what they have to say and you are ready to speak, offer your thoughts respectfully. Follow the guidelines for effective communication you've been practicing throughout this chapter.

◇◇

Something important to note in this section is that active listening is intended for someone who is speaking respectfully to you and trying to share their perspective and find solutions. Unfortunately, active listening is *not* productive in a relationship where the other person repeatedly uses your time to complain, dump their negative feelings onto you, or disrespect or verbally attack you. You don't need to actively listen to someone who is doing this; it is okay to cut off a conversation that isn't serving you or the other person.

◇◇

The Gottman Method

The Gottman method is an empirically researched method of couples therapy developed by Drs. John and Julie Gottman and based on the sound relationship house theory (The Gottman Institute, 2023). The techniques in the Gottman method are designed to help people in intimate relationships increase closeness and friendship, address how conflict is resolved, and create shared meaning in life.

Conflict is natural even in healthy relationships. In fact, conflict can have a positive impact on a relationship when it's managed well. For that reason, in our practices we prioritize managing conflict over resolving disputes.

When managed well, conflict can help the people in the relationship understand that there is a critical difference between them while at the same time creating an atmosphere that encourages each person to talk openly and honestly about their hopes, values, and aspirations. The individuals in the relationship can craft visions, narratives, and metaphors about their relationship, creating shared meaning. Shared meaning helps to increase communication and trust, maximizing and strengthening your relationships. This means believing that your relationship is a journey—it will have its high and low points, but you both will commit to continuously trying to improve your relationship by nurturing each other.

The nine components of the Gottman method can help us learn to replace negative conflict patterns with positive interactions and create the space to repair past hurts through understanding the other person's inner psychological world, personal history, worries, joy, stresses, and hopes. A few of these components—Gottman's ideas of repair attempts, bids for connection, and accepting influence—are summarized in the following sections.

REPAIR ATTEMPTS

Before two people can come up with a mutually satisfactory resolution to a conflict, they first must defuse the tension and negativity so that the communication gets back on track. John Gottman defines a *repair attempt* as "any statement or action—silly or otherwise—that prevents negativity from escalating out of control" (The Gottman Institute, 2023). He includes silliness in this definition because a repair attempt does not always have to be serious or somber. In some cases, a bit of kind, gentle humor or playfulness can be very effective, as long as it's for the benefit of your loved one (never at their expense).

Repair attempts require three important elements:

- **Time:** On a given day, how many hours do you think you spend with this person? Of those hours, how many do you spend working on the relationship? To start a repair attempt, you must be willing to invest in spending more time together, learning how your loved one receives love and what they need to repair from conflict. Knowing this is like having a secret weapon tailored to your mutual happiness.

- **Collaboration:** Each person in the relationship must come up with ideas and then pick the ones that will work for them. This not only starts restoring the communication but also enhances the connection.

- **Creativity:** Each unique relationship circumstance presents an opportunity to try infinite repairs. There are so many different ways to work on repairing conflict; you can choose what is helpful and unique to your relationship.

For more information about repair attempts, see Gottman's "repair checklist" (which you can find at https://www.gottman.com/blog/r-is-for-repair/). It's a list of helpful phrases that are placed into different categories, such as apologies, expressions of appreciation, and deescalating arguments. You can turn to this list for ready-to-use examples and as inspiration for your own repair attempts.

One way to begin a repair attempt is for each person in a relationship to look at what is happening to them individually and together. Healthy relationships require us to understand that more than one reality can be valid. When you recognize how fixated you have become on your truth, you can step back, start to acknowledge your loved one's truth, and become curious about how they developed it. Next, you can look for similarities in the thoughts, feelings, and behaviors that come from your unique viewpoints. This will allow you to start seeing things in more than one way, rather than being locked into your position, and help you to listen deeply without judgment.

The following reflection prompts will help you get into the right mindset to make healthy repair attempts in your relationships.

Think of a conflict you're currently having with a loved one (or perhaps a conflict that you're worried will occur in the future). What is your perception of the situation?

_____

_____

_____

_____

Now try to put yourself in your loved one's shoes. How might they perceive the situation? What do you know about their past experiences and other relationships that might be shaping their truth?

_____

_____

_____

_____

Can you find any common ground with your loved one—in your thoughts, feelings, or behaviors? How might this help you work with them to find a solution?

_____

_____

_____

_____

List a few repair attempts that you'd like to try with this person. How would you like to approach them to restore connection and invite them to problem-solve with you?

_____

_____

_____

_____

The more you practice repair attempts, the more it becomes a habit, a part of your relationship routine. Instead of thinking about it with dread and defensiveness, you will mentally associate it with growth and a positive relationship experience. Needless to say, it's beneficial to practice the repair skill early and often in every relationship.

BIDS FOR CONNECTION

We are all biologically wired for connection, yet many of us feel shame for needing it. A *bid for connection* is a request for another person's attention, affection, support, or any other positive form of connection. Bids for connection can appear in subtle and simple ways, like a smile or a wink, or they can be more complex, like a specific request for help or advice. In general, women tend to make more bids for connection than men, but in healthy relationships, each person should be comfortable with it.

Bids for connection can be missed at times, so it is crucial to pay attention. For example, your child's bid for quality time might sound like "Can you color with me?" while your partner may say "How do I look?" as a way of gaining positive attention. By actively listening to and observing your loved ones, you can learn to recognize the bids you are receiving and understand what they mean. Responding to bids for connection trains both people in the relationship to turn toward each other rather than away from each other in moments of vulnerability. Turning toward each other increases emotional connection and trust. For couples, it also enhances romance and sex. In any relationship, it effectively stores up an emotional "bank account" that can sustain your relationship through times of stress.

Most of the time, fights happen due to resentment and distance that build over time when one person in the relationship continually turns away from the other's bids for connection. The most vital relationships stay strong through daily efforts to make and accept bids for connection.

To learn to recognize your loved ones' bids for affection, try keeping a log over the next week. How does each person express, through words or actions, that they would like to connect with you? What types of connection are they seeking? Do you notice any themes or patterns in each person's bids for connection?

ACCEPTING INFLUENCE

Most relationships work best when both parties accept and have influence. Gottman's research with Neil Jacobson found that men who accept influence from their partners have happier, more fulfilling relationships (Jacobson & Gottman, 1998). (This is true for people of all genders; however, the research focused on men because they are often less willing to accept influence from their partners.) And, while it may seem paradoxical, the research showed that the more influence a partner was open to receiving, the more influential that partner was in the relationship altogether.

Here are some suggestions for learning to accept influence in your relationships:

- **Focus on your reaction.** Self-awareness is always essential when learning to have and accept influence. Most of us don't knowingly shut down our partners, friends, or coworkers but inadvertently do so when we fail to listen or are quick to speak. This can sound like "I don't agree; let me tell you what I think about it," which leads to the other person thinking "I guess my ideas don't matter." Consider whether you are open to the views of others and whether you are listening to genuinely learn about them or only listening to respond.

- **Ask questions.** Asking questions for clarification is crucial to any relationship. If a comment or viewpoint triggers you, check in with a question to see if you understood the other person correctly. It is much harder to do this when you disagree, but the solution you can ultimately come to will feel much better if both of you feel understood.

- **Don't say no so quickly.** There is a benefit to yielding a bit, not being defensive, and being open to seeing that other people have interesting perspectives even if you don't share them. Think of it as looking for ways to say yes. This can consist of a simple acknowledgment, such as "I see your point of view." For many, this can be a challenge, but you have to ask yourself whether you simply want to be recognized as correct or if you want to improve your relationship.

Do You Overreact or Underreact?

As you have been exploring your triggers and tensions in relationships up to this point, you may have noticed whether your responses tend to be more or less intense than the situation warrants. Overreacting and underreacting can be both the result of past and present trauma or extremely stressful situations.

Overreacting can happen when we think someone is blocking our progress, pushing our buttons, or treating us inappropriately. When we are in the middle of an extreme reaction, we might know there is a better way, but the overwhelm we're feeling limits our ability to think through the problem and course-correct. Afterward, we often feel embarrassed by our actions, sometimes to the point that we minimize the other person's feelings about our reaction or even blame the other person for it. This can lead to the other person feeling they cannot count on us and choosing not to confide in us in the future out of fear of our reaction.

Many of us don't think or talk about underreaction as a problem. But while someone who underreacts might seem calm and collected under stress, they are just as reactive as someone who overreacts. When we underreact, we're trying to avoid or escape conflict rather than truly addressing it, so we don't learn to manage difficulties or ease our anxiety. People who typically underreact to challenging situations tend to have more physical symptoms and can unknowingly place themselves in danger by avoiding and ignoring issues that should be faced, like paying their bills on time or dealing with a health diagnosis.

No matter what you feel in each moment, you can learn to respond in healthier ways that don't create lasting damage to your relationships or personal life. Being appropriately responsive to situations that raise your anxiety actually helps you manage the anxiety better. Instead of getting overly involved with the problem or avoiding it altogether, try to keep the facts in mind as you respond. To work on this, consider the following:

- **Identify when you're overreacting or underreacting.** Why are you so reactive to or frustrated by this person or situation? What is it that you tend to under- or overreact to?

- **Pay attention to your internal voice.** What is this stirring up inside of you? Is this feeling connected to your past? Does the content of this relationship feel familiar?

- **Sit with the feeling.** Be curious, open, accepting, and loving toward whatever comes up for you.

- **Take responsibility.** Acknowledge the role you are playing or have played in the situation.

- **Practice collaborative communication.** Practice active listening and empathizing with others and yourself while you find a way to communicate your thoughts and feelings.

Calming the Brain's Reactivity

A primary goal of our emotional reactivity is to motivate action that aids our survival. Emotions drive the brain to seek pleasure and rewarding experiences that make us feel like we can thrive. They encourage us to seek rest and self-care to recover when needed. On the other hand, when we are faced with a possible threat, the brain receives information from the emotional system that activates the amygdala to initiate behavioral reactions like the flight, fight, freeze, and fawn responses that aim to deescalate a threat.

We must not attempt to suppress these "fear" or "threat" messages from our emotions but rather embrace and manage them. This will help you understand your feelings without needing to react to them immediately. Some situations do require immediate emergency reactions, but for those that don't, it's best to calm our brain's response so that we can accurately assess the perceived threat and deal with it appropriately.

Meditation is a great way to help bring more calmness into your life (and into anxious or seemingly threatening situations in particular) by generating warmth, love, empathy, and a sense of peace throughout your body and mind. For the following meditation, find a comfortable space where you can become still and centered, then take a moment to welcome some calming self-compassion into yourself with these simple steps:

- Start by following the rhythm of your breath.

- Take a deep breath in and imagine compassion and love filling your body and mind with warmth, starting at your toes and flowing up to the top of your head.

- When you feel the warmth of love and compassion has filled your body and mind, radiate kindness outward as you exhale.

- Be mindful of taking this peaceful energy into your day whenever you find it hard to calm yourself.

Showing Appreciation

Feeling underappreciated is one of the biggest complaints we hear from our couples therapy clients. Many people do not feel valued in their relationships while also taking those relationships for granted. We underestimate how much showing we care matters to someone else. Moreover, we rarely notice when we aren't showing appreciation and thus tend not to show it until something drastic—like an argument, withdrawal, or even an affair—happens and wakes us up.

The good news is that you can become better at showing appreciation, starting right now. You don't need to make a large gesture to show that you appreciate someone. You can start by saying "thank you" for the seemingly small, everyday ways that they contribute to your life: "I appreciate it when you fold my laundry." These expressions of gratitude show appreciation and value for their time. Sending a quick text message to let someone know you are thinking of them, spending time with them, and paying attention to their experience are other ways to help them feel like they are not being taken for granted.

Actively appreciating each other creates a daily refresh within any relationship, increasing the love already there and bringing greater awareness of the potential of the relationship. It creates opportunities to be playful and have fun while subtly encouraging each person to take more responsibility for the relationship's growth.

Moving On from Conflict

What we tell ourselves about someone else and their intentions can affect whether we stay angry or move on from relationship issues. If you believe people are mostly unaware of how their actions impact others (instead of intentionally doing things to hurt others), it will significantly influence how you respond to them. The same is true when you are the one who has hurt someone else. People will never know your true motives, thoughts, or feelings unless you clearly communicate them.

Think about how you tend to communicate and express yourself, then ask yourself the following questions.

Have I been open and honest with the people in my life?

_____

_____

_____

When I have been hurt by others, have I told them how I feel?

_____

_____

_____

Do I tend to give people the benefit of the doubt or assume that their intentions are bad?

_____

_____

_____

How do I usually communicate what I am thinking and feeling when I disagree with someone? How might I communicate more effectively?

_____

_____

_____

_____

_____

_____

_____

_____

◇◇

Chapter Takeaways

How you choose to behave, think, and communicate during conflict are all expressions of who you are. When you avoid conflict or become overly reactive, you deny yourself the opportunity to experience who you can be in different situations and circumstances. Try to see difficulties in your relationships as opportunities to decide who you are and to communicate more effectively.

In this chapter, you:

✓ Learned about different types of conflict and how they occur

✓ Considered counterproductive ways of expressing anger

✓ Worked on taking others' actions less personally

✓ Learned how to listen actively and communicate effectively

✓ Identified whether you tend to over- or underreact to conflict

In the next chapter, we will discuss the benefits of vulnerability, how to let go of our fear, and what we can do to show up in our relationships authentically.

◇◇

CHAPTER 7

Stage 5: Vulnerability

The brave decision to be vulnerable can transform your relationships. When you let go of what is holding you back from living authentically in your relationships, you are consciously choosing to be more of yourself. This chapter explores what it means to be vulnerable in our relationships and why it is essential to let go of our fear of vulnerability.

What Is Vulnerability?

Vulnerability is opening ourselves up to something that can feel harmful or dangerous to us. It involves putting our genuine selves out in the open, knowing very well we may not be accepted, and being honest about our feelings and thoughts, even if others might not receive them well, because we know that we will be better off living in our truth.

Many people avoid or distance themselves from vulnerability. After all, it is anxiety-provoking to open yourself up to something that can harm you. Moreover, vulnerability has a negative implication in many cultures. However, the mental health field has reclaimed the value of being vulnerable. As self-help author Mark Manson (2023) writes, "Vulnerability is consciously choosing to not hide your emotions or desires from others," making it a subtle form of strength.

Indeed, it takes courage to physically and emotionally show up when you do not know what the outcome will be. The thought of going on a job interview, saying "I love you" first, disagreeing with the popular opinion, or setting a boundary with someone might fill you with apprehension and even fear. However, vulnerability is a natural part of living an authentic life, and practicing it will allow you to experience more fulfilling relationships. According to social researcher and best-selling author Brené Brown (2012), vulnerability is what allows a person to connect deeply with others and experience their own emotions fully.

The urge to shield ourselves from the pitfalls in life or the judgments of others can make us view our feelings as something to be ashamed of. Because many of us see ourselves as fragile when we are emotional, we believe that we need to armor up each day to protect ourselves from our insecurities. Not wanting to admit that we struggle or to burden those we care about with our feelings, we hide our shame, anxiety, fear, and uncertainty, telling everyone we are fine. We think that we are showing strength by hiding what hurts us. However, when we live to protect ourselves from the potential danger of our emotions, we are robbing ourselves of meaningful connections and support. When we don't practice vulnerability, we miss out on showing up and being seen.

Depending on your family and culture, you may have received the message that it shows weakness to cry, that it isn't okay to struggle, or that it's best to bottle up how you feel. However, our feelings are not our enemies; they are essential messengers with a lot to say about our lives. They let us know what we enjoy and what we don't like so much. They open us up to our passions and let us know what is not okay with us. They help us set boundaries and tell us when it's time to take it easy.

In short, vulnerability is not just about being honest with others about your feelings; it is about being honest with yourself. When you practice vulnerability, you no longer invalidate your personal experience but instead allow it to exist without judgment. The following example illustrates the power of practicing vulnerability in our relationships.

A Story of Vulnerability

Taylor, a 15-year-old girl, went with her mother Kariyah to see Dr. E about the increased arguments they were having at home. Kariyah wanted Taylor to do more around the house and take responsibility for her behaviors. Taylor felt like her mom was not listening to her and was only concerned with what she was not doing well. In an individual session, Taylor told Dr. E how hard it was for her to be open with her mom. Because she felt emotionally shut down by her mother, she had simply stopped talking to her.

In a joint session afterward, Dr. E asked Kariyah if there was a time that she felt connected to her daughter. Kariyah explained that she and her daughter were like best friends not too long ago, and she was unsure why

Taylor was pulling away. When Dr. E asked how she expressed her love for her daughter, Kariyah replied, "I buy her what she wants."

Dr. E continued gently, "And how do you show up for Taylor emotionally?" Kariyah went quiet and, after reflecting, began to cry.

Taylor, looking surprised, shared that this was the first time she had seen her mom express so much emotion. Kariyah apologized for "getting emotional" in front of her child; crying in front of others was frowned upon in Kariyah's family of origin, and she believed she must hide how she truly felt or at least put a positive spin on her negative emotions. However, Dr. E assured her that there wasn't anything to be ashamed of and encouraged her to stay with her emotions.

"It's okay, Mom," Taylor offered. "I don't mind if you get all emotional. Actually, it makes me feel better! Like I don't have to hide from you either." Much of the time, if we just allow ourselves and others to feel whatever feelings arise, we have a better chance of them opening up to us. Kariyah's emotional vulnerability gave Taylor the space to share her own struggles and allowed Kariyah to hear her daughter's struggles without trying to fix them. They decided to create weekly time to have a "share talk," an intentional and safe emotional space in which they could communicate and connect. Being emotionally open with each other not only improved their relationship, but also changed the family pattern around vulnerability, as they later reported back to Dr. E.

Your Emotions Aren't Wrong

We explain to many of our clients that there is nothing inherently wrong with any emotion. The only thing that makes emotions "wrong" is the belief that we shouldn't be having them. While you may not wish to experience a specific feeling in response to a particular trigger, beating yourself up will not help. Instead, take a breath, and try to meet the emotion with curiosity and compassion. Recognize it as part of a complex system with many patterns of conditioning. Ask the feeling what it's trying to tell you and how it's trying to serve you.

This allows you to converse with the emotion, assessing if it brings any practical value in the context where it's arising or if it's just a habitual response that was once necessary to protect you, such as in childhood, but is no longer needed where you are today. Giving the emotion space to be felt, heard, and respected goes much further in reconditioning your emotional responses than dismissing the emotion as "wrong."

What Is Holding You Back from Being Vulnerable?

Anytime we do something different from our status quo, even if it is good for us, feelings of resistance will come up. This is especially true when it comes to working on becoming more vulnerable. In our therapeutic work, we have found that specific ideas and thoughts hold some people back from being vulnerable. The things we tell ourselves can make a big difference in our decisions to open up to others.

Following are some beliefs our clients have expressed. Check off the ones that resonate with you—the ideas holding you back from being vulnerable.

☐ I'm scared that others won't understand my feelings or perspective.

☐ Not sharing my pain gives me a sense of control over a situation I cannot control.

☐ My feelings have never really been validated by anyone else and I'm scared they won't be validated this time either.

☐ I don't want to burden other people with my feelings.

☐ I don't open up to people when I think they might criticize me.

☐ I will open up when I am ready.

☐ When I feel deeply hurt, I cannot trust anyone with my feelings.

☐ It isn't safe or possible to share my honest thoughts and feelings with others.

☐ If I open myself up to people, they will not like me.

☐ I'd rather avoid someone who has hurt me than have to talk about what bothers me and set boundaries.

☐ If a person hurts me, I can't undo what they did, so there is no point in telling them how I feel about it.

What are some other beliefs that may be holding you back from being vulnerable?

_____

_____

_____

_____

Now that you have identified the thoughts that are holding you back from practicing vulnerability, consider how you might reframe those ideas to better fit with your progress to this point. For example, you can reframe the statement "I'm scared that others won't understand my feelings or perspective" to "Just because others might not know exactly how I feel doesn't mean I can't try to explain my experience to them. And if they don't understand, it doesn't mean that my experience is not valid."

Write down your own reframes here:

_____

_____

_____

_____

_____

_____

_____

Choosing Whom to Be Vulnerable With

"I don't care about what other people think" is a phrase we have all said or heard at some point. However, that phrase isn't accurate; we are all neurologically wired to care about what people think. Whether we admit it or not, we care what others think about us, especially if that person is special to us . . . and there is nothing wrong with that!

Instead of pretending we don't care (or the opposite: overly focusing on what others think about us), we should question whose opinions truly matter to us. These should be people we deem significant in our lives, whose perspectives and feedback we trust. We are not obligated to include the people we think "should" have meaningful commentaries just because they have a particular role in our life, like our parents, siblings, friends, or teachers. Instead, being vulnerable requires us to thoughtfully decide whom we can be ourselves around. In general, vulnerability is best practiced with people who genuinely matter in our lives because they show up as authentically as possible for us.

It's helpful to understand attachment when determining whom we will be vulnerable with. As we mentioned in chapter 2, attachment refers to the close emotional bond between a child and their primary caregiver during early development. Humans must attach in order to develop emotional and stress regulation, adaptability, and resilience. For that reason, early attachment is an essential aspect of all relationships. When a young child is made to feel safe, secure, and protected early in life, they develop *empathy*, the ability to understand and share another person's feelings. According to attachment theorists, individuals who learn healthy attachment early in life transfer those skills to later relationships, creating connections that feel safe and stable, in which they can thrive. Those who are not supported in learning how to attach can develop difficulties getting along with others and feel a lower sense of trust and confidence in having relationships.

Your individual attachment style can make it easier or harder to be vulnerable with people, even the ones you consciously choose. The following pages will explain the different attachment styles: *secure, ambivalent, avoidant,* and *disorganized*. As you read, please identify which attachment style most resonates with you and your experience.

The Attachment Styles and Their Characteristics

Mary Ainsworth—a protégée of attachment theory pioneer John Bowlby—and her colleagues (1978) created a study for observing attachment differences in children called the "strange situation." This situation involved a series of steps to see how young children would respond to being separated from their caregiver for several interludes while in the presence of a friendly stranger. The way in which the caregiver and stranger enter and leave the room was designed to recreate the flow of familiar and unfamiliar presences in the child's life.

Ainsworth observed differences in how children reacted to this scenario, including:

- What happened when the stranger entered the room
- What happened when the caregiver left the room

- Whether the child exhibited separation anxiety

- What the reunion behavior looked like when the caregiver returned to the room

- Whether the child stayed close to their caregiver or explored the room

SECURE ATTACHMENT

In the study, securely attached children showed distress when their caregiver left the room but were happy upon their return. They avoided the stranger when left alone with them but became friendly with them when their caregiver was present. They used their caregiver as a "safe base" but were willing to explore the room.

Securely attached people grow up feeling safe emotionally and physically, and thus tend to engage with the world and with other people from a healthy space. They tend to have high self-esteem and are generally positive people who can regulate their emotions, easily trust others, and connect well with others. Securely attached individuals can communicate effectively, manage conflict well, and self-reflect in relationships. They are comfortable being alone as well as in close relationships. According to attachment research, about 50 percent of the population fits this attachment type.

AVOIDANT ATTACHMENT

Children with an avoidant attachment style would display no distress when the caregiver left the room and little interest when the caregiver returned. Moreover, these children were not anxious when the stranger was present, whether their caregiver was present in the room or not, and they could be comforted equally by either their caregiver or the stranger.

Individuals with an avoidant attachment style tend to be very independent, both physically and emotionally. They do not seek contact with others when they feel distressed, making physical or emotional intimacy difficult; they may have trouble building close relationships. It is theorized that this attachment style develops when a child's caregiver is insensitive and rejects the child's needs. Expected to be independent and to self-soothe even when their basic needs were not met, these people grew up learning to fend for themselves.

AMBIVALENT ATTACHMENT

In the study, children with an ambivalent attachment style displayed intense distress when the caregiver left the room but resisted contact with the caregiver upon their return. These children would avoid the stranger as well and even show signs of fear of the stranger. In general, these children would cry more and explore less than children with other attachment styles.

People with an ambivalent attachment style have a fear of rejection and abandonment. They have difficulty understanding others and have no security about what to expect from others. This is a result of parents who were inattentive, often unstable, and quickly overwhelmed, and who made their children responsible for their needs. These individuals tend to struggle with codependence in their relationships, are highly sensitive to criticism and require the approval of others, and have difficulty being alone.

DISORGANIZED ATTACHMENT

The disorganized attachment style was discovered by Mary Main and Judith Solomon (1990) some years after Ainsworth's "strange situation," using her same procedure. Individuals with this attachment style show signs of both the avoidant and ambivalent styles. They tend to have trouble regulating their emotions, display contradictory behaviors, and have difficulty trusting others. These confused and disorganized behaviors are most likely the result of the person being neglected, abused, or exposed to another type of childhood trauma. While these individuals sincerely seek love, they can also push their partners away out of fear of love and abandonment.

Creating a safe emotional bond that offers a secure retreat from the outside world and a way to be comforted is a buffer against the stress of life and is central to solid relationships. Particularly in times of conflict, our attachment style can put us in a more sensitive or uncomfortable position in our relationships. Without a feeling of safety in our relationships, it's difficult to practice vulnerability. Therefore, identifying your attachment style will help you understand how you learned to form early relationships, increase your comfort level with vulnerability, and create healthy emotional bonds where you can express your authentic self.

Which attachment style best describes your experience?

Reflect on your interactions with your parents or caregivers while growing up. How has their influence affected your attachment style?

_____

_____

_____

_____

_____

Connection Instead of Protection

When we are in close relationships with others, we might assume that we will always stay connected based on biology, familiarity, or romantic feelings. In reality, though, it is being intentional about vulnerability that fosters a long-lasting emotional connection.

When we don't feel safe to be ourselves or let our guard down, we create superficial relationships at best where we're focused on protecting ourselves from hurt or disappointment. But when we do feel safe to open up, we foster connection within our relationships and demonstrate genuine care about each other's needs, which creates happiness and long-term emotional intimacy.

In relationships riddled with protection, we are always calculating whether, when, and how we will share information. This calculus diminishes our ability to authentically connect. When you operate from a place of seeking protection over connection, your amygdala is on constant alert. This makes the relationship feel like you are constantly drifting apart. Particularly when the relationship has its natural conflicts or low points, it makes you feel lonely, sad, and even helpless.

When we talk about emotional connection, we're referring to a natural feeling of intimacy between people that creates a deep and meaningful alignment. This type of connection provides a layer of security that holds even during times of tension. When we feel connected to others, it helps us to effectively self-regulate and be less emotionally reactive. This dynamic works in the other direction too: We find it much easier to emotionally connect when we are calm and collected, and more challenging when we feel upset or threatened. At those times, we may resort to defensive moves like withdrawing or verbally attacking to manage our anxiety, and that doesn't help our relationships. However, learning to control ourselves when we feel like retreating into protection and instead leaning into connection can make a significant difference in our relationships.

One way to disarm your protective stance in your relationships is to ask yourself if the threat you perceive is real. Much of the time, the threat we feel during a relational conflict is brought on by our past experiences, rather than being based on the actual behavior and intentions of the person we are with here and now. When we respond from a place of fear, we are operating in protection mode and there is a higher chance that the people in our lives will respond to us similarly.

Self-Regulating Toward Connection

Intellectually, many of us know we need to calm down and self-regulate if we want to respond better to others in times of disagreement and stress. We aren't going into protection mode on purpose; we want to move forward and lean into connection. But our more emotional parts don't always get the memo.

Self-regulation isn't something you do once. It's a continuous process that starts with a conscious decision and commitment to working on it. Retraining your emotional brain can teach you to think more logically, even in your most self-protecting moments. Self-regulation allows you to decide to let go of a moment of reactivity, and it creates a sense of self and well-being. It develops your ability to understand and manage your responses to strong emotions like frustration, excitement, anger, and embarrassment, as well as to things happening around you.

Think about a situation that happened recently in which you felt threatened. What was the situation?

_____

_____

_____

How did your protective brain feel in this moment?

_____

_____

_____

What does your logical brain think about this situation?

_____

_____

_____

Once your thoughts are written out, reread each section and decide which ideas will help you to connect more with others. More than likely, you will find it's the ideas that come from your logical brain.

Assessing Vulnerability

Avoiding vulnerability keeps us from taking risks and connecting in our relationships. Our fears want us to maintain the status quo. However, when we listen to our anxiety over what we truly want in our relationships, we miss out on stronger connections and deeper intimacy. To be vulnerable, we must release the idea that exposing our real feelings and thoughts is a weakness. Answer the following questions to gain clarity and understanding of what vulnerability means to you.

What is your definition of vulnerability?

_____

_____

_____

_____

What messages were you given about vulnerability from your family, friends, culture, or others?

_____

_____

_____

_____

_____

_____

Describe a time when you practiced vulnerability.

_____

_____

_____

_____

Whom do you allow to see your vulnerability?

_____

_____

_____

_____

Relational Hurt and Attachment Injuries

When couples or families come to therapy, it is often because of an experience or pattern of incidents that created hurt for one or both parties. They decide to pursue treatment because they have difficulty resolving this hurt to feel safe and vulnerable with each other again. When working with these clients, we seek to understand the nature and significance of their pain before moving toward resolution. There are two levels of pain: *relational hurt* and *attachment injuries*.

RELATIONAL HURTS

Painful experiences like forgotten birthdays, insults, and big fights sneak into any relationship. When the people involved can share their hurt feelings, hear and empathize with each other, and give each other comfort, they can move on in the relationship with trust, security, and safety despite the negative experience. When the individuals in the relationship are securely attached, they can often heal from relational hurts without professional help. Because they feel they can depend on and be vulnerable with each other in times of need, they find these situations relatively easy to navigate.

In our therapy sessions, it's common for people to share their feelings of sadness, anger, hurt, and pain in response to a relational hurt. However, when we ask if they feel that the other person loves and cares for them, many say yes. The relational hurt hasn't significantly changed how they view each other or their relationship.

ATTACHMENT INJURIES

An attachment injury can be defined as "a feeling of betrayal or abandonment during a critical time of need" (Johnson & Greenberg, 1992). After an attachment injury, a person may view their loved one and the relationship differently than they did before.

An affair is an obvious example of an attachment injury, in that one person used to see their partner as trustworthy but now wonders, *Can I trust them again?* There are also more subtle attachment injuries. Consider the example of a husband grieving the loss of his job. While sitting with his upset emotions in the living room, he sees his wife walk by, talking on the phone. Caught up in her phone call, she sees that her husband is upset but doesn't return to check on him. As a result, he decides he is unimportant to her and must go through his pain alone. From that moment, everything changes in how he views the relationship and his wife. He was in need but she was not there for him.

Attachment injuries require a lot of care and consideration; often, people find they need guidance from a therapist. This is because they can feel stuck when they try to respond to attachment injuries as if they were merely relational hurts. Not recognizing the significance and impact of the damage, the person who caused the injury often feels frustrated and reacts in a way that causes even more pain, creating intense distress in the relationship. However, healing and reconnection are possible when the people in the relationship learn how to comfort and validate each other's pain.

There are three ways to tell whether an attachment injury has been caused:

- The person who was hurt continues to bring up the painful experience even after the other person has (sincerely) apologized.

- The hurt person is reliving the painful experience—they feel the hurt like it just happened.

- There has been a significant shift in the relationship that one or both parties trace back to a specific incident.

If you feel like there has been an attachment injury in one or more of your relationships, we encourage you to work through the following activity. If this doesn't apply to you, feel free to skip to the next section.

When dealing with an attachment injury in your relationship, here are some helpful questions to consider. If you believe you are the one who caused the attachment injury, answer the questions based on what your loved one has shared with you about their experience.

How has the attachment injury affected the way you see yourself? How has it affected the way you view your loved one or the relationship?

_____

_____

_____

_____

_____

What is your experience when you recall the painful situation? What do you feel, both physically and emotionally? What do you think about it?

_____

_____

_____

_____

_____

What would you like your loved one to do when you are feeling this way? Offer physical touch like a hug or cuddling? Provide emotional comfort such as validation, understanding, and no judgment? Simply listen to you?

_____

_____

_____

_____

How to Let Go of Controlling Others

Do you know someone who always needs to be in control—someone who manages their anxiety by ensuring they have everything their way? Are *you* that person?

For many, controlling others is a way of managing relationship tension. They might avidly offer advice to others on how they can have a "better" life or even jump in to "fix" things themselves. The thinking behind that impulse goes like this: *If you do what I say, there won't be any issues between us, and your life will be how I thought it should be, so I no longer have to worry.*

People displaying control in their relationships aren't always aware of how their actions come off to others. The things they see as wise or caring can feel overbearing and selfish to the people they care about. Selfishness does not mean living as you want; it means wanting others to live as you expect. In other words, selfishness is about trying to control the people you're in relationship with. If you hold on to an expectation that others should listen to, value, and apply your advice, you may be more controlling than you realize.

Letting go of control can help you step back and consider how you may have been unintentionally sabotaging your relationships. Think about how you feel when you are in a relationship with someone who always needs to have things their way or pushes you to be different so that they can feel better. We're certain this isn't what you wish to put your loved ones through either!

Or you might be someone who always goes with the flow to avoid conflict. Over time, this can turn into living a life dictated by what others expect from you. In contrast to the emotional safety that comes when we can just be ourselves around the people closest to us, we can feel suffocated when we think we must go along with what others say or they won't love us. When we lose ourselves to keep conflict out of our relationships, we are actually using a different form of control. This method of control involves monitoring how the other person responds to us and changing how we present ourselves out of fear of their reactions. When we change ourselves by trying to be extra nice or easygoing, we manipulate the other person's response by doing what we can to get a "better," not more authentic, response from them.

When we try to control our relationships too much, it creates a sense of obligation that leads us to worry over every single problem faced by the people in our life—and, often, to figure out how to fix it for them—all at the expense of our energy and priorities. Eventually, we distance ourselves from these relationships because they get overwhelming or start to feel like a burden.

We all want to be part of relationships that make us feel empowered, not those we are controlled in or are controlling in. When you learn to let go of the need to control others' actions or reactions, you create a safer environment for your relationships, which leads to a feeling of empowerment and confidence in yourself and in the other person. Since we do not have all the answers, and neither do other people, we should really only be focused on ourselves and on showing up intentionally in our relationships.

Letting Go of What You Can't Control

You can't control what you naturally feel and you can't control others; the only thing you can control is how you respond to situations. This is why you must take initiative for what is important to you in your life.

How would you like to respond to your vulnerabilities?

_____

_____

_____

_____

What can you do to stop expecting others to change so you can focus on yourself?

_____

_____

_____

_____

Once you focus on what you can control, how can this open up your life and future possibilities? How will it free you from your past patterns?

_____

_____

_____

_____

"Helping" to Avoid Vulnerability

Many of us become overly invested in other people's lives because we are anxious about their suffering, as well as our own. When we fail to come to terms with suffering as a natural part of life, we can stunt the growth of ourselves and our loved ones.

Giving and receiving help is part of all personal relationships. But are we truly being helpful when we step in to prevent someone from being vulnerable or push them to follow our advice over finding their own solution? It is essential to tackle these questions and find out what genuinely being helpful means, so we don't use "helping" as another way to avoid being vulnerable ourselves.

WHAT BEING HELPFUL TRULY MEANS

Being in the presence of another person's afflictions and needs provokes a profoundly emotional response from human beings. Like many who go into a helping profession, we became therapists to help people; however, our idea of what constitutes help has changed over the years. Sympathy and the desire to relieve someone's distress are natural responses. Even Darwin wrote about them as part of the social instinct humans and animals share—we take comfort in one another's company and in protecting and defending each other against threats.

When we jump in to help others, we operate from a purely instinctual place. What we often don't realize is that this instinct is largely anxiety. Operating from that anxiety means we can't access the calm and rational responsiveness that is appropriate and necessary for meeting the long-term needs of others and ourselves.

Our efforts to be helpful might be based on good intentions, but those good intentions don't always provide good results. Trying to help based on knee-jerk reactions, instead of coming from a place of reflection, vulnerability, and objectivity, can do more harm than good. The ability to manage our own emotions in the highly anxious or distressed presence of another, especially a loved one, is not easy to develop. But when we can practice this, we can indeed be present and accountable without needing to control or fix anything. This is what we believe is genuinely helpful in relationships.

In our own journeys to find out what it means to be truly helpful, we have found some tools that we keep in our back pockets when the going gets tough. If you are the helper, fixer, or people-pleaser in your relationships, pay close attention to this section.

- **Stay in touch.** This isn't easy to do in the presence of someone who is feeling very anxious or upset. Sometimes we instinctively create distance when anxiety is high. Thinking that you can't help or that the situation is too large can lead you to run in the other direction. Still, you can commit to staying in contact with the people you care about, even if their problems are big or unsolvable, like having a chronic illness. Staying in touch gives us the opportunity to practice regulating ourselves in the presence of others' pain and accepting people as they are.

- **See past the problem to the person experiencing it.** When we walk around with a hammer, we see everyone in our lives as a nail. There is more to the people we love than the issues they face, but anxiety often prevents us from relating to them as whole people. People are more resilient than we tend to think. Rather than seeing your loved one as a problem you must fix, look for their strengths and trust their ability to solve their own problems.

- **Respect others' boundaries.** Many people feel vulnerable when they face life's stressors, and some look to others to solve their problems. It's important to respect other people enough to let them come up with their own answers while staying in their vulnerability (without thinking it's a bad thing). To support their autonomy, focus on being there for them emotionally but stay out of the way when your opinion isn't needed or asked for. Determining how much to say in a given situation is not an exact science, but in general, we recommend offering helpful information without telling them what to do and making sure that any ideas for possible solutions come from them.

- **Know your limitations.** Grandiosity tends to get triggered in the helping relationship, making us believe we can do the impossible. It is humbling to find out how little control we have over the way others decide to live their lives. The two of us have learned the hard way that our limits were often reached before other people's needs were met. We must change our thought process from thinking we know what is best for our loved ones to defining what we really can and can't do for them. This makes our responses to them clearer, especially regarding how available we can be to others.

- **Become more objective.** It is hard to think clearly and objectively about our meaningful relationships. In intense emotional situations, it's easy to get pulled into the minutiae and feel pressured to do something instead of taking a step back and seeing the bigger picture. With each difficult situation we encounter, we must work on getting more objective about it, reflecting on how we can remain calm and resist the urge to solve anything immediately.

- **Work toward being open and honest.** To be seen, heard, and understood is crucial for people in any relationship. However, many people aren't available and honest in their relationships. When we try to solve and fix everything, we aren't connecting with others at a deeper level; we're acting as if we're above them. When we instead meet our loved one where they are, see them as a whole person, and let them see us open and honestly, it can be healing and calming.

The biggest lesson we've learned is that we weren't helping anyone by swooping in to solve every problem before looking at the bigger picture. When our "helping" is rooted in anxiety and an urge to smooth things over, it isn't coming from a genuine and vulnerable place. It's okay not to have all of the answers. It's okay to take your time to think things over. It's okay to throw your hands up and say, "This situation stinks right now, and it's going to be hard for a while." Not all problems can be fixed. Not every struggling person needs saving. Knowing that, and accepting it, might be the most helpful thing you can do for those you love.

Creating Your Own Definition of Help

So, what is help? To answer this question, we each need to reflect, deliberate, decide, and act in the context of each situation we face. We've described some of our personal experiences to get you thinking, but there's no one-size-fits-all method for determining what help is.

How do you define help?

_____

_____

_____

_____

In what ways would you like to change when it comes to helping others?

_____

_____

_____

_____

Letting Go of Fear of Vulnerability

We can imagine it hasn't been easy for you to face your vulnerabilities in this chapter. While we know that ignoring our feelings doesn't allow us to move forward, we also don't want to get stuck in our fear, unwilling to experience and express our vulnerabilities. Finding a way to express ourselves in words can empower us to finally let go of our fear of vulnerability.

In the following space, write about the vulnerabilities you want to continue working through.

The emotions that scare me the most are . . .

_____

_____

_____

_____

_____

I am scared that my emotions will . . .

_____

_____

_____

_____

I am scared that people will . . .

_____

_____

_____

_____

_____

I find it hard to move on from the fear . . .

_____

_____

_____

_____

_____

The people whom I fear the most to open up to are . . .

_____

_____

_____

_____

Read these fears aloud and say, "It's okay that I'm scared, but I am letting go of this fear now."

If you'd like to reflect upon additional thoughts and feelings that you have, use the space below:

_____

_____

_____

_____

_____

_____

_____

_____

◇◇

Chapter Takeaways

We have the choice to hide our true thoughts and feelings or to let go of the fear of being vulnerable. In this chapter, you:

- ✓ Defined vulnerability and its risks and benefits
- ✓ Identified your attachment style
- ✓ Learned about relational hurt and attachment injuries
- ✓ Worked on letting go of control and the fear of vulnerability

The next chapter discusses why self-reflection is needed for better relationships. Self-reflection is a means of becoming aware of your intentions. It will help you live a more autonomous life filled with authentic connections.

◇◇

CHAPTER 8

Stage 6: Self-Reflection

When we can find a way to look at ourselves and the part we play in our relationship triumphs and struggles, we open ourselves up to more profound, meaningful connections. When we choose to be honest with ourselves, we invite inner peace and close the door to future triggers from unresolved emotional attachments. By developing our ability for self-reflection, we are healing ourselves and our relationships with others.

Self-reflection is about enhancing all aspects of our experiences, clarifying our thinking, and focusing on what truly matters. Whatever our histories might be, our experiences are ours to interpret and deal with however we see fit. No one but you can decide what is best for you or how you should handle your relationships.

This chapter on self-reflection will help you live from a place of gratefulness, mindfulness, and intention and encourage you to be a more compassionate version of yourself. This final stage of building healthy relationships offers an opportunity to assess your development for yourself and to think mindfully about how you want to move forward.

What Is Self-Reflection?

Self-reflection is witnessing and evaluating our cognitive, emotional, and behavioral processes. It plays an essential role in our personal growth and our relationships by helping us absorb all aspects of our experience, such as why something took place, the impact it had, and whether it is something we would like to repeat or change in the future.

Practicing self-reflection in our daily lives takes intentionality and discipline. It requires pausing amid the chaos of life to honestly think about our choices and consider the bigger picture. When we don't self-reflect, we float through life without intention or agency, drifting from one situation to the next while trying to keep our heads above water. Without self-reflection, we fall into decisions without evaluating what we truly want, what the consequences might be, what is going well versus isn't working for us. This is how we end up feeling stuck in a situation or a life we don't want, repeating the same behaviors even when they aren't producing the results we hope for.

In contrast, when we practice self-reflection, we maintain thoughtfulness and intention behind our behaviors and decisions. The more reflective we are about the actions we take, the more our lives will align with who we want to be.

Practicing Self-Reflection

When a situation arises that you want to reflect on, ask yourself to observe the situation objectively. Being objective means accepting things as they are without projecting your fears, ideas, and past experiences onto the experience. Looking at problems objectively involves resisting an immediate reaction and instead taking in the information as if you are outside the situation. This allows you to see the situation for what it is and make better choices about how to respond to it. It helps make you aware of how your behaviors might occur in the situation, empowering you to evaluate whether those behaviors align with who you are and want to be.

When an opportunity to self-reflect arises, first work on stepping back from your immediate reaction to take an objective look at the situation, then ask yourself the following questions.

What would my autonomous self like to do right now?

_____

_____

_____

What actions would make me feel happier and more fulfilled?

_____

_____

_____

What kind of person do I want to be in this situation? What actions fit best with my values?

_____

_____

_____

You can learn to take obstacles, situations, and interactions with people as opportunities to self-reflect. Over time, you will likely notice that reflecting before reacting will help you act in ways that better fit with your long-term goals.

Why Is Self-Reflection Needed for Better Relationships?

Self-reflection is a means of becoming aware of your emotions and intentions. Having this awareness is essential to any relationship, especially during a conflict or disagreement. As therapists, we have seen countless times that a couple's argument over a minor issue, like when to wash the dishes, isn't just about the dirty dishes or even about housework in general. When a trivial disagreement brings up a big reaction from one or both partners, it shows that their reaction isn't reflective of the current situation. Instead, the intense emotions are likely connected to a deeper issue in the relationship. Self-reflection is vital in evaluating these tense moments and improving self-awareness, self-compassion, and emotional regulation.

Identifying Sensitivities

Our past experiences are like short stories etched into our nervous system. When past sensitive experiences are touched upon, they can bring up old emotional pain. In our times of conflict, specific sensitivities trigger our nervous system to produce intense reactions. We are often unaware of these "sore spots," which makes it easy for them to be provoked without our even realizing what is happening. Self-reflection and internal dialogue are necessary for exploring the source of the pain so that we can identify our sensitivities and change our pattern of reacting to them.

Reflecting on the Past

Recall a critical moment in your life—a situation or event that helped shape you. This moment can be significant, like a traumatic event, or seemingly smaller, like a positive interaction with a caregiver or essential advice from a mentor. These events become landmarks in our stories, shaping our view of ourselves, others, and the world around us. Needless to say, they also have an impact on our relationships.

Reflect on how the moment you selected has affected you by considering the following.

How did this particular moment or event change you as a person?

_____

_____

_____

How was this event impactful to your view of yourself, others, and the world around you?

_____

_____

_____

What did you learn from this experience?

_____

_____

_____

How has it affected the important relationships in your life today?

_____

_____

_____

For example, if you witnessed violence, it might have changed your sense of safety, leading to a general feeling of anxiety. You may now have strict routines and keep your home impeccably organized as a way of coping with the anxious feelings. But if your spouse is carefree and less regimented, there may be tension in your relationship around everyday routines.

Relationships as Templates

Another essential step in self-reflection is to continue to look closely at the early significant relationships in your life. As we have said, your early relationships provide a template for all your intimate relationships. Our early interactions teach us who we are expected to be and what we can expect from others—the good and the bad.

For example, if you rarely saw your father when you were a child, you might place a high value on being dependable and present as an adult, and thus may feel intensely angry or hurt if your partner shows up late to dinner. These emotions are rooted in the past and don't necessarily reflect what's actually happening now.

Think about your caregivers and the other people who were significantly involved in your early life—this might include close relatives, mentors, friends, and siblings. Consider your role in those relationships and the parts that other people took on. As you reflect on your past relationships, ask yourself the following questions.

What behaviors do I expect from others, and what do they expect from me?

_____

_____

_____

_____

_____

What did I learn about how to best connect with others?

_____

_____

_____

_____

_____

What needs of mine went unmet?

_____

_____

_____

_____

_____

What fears do I have, or did I have, that I need reassurance about?

_____

_____

_____

_____

_____

When we identify our essential experiences in relationships and why we have heightened reactions in specific situations, we can begin to separate our interactions today from sensitivities created by our past. It's important to share this backstory with our loved ones if we do find ourselves overreacting, as it offers them deeper understanding of what we're going through in these situations.

Reflect on Your Experiences with Mindful Breathing

If you have tried mindfulness a couple of times and thought it wasn't for you, we encourage you to try it again! Individuals who practice mindfulness are happier, healthier, and more self-aware than those who don't. But like any skill, mindfulness takes practice.

Many times, the only thing standing in our way of being mindful and self-aware is a little bit of direction. The following steps will guide you through some mindful breathing for self-reflection.

1. **Get out of autopilot mode and bring awareness to your actions, thoughts, and sensations at this moment.** When you find yourself feeling unusually

hurt or angry about an otherwise moderate situation, pause. Find a comfortable and relaxing position where you can be still and quiet. Become attuned to yourself and your current state. Take note of the thoughts that come up and accept your feelings, then let them pass.

2. **Bring awareness to your breathing for six breaths or one minute.** In your relaxed position, focus your attention on your breath. Become aware of the movement in your body with each breath you take: your chest rising and falling, your stomach pulling in and out, your lungs contracting and expanding. Recognize your breathing pattern and anchor yourself in the present moment with awareness, reflecting on experiences that create heightened sensitivity for you as you breathe.

3. **Expand awareness outward through the body.** Now, let your awareness expand throughout your body. Take note of the sensations you are experiencing, like aches, tightness, or lightness in your face or shoulders. Think of your body as a whole, complete vessel for your inner self. Next, pull your attention to the types of experiences that bring up tension in your body. Observe your feelings, sensations, and thoughts without judgment.

When you've finished the exercise, try to carry that mindfulness with you daily. When we are willing to take the time to reflect on our experiences through mindfulness, we are better able to self-reflect during times of heightened stress.

A Story of Self-Reflection in Therapy

Debra came to therapy feeling anxious in her daily life, which she attributed to her marriage. She didn't feel like she could be herself around her husband, Jonathan. On the rare occasion that Debra told him what she wanted, Jonathan would get upset if it didn't align with what he wanted and would tell her that she made him feel distant and unloved. She took this personally and began to believe that his hurt feelings were all her fault. It was common for her to be the one to apologize, even when she didn't do anything wrong. This way of thinking spilled into many of Debra's other relationships, resulting in her keeping her true thoughts and feelings to herself.

Eventually, though, Debra found that she couldn't live tiptoeing around her husband's feelings forever. After much thought and self-reflection, Debra realized that she needed to work on her inability to tolerate hurting other people's feelings.

When Dr. Ilene gained more details from Debra, she realized that in most of Debra's relationships, she worried more about how she affected others than about her own feelings. While Jonathan might have been more sensitive to feeling hurt, Debra's unwillingness to express herself, for fear that she would hurt him, also contributed to their relationship's difficulties. Debra had never considered that it was impossible to be in a relationship with someone without hurting them at some point; she couldn't wrap her head around the idea. For her, it felt natural to suppress her feelings and thoughts to avoid seeing someone she loved in discomfort.

Dr. Ilene asked, "Debra, where did the idea come from that it isn't acceptable to hurt someone you love?" This led them to discover a core belief Debra held: that when people feel hurt, they're always deeply wounded.

Debra mentioned that when she was growing up, her father would easily get hurt by minor things. She shared one particular memory of her father yelling at her about how hurt he was when Debra didn't like that he made fish for dinner. He screamed that she failed to appreciate all the time, money, and effort it took him to feed her. Debra remembered how scared she was when her father was angry and how much humiliation she felt about not liking the food he had cooked. She became mad at herself for not enjoying fish and ate it to appease him. From that moment, Debra began to make the connection that the prospect of hurting someone's feelings created deep anxiety for her.

As a young girl, Debra wasn't aware that she didn't need to internalize her father's overreactions. She always believed it was her responsibility to make her father happy, so she focused on his needs to avoid making him angry. As she became aware of this in therapy, Debra realized that her dedication to keeping her father happy and avoiding his anger led her to overlook her own best interests.

This helped her see how she was recreating that relationship dynamic with Jonathan. Her anxiety about hurting Jonathan whenever their desires didn't align strengthened her belief that she shouldn't voice her opinion. She realized that although Jonathan's reactions weren't as intense as her father's, she was replaying the same patterns with him. Ultimately, Debra came to recognize that she isn't responsible for other people's feelings, that it isn't wrong for her to speak up about what she wants, and that she is only responsible for using her voice.

Once she became aware of all this, she started working on breaking free from her pattern of absorbing other people's anxiety by overly focusing on them instead of herself. By working to become more comfortable expressing her thoughts and feelings, and then dealing with the impact this had on the people around her, Debra was able to bring herself to life. No longer believing that she was to blame for others' reactions made her better at dealing with conflict and helped her worry much less about being a bad person. She gained confidence in herself and her ability to speak her mind. By simply looking at her history and better understanding her part in an anxious family system, Debra made real and meaningful changes in her own life and in her marriage.

Debra's case offers one example of how self-reflection can help you to see how anxiety in your family of origin plays out in your life and future relationships. When we become anxious about our effect on others and silence ourselves or alter our behavior to ensure we don't hurt anyone's feelings, we operate as a non-self. If we take time to self-reflect, whether in therapy or on our own, we can nourish our own development and improve our relationships as a result.

Responding Intentionally

In general, people who self-reflect are more intentional in their lives. Intentional people aren't highly affected by the people around them. Instead, they observe their own emotional state, operate directly from it, and find ways to respond based on their values and beliefs.

When we respond with intention, people change how they interact with us. When we learn to use wisdom and care in choosing our responses to the world around us, we create a better life and more meaningful connections.

How can you respond more intentionally to the people in your life? We've included some examples below to help you get started:

- I can take a deep breath before I answer someone.

- When I notice I'm angry, I will take a quick meditation break.

- I will consider my words carefully before sending text messages.

_____

_____

_____

_____

_____

Acts Showing Progress

It's important to honor yourself by noticing the strength and willpower it has taken to work on your relationships. Many of us tend to work on something, then quickly move on to the next project without recognizing how far we've come. We frequently encourage our clients to celebrate themselves and their progress, no matter how small they think it is. You have shown strength by making it this far in this book, and that deserves to be honored.

Reflecting on your progress and the positive changes you've already made will give you the motivation you need to continue this journey. The following questions will help you take note of your successes in handling challenging encounters with others.

Describe some recent experiences or encounters that you found difficult, frustrating, or triggering. (Examples might include your father being critical of you, someone cutting you off in traffic, or your child not listening when you told them to do their chores.)

_____

_____

_____

_____

_____

Recall how you responded to these situations. In what ways were your responses different from what your reactions might usually have been before you began this journey? Did you feel less overwhelmed by emotions? Did your perspective on the situation change? Were you able to recognize the patterns from your past that were coming into play? Were you able to choose your words and actions thoughtfully?

_____

_____

_____

_____

_____

_____

_____

_____

Reflecting on How You Manage Relationship Anxiety

Families and individuals aren't creative or unique in how they handle stress. In fact, there are a handful of well-documented approaches we see utilized over and over again in our therapy practice. Understanding these automatic strategies and the generational patterns they're based on will support you in your self-reflection. We've listed the most common patterns for managing anxiety in the following paragraphs—take note of the ones you tend to engage in.

CONFLICT

How often have you found yourself in a fight with a loved one without knowing how or why it started? It's no secret that conflict is more likely to arise during times of high stress and anxiety, including anxiety that doesn't even originate from the relationship! Any anxiety can trigger conflict with someone you love and care about, whether it's related to work, health, or other aspects of life.

When we're anxious and upset, we often get overrun by a sense of urgency. We feel like we need to blurt out everything we're feeling in that moment or else we'll explode. We also tend to display these behaviors, which lead to conflict with others:

- We become more critical of others.

- We blame them for the problems we're facing.

- We project our issues onto the other person.

- We focus outward instead of on ourselves.

- We escalate existing arguments and pick fights.

Strangely, getting into a conflict can have an initial calming effect. It serves as an outlet for our anxiety and offers a sense of reassurance that we aren't at fault for what's happening to us—that we are right and the other person is wrong.

Conflict also provides a feeling of having "done" something about the problem. The trigger that starts the conflict can feel like an electrical current moving through you, jolting you into action. It's hard to resist, even when you know from experience how it's likely to turn out. After all, despite the initial reassurance it provides, conflict isn't a particularly helpful or advisable way to manage your anxiety.

You don't have to indulge those urges to pick a fight. Instead, you can see those instincts for what they are and take the time you need to access your more logical self. Once you've centered yourself within your rational brain and your values, you can reflect on your part in the situation and decide how to approach others reasonably, even when they (or you) are anxious or intense.

DISTANCE

Some people experience their emotions so intensely that they believe they have no choice but to deny or create distance from the problems and people they see as the cause of their feelings. This distance feels like the only way they can maintain control of themselves and their reactions. Most of the time, they do this subconsciously. For some people, creating emotional distance becomes so automatic that they lose touch with how they truly feel about anything.

Some possible ways that emotional distancing can manifest include:

- Going long periods without talking to others

- Overworking

- Using drugs or alcohol

- Spending extreme amounts of time on hobbies

- Suppressing your feelings when you're upset or anxious

- Feeling disconnected from your loved ones in general

- Avoiding emotionally loaded topics

Distancing can provide some relief from the emotional intensity of a relationship, offering an opportunity to collect yourself and gather your thoughts. Couples often create distance by seeking space or time apart, seeing it as a way to maintain their individuality. It might not seem like a problem in your relationships until your partner, family member, or friend gets jealous or feels ignored and unloved. Over time, engaging in this behavior without awareness can inflict irreparable damage on the relationship.

For example, a couple engaged in distancing might appear from the outside like two individuals with their own respective lives. However, because they're avoiding their problems indefinitely—as opposed to cooling off briefly before attempting repair and connection—they remain hyperfocused on each other and on the hurt they're feeling. We have found that distancing only creates more tension and emotional reactivity in a relationship.

If you tend to use distancing as a way to manage your emotions around someone, you can start finding other ways to calm yourself amid intense emotions. Instead of trying to dodge conflict and confrontation, resolve to bring up important issues even if they make you anxious. This will help you build confidence in your ability to think through emotionally intense conversations, which in turn helps you push through the instinct to distance yourself from troubling issues or people.

CUTOFF

Breaking off a significant relationship, also known as *cutoff,* is not an uncommon method of managing intense anxiety within relationships. While divorce and breakups are the most widely recognized forms, cutoff can happen in many different ways. For example, an estimated 67 million Americans are currently estranged from a relative (Pillemer, 2020). You may have experienced this yourself or noted while creating your family genogram in chapter 3 that some of your relatives were cut off from each other.

In a family system, cutoff can lead to a generational pattern of responding to intense feelings by severing connections with the people who trigger them. If your family has a history of cutoff under stressful circumstances or over issues such as financial strain, religion, or politics, you may be more likely to consider cutoff when you're experiencing relationship difficulties, or even to have it cross your mind during minor disagreements and moments of frustration.

Like distancing, cutoff tends to relieve relationship anxiety in the short term, but over time, it might lead to more anxiety and emotional intensity in your other relationships. For example, someone who is estranged from their family of origin may look to their partner to meet all of their needs, and as a result expect too much of their partner or suppress their own needs out of fear of jeopardizing that relationship (The Bowen Center for the Study of the Family, 2023). These cascading effects can explain why people who seek therapy for anxiety or depression often have a history of cutoff in their relationships.

It's important to note that while cutoff is not an "easy way out," sometimes it may be the healthiest option, such as when abuse is involved. Given the intensity of a relationship that leads you to consider cutoff, you should not stay in the relationship simply for the sake of reversing a pattern. It's better to first spend time thinking about the forces that contributed to the pattern and what you want to accomplish in addressing it. You can still work toward addressing the pattern in your other relationships, even if you find that ending one or more specific relationships is necessary for the safety, health, and emotional well-being of yourself and others.

Some cutoffs can be repaired when we take responsibility for our part in the relationship rift, learn to manage our anxiety around intense relationships, and become more differentiated. As you work on your relationships, it will be helpful to get curious about any history of cutoff in your family. This will help you gain more objectivity about how the cutoff pattern plays a role in your past and current life. (We'll talk more about this in the next chapter.)

Over- and Underfunctioning Reciprocity

It's common for one person to take on more responsibility in the family when another seems less capable. This results in a pattern of *overfunctioning* and *underfunctioning*. It often happens in marriages, but children can also overfunction for their parents or siblings.

If you're an overfunctioner, you're likely to:

- Think you know what's best for the other person

- Worry a lot about the other person

- Give a lot of advice

- Perform tasks for others that they could do for themselves

- Think you're responsible for others' feelings and choices

- Do most of the talking

- Set goals for others that they haven't set for themselves

If you're an underfunctioner, you're likely to:

- Be indecisive

- Ask for others' advice when you should think things through on your own

- Ask others to help with things you can do for yourself

- Often make irresponsible choices

- Do most of the listening

- Not have goals for yourself

- Not complete tasks that you start

- Regularly become mentally or physically ill

- Easily become addicted to substances

While the underfunctioner is usually labeled as the problem partner/child/sibling because they have trouble completing tasks or doing things for themselves, the reality is that everyone in the relationship or family system plays a part in this pattern. After all, underfunctioners go through life by getting others involved in their problems. The underfunctioner does this because they underestimate their abilities. They resort to having others do things for them that they could do for themselves because it temporarily relieves their anxiety . . . and, to be blunt, it's just easier. Why learn to do the laundry when your mom or wife will do it for you?

Overfunctioners tend to become anxious about underfunctioners' lack of enthusiasm and initiative to complete tasks. Many overfunctioners believe that if something is going to get done, it's up to them to do it. The truth is, sometimes it's easier to do something for someone than to watch them struggle with a task and get frustrated or upset.

Becoming aware of this pattern isn't about assigning blame. It's about recognizing our contribution to the relationship pattern so we can learn how to become more responsible for ourselves. With awareness of this pattern, you can work toward establishing an equal balance of functioning within your relationships. If each person can learn to take responsibility for themselves—and only themselves—within the relationship, their relationship anxiety will diminish.

How Does Your Family Manage Relationship Anxiety?

It's important to remember that the behaviors we engage in to manage our anxiety don't make us bad people; they make us human. Our work is simply to become fully aware of how we manage our relationship anxiety and, with the objectivity that comes with this awareness, choose to respond differently to our family and friends.

For this activity, you will be reflecting on the patterns of managing relationship anxiety that you recognized in yourself while reading this chapter. Then you will look back two generations in your family—to your parents and your grandparents—to gather information that can shed light on how these patterns came about.

How do you and your partner, spouse, or coparent handle disagreements in your relationship?

_____

_____

_____

_____

How do you manage stress and anxiety in your relationship? Do you fight a lot? Avoid talking about what bothers you? Lead separate lives?

_____

_____

_____

_____

Who takes care of most of the household responsibilities? (Keep in mind that this could be driven by practicality or thoughtful agreement as well as anxiety.)

_____

_____

_____

_____

Are you or your partner cut off from anyone else in the family? If so, what happened?

_____

_____

_____

_____

How do you show love and affection to each other?

_____

_____

_____

_____

If you have children, how do you show love and affection to them?

_____

_____

_____

_____

How do you each express and manage anxiety?

_____

_____

_____

_____

    Now consider the relationships between your parents and your grandparents. The genogram you created in chapter 3 can help you with this; you may also wish to talk to one or more of your family members to gather more information.

    We understand that your grandparents or parents might have been unmarried or single. However, it can still be helpful to reflect on these family members, since the lack of a partnership may point to cutoff and distancing. It may also be helpful to consider what your parents' or grandparents' relationships were like with any others who were significantly involved in caring for their children or managing the household (for example, maybe your grandmother lived with you and your father and helped raise you).

How did your parents handle disagreements in their relationship with each other (or in their relationships with their other partners or spouses)?

_____

_____

_____

_____

How did they manage stress and anxiety in their relationship? Did they seem to fight a lot? Avoid talking about what bothered them? Lead separate lives?

_____

_____

_____

_____

Who took care of most of the household responsibilities? (Keep in mind that this could have been driven by practicality or thoughtful agreement as well as anxiety.)

_____

_____

_____

_____

Were they cut off from anyone else in the family? If so, what happened?

_____

_____

_____

_____

How did they show love and affection to each other?

_____

_____

_____

_____

How did they show love and affection to their children?

_____

_____

_____

_____

How did they each express and manage anxiety?

_____

_____

_____

_____

How did one set of your grandparents handle disagreements in their relationship with each other (or in their relationships with their other partners or spouses)?

_____

_____

_____

_____

How did they manage stress and anxiety in their relationship? Did they seem to fight a lot? Avoid talking about what bothered them? Lead separate lives?

_____

_____

_____

_____

Who took care of most of the household responsibilities? (Keep in mind that this could have been driven by practicality or thoughtful agreement as well as anxiety.)

_____

_____

_____

_____

Were they cut off from anyone else in the family? If so, what happened?

_____

_____

_____

_____

How did they show love and affection to each other?

_____

_____

_____

_____

How did they show love and affection to their children?

_____

_____

_____

_____

How did they each express and manage anxiety?

_____

_____

_____

_____

How did your other set of grandparents handle disagreements in their relationship with each other (or in their relationships with their other partners or spouses)?

_____

_____

_____

_____

How did they manage stress and anxiety in their relationship? Did they seem to fight a lot? Avoid talking about what bothered them? Lead separate lives?

_____

_____

_____

_____

Who took care of most of the household responsibilities? (Keep in mind that this could have been driven by practicality or thoughtful agreement as well as anxiety.)

_____

_____

_____

_____

Were they cut off from anyone else in the family? If so, what happened?

_____

_____

_____

_____

How did they show love and affection to each other?

_____

_____

_____

_____

How did they show love and affection to their children?

_____

_____

_____

_____

How did they each express and manage anxiety?

_____

_____

_____

_____

Opportunity to Grow with Self–Reflection

Imagine a world where, instead of directing our energy toward avoiding others, trying to change others, or overthinking how others see us, we direct our energy toward changing how we see ourselves. Imagine a world where you don't need others to accept you so you can feel good about yourself but instead feel sure of who you are, regardless of the views of others. In this world, you'd experience a sense of freedom that would help you manage your anxiety instead of feeling like it controls you.

As we mature and grow, we come to notice that a good life isn't without hardships. When we live intentionally and use self-reflection, we find ways for our difficulties to work in our favor instead of letting them push us off course. We don't shy away from the struggles in life but rather see them as opportunities to grow into who we want to be. We notice what we tend to do when we feel anxious and stressed, and instead of repeating patterns we thoughtfully do something new.

◇◇◇

Chapter Takeaways

Self-reflection allows us to live our lives with intention and build healthier relationships with ourselves and others. In this chapter, you:

- ✓ Learned about self-reflection and its benefits
- ✓ Explored how your past experiences have shaped your current relationships
- ✓ Identified how you and your family have managed relationship anxiety
- ✓ Practiced responding intentionally rather than reacting automatically

In the final chapter, we'll conclude this book by further explaining how to do the work toward better and more fulfilling relationships. The lessons you have learned so far have encouraged you to change how you think about yourself and your relationships, but the next level of change comes from doing the work in real life.

◇◇◇

CHAPTER 9

Doing the Work

It's no secret that working on our relationships can be challenging. Moreover, doing the work unfortunately does not guarantee success in all your relationships. Sometimes we must learn when to walk away from a relationship or the idea we had about it. In this final chapter, we will explore when it is time to end a romantic relationship or make the difficult decision to cease contact with a family member. We'll also work on letting go of the idea that there is a perfect relationship and rethink our motivation to continue improving our relationships without that ideal goal in mind.

Creating Yourself Within Your Relationships

If you think about our solar system and only see planets acting independently out in space, you're missing the bigger picture: that each planet works as part of a greater system in which everything influences everything else. Gravity is the powerful force that keeps this system together. It holds the planets in orbit around the sun and the moons in orbit around the planets. We would float into the sky without gravitational forces keeping us grounded on Earth. So it's safe to say that gravity—the mutual influence that holds everything together—plays a significant role in our survival.

This same idea applies to how we view ourselves and other people. When we think that being an individual means operating as a single entity with no influence from the outside world, we fail to see that each individual is part of a system of relationships that influence each other. Real change happens with the awareness that we create our sense of self within our relationships, not apart from them, and that problems do not reside within individuals but in the interconnections between them.

Through your work in this book, you have become more aware of how interconnected you are to those you care about, what that means for you, and the changes you can make in your relationships. Many of our clients see this interconnection only in the context of their sensitivity to the discomfort in others, which triggers them to try to fix the other person's problem, lecture the other person to make themselves feel better, avoid the person, or not feel like they have room for their own feelings. However, the same interconnection is at work when we're around someone happy and upbeat who makes us feel good and helps us respond accordingly. No matter whom you choose to be around, paying attention to what the relationship means to you and what it does to you internally and externally is always helpful.

It isn't necessarily good or bad that we are part of a system of relationships that influence each other. Being aware of the invisible lines that connect us can help us decide how to respond more thoughtfully to others in any situation.

When we are in the middle of surviving our busy lives and navigating our relationships, we might forget what is valuable and important to us. In the following activity, you will create a relationship vision that maps how you want to connect and respond in your relationships. This vision will help you remain grounded in who you are while being accountable for how you behave with others.

Your Relationship Vision

People with a vision can think about and plan their future. You don't have to wait for your dream relationships to show up; instead, you can become conscious of what you envision for your relationships and hold yourself accountable for achieving it.

In this activity, you will create a vision for how you want to experience the relationships in your life and brainstorm a few ideas for how you can contribute to the kind of relationships you envision. This list will guide your work in improving the relationships in your life. To get you started, here are a few examples:

Vision: I want to create more meaningful moments for myself.

Actions:

- Build self-awareness by continuing to meditate and journal daily.
- Create a list of affirmations to use as positive self-talk.

Vision: I want to stay intentionally connected with my partner.

Actions:

- Stay present and mindful during our conversations using active listening.
- Plan a weekly date night for some one-on-one time.

Vision: I want to give my children a safe space for feeling their emotions.

Actions:

- Practice patience when my children are struggling—determine whether they need my help or would benefit from figuring it out on their own.
- Limit their screen time, which they might use to distract or numb themselves.

Vision: _____

Actions:

- _____
- _____
- _____

Vision: _____

Actions:

- _____
- _____
- _____

Vision: _____

Actions:

- _____
- _____
- _____

Healthy Relationships Aren't Perfect

The idea that good relationships shouldn't have any difficulties can lead people to let go of a relationship at the first sign of turbulence. When we get stuck in the idea of perfection, we cannot see that it's normal and okay to have trouble in our relationships.

A Story of Friendship

Kaeden and Moises have been best friends for three decades. For most of that time, their lives were usually in sync and their ideas in agreement, from choosing the same college, to moving to the same city after graduation, to getting engaged to their girlfriends in the same year. They were so compatible that they always thought of their friendship as perfect.

But then Moises's fiancée got a job in Miami and he moved there with her. Meanwhile, Kaeden stayed in Chicago. With this significant life transition, communicating and connecting became much more challenging. Unlike before, when they had their weekly golf tee times, their relationship now included some conflict. They would schedule guys' trips to reconnect, but Moises often canceled due to work scheduling or family responsibilities. They began to disagree about the way the relationship was going. While Moises thought everything was fine, Kaeden started to question whether their perfect friendship was working anymore.

Kaeden needed to acknowledge that friendships come with changes and conflict, that differences of opinions and priorities do not mean the end of the relationship. He needed to let go of the "perfect" friendship as he understood it and accept the friendship as it now existed. To his surprise, working through the conflict with Moises allowed Kaeden to become even closer to his friend than before.

In any relationship, it's important to realize that you can love someone and feel close to them even while experiencing times of distance and stress. In fact, perfectionism is incompatible with true intimacy. To have the most intentional and healthy relationship, you must work through difficult moments rather than expect that they will never happen. Living in that reality will create a safe space to foster deep connection, where imperfect people create their own version of "perfection" together.

While Having Romantic Relationships Matters, So Does Ending Them

Most of us do not like to lose things, especially relationships. After all, relationships are the most critical aspect of our lives, as essential to human existence as our need to breathe. But sometimes, no matter how hard we try, a relationship just doesn't work. We have all been taught that love should win out if we work hard enough at it. However, some people do not belong in each other's lives, even when they have the best intentions and relationship tools. One of the most complex decisions we must make as humans is when to stay in a relationship and when to let it go.

As we have said, every relationship has both good and not-so-good times. However, if you notice that over time, you often feel distressed thinking about or interacting with a person you are in a relationship with, this is a sign that the relationship may need to end. When you cannot sort out the differences between you with mutual respect and support, there is no room to collaborate. This indicates that your differences outweigh your connection.

People often stay in relationships even after they have proved incompatible because they feel they have invested too much to leave. Maybe you tell yourself you should have left earlier but now you're in it too deep. Maybe you've bargained with yourself, saying things like, "If this or that happens, then I can go."

To be frank, staying in an unhappy relationship because you've already stayed in it this long is a terrible reason for sticking it out longer. If you believe you have to dim your light, hide your interests, or suppress your opinions to maintain the relationship, your relationship isn't helping you to be more of yourself. Instead, it's causing you to slowly lose yourself—a much more significant loss than the end of a relationship.

Instead of fighting for someone to be in our lives or for something to turn out a certain way, we must let go of the desire and accept what is actually happening (or needs to happen). True acceptance means actively embracing your thoughts, feelings, and experiences as they are. To do this, there are two questions you can ask yourself:

- Do I like who I am in this relationship?

- Will I be okay in this relationship if nothing changes?

Four Horsemen of the Apocalypse

According to Gottman, there are four primary communication styles that strongly predict your relationship is ending (Lisitsa, 2022). These "four horsemen of the apocalypse," as he calls them, are criticism, defensiveness, contempt, and stonewalling.

- **Criticism** means speaking badly about someone's character rather than their behavior. When criticism becomes pervasive, bringing up important issues becomes a considerable relationship divide. Unlike complaining, which focuses on a situation ("I wish you would help me with the housework rather than stay in bed"), criticizing involves being talked to from a superior point of view, often with sarcasm or name-calling in the mix ("You're so selfish; you never think about anyone else").

- **Defensiveness** is typical in any relationship when a person perceives they are being criticized. We can all get defensive at times when we are feeling verbally attacked. However, if you are always shifting the blame onto your partner rather than taking accountability, you may live in an ongoing state of defensiveness that harms your relationship. No one likes to be told they are doing something wrong or being hurtful to others, but refusing to ever take responsibility for your role in a situation can cause the other person in the relationship to feel chronically unseen and unheard, leading to an erosion of your connection.

- **Contempt** refers to treating others with disrespect, either passively (such as rolling your eyes, mimicking others, or using sarcasm) or directly (insulting or belittling another person). Contemptuous behavior diminishes the other person, making them feel unworthy. It's a major relationship red flag that implies you've stopped respecting the other person and creates a dominant stance that causes resentment to build. When there is no respect between two individuals, there is little chance the relationship can be salvaged.

- **Stonewalling** happens when someone in the relationship avoids listening, limits contact, withdraws, shuts down, or stops responding to communication. Given how important honest communication is for a healthy relationship, when a relationship reaches a point where someone dreads conversations, it is tough to recover.

We have all experienced one or more of these horsemen in our relationships at times, but when any of these behaviors consistently shows up in a relationship, it is a definite sign the relationship is on its way to an end, especially without professional help from a marriage and family therapist.

When a Relationship Ends (and What Comes Afterward)

One reason the decision to let go is so hard is that you may feel like you know yourself as a specific person within that relationship, and the uncertainty of who you'll be or how you will feel without the relationship is scary. It can also be challenging to let go of a specific idea of how you thought your future would turn out with this relationship in your life. But probably the most challenging part of letting go is releasing your connection to the past, especially the memories you hold of someone and your relationship with them. Allow yourself to grieve the change process, knowing that it is okay to miss the person or long for the version of them you once knew.

No matter who decides to let go of the relationship, remember that you are not solely responsible for the entire relationship's success or longevity. Give yourself permission to understand that it is okay and even natural for relationships to end—this will help you release any blame and guilt you may be carrying, as well as sadness, anger, or lack of closure over the loss. Practice self-compassion, offer yourself and the other person forgiveness for any mistakes that were made, and accept your needs as they are.

After you've ended a relationship, it's important to be open to a new network, new projects, or even new relationships. Try to focus on the good things to come. If we focus on the fact that one relationship ended, we are more likely to be unsuccessful again, whereas if we expect the best from our future, we attract and align the best for ourselves and our relationships. Additionally, the work on yourself that you've done with this book will support you in attracting (and being attracted to) more compatible partners.

Making the Decision to Cut Off Family

As we've discussed earlier, *cutoff* describes how people manage their unresolved emotional attachment with parents, siblings, or other family members by cutting off contact with them. It can happen as the result of abuse, conflict, differences in core values and beliefs, or any other reason that is significant to the individuals involved. The way in which cutoffs occur also varies—people may stop communication all at once or they may gradually decrease contact first, such as by moving farther away or visiting less frequently over time.

Lately, we have seen a greater willingness of our clients to cut off family members. Some people say they get overwhelmed with their family, that their family members are critical, judgmental, controlling, angry, disrespectful, or uncaring to the point that the person is unable to handle it. For these individuals, cutoff can provide relief from the emotional reactivity. This is the preservative side to cutoff, the aspect that leads many people to do it because they cannot figure out what else to do.

However, there can be a cost to achieving that relief. As we've shown, it's a reality of human life that we need other people, and the family is crucial in how we develop. To cut off from your family might mean losing a foundational relationship system. Ending contact with one relative may affect other relationships within the system or even your connection to the family as a whole. And, of course, if the person you'd be cutting off is currently providing you with any kind of emotional, physical, or financial support—perhaps by serving as an emergency medical contact, cosigning a loan, offering parenting advice or childcare, and so on—you'll need to be prepared for that support to end. It will be vital to identify other people, such as your partner and friends, whom you can turn to for support in those areas.

We are not saying that cutoff is inherently wrong; our goal here is to clarify some of the pros and cons to help you think about what's important in your particular situation. You may decide that cutoff is the best course for you, and if you do, you can still work on becoming more objective and understanding of what fueled the cutoff and, potentially, who else in the family you can remain connected to.

When you look at your family history on your genogram, you may see a pattern of cutoff in each successive generation. This can have implications for the family that you create on your own. We have found that a family pattern of cutoff isn't necessarily fueled by irreconcilable differences between members, but rather by intense reactivity to circumstances: "If you and I don't agree on something, we just aren't going to talk to each other." If your family has a history of cutoff, it is helpful to explore what is fueling this pattern and how you manage tension in your own relationships.

If cutoff has become a pattern in your family, or if you feel deep down that repairing the relationship is possible and desirable (though it may also be difficult), then it is worth taking some more time to reflect on the relationship and consider what other options may be available to you. Ask yourself the following questions.

How can I get less caught up with who my family thinks I should be?

_____

_____

_____

_____

_____

How can I work on being my own individual self while trying to stay connected to others?

_____

_____

_____

_____

_____

Is there a way for me to get a little more comfortable with how my family functions without letting that functioning determine who I am and how I react to my family?

_____

_____

_____

_____

_____

Your answers to these questions can help you become more thoughtful about how you would like to move forward. You very well might decide that certain people are not going to have access to you because they are abusive, toxic, or a negative influence. We never tell our clients whom they should or should not have in their lives. We just want to support you in making decisions from what you truly need instead of what may be dictated by a family pattern of cutoff.

Bridging Cutoff

Knowing the broader implications cutoff has for you, your family, and the other relationships in your life, you may wish to bridge cutoff when you can. You can't control other people, but bridging cutoff can help improve your emotional flexibility within your relationships. Studies show that the more positive contact we have with family, the better we do in general: less stress, reduced depression, boosted self-confidence, and lengthened life expectancy (Vangelisti, 2004).

Whether the cutoff was one that you had enacted, one that you were subjected to by your family, or one that occurred when you were a child or even before you were born, trying to reconnect can be daunting. You can start by trying to build one-on-one relationships with each person on the other side of the cutoff. Try to get to know them for who they are, not through other people or what you have been told about them. Rather than getting into the past conflict, start small and casually. You might reach out to simply say hi and slowly build contact from there.

If you are seriously considering bridging a cutoff but are unsure how to proceed, an informative book is *Fault Lines: Fractured Families and How to Mend Them* by Karl Pillemer (2020). It includes wisdom from people who have healed rifts within their families and clear, practical steps that you can take.

The most challenging part is the initial contact. Some family members may be happy to reconnect and get to know you better; others may not be so warm and welcoming. It is hard to put yourself out there and try to restore the relationship. If you aren't up for the challenge, that is okay too. Regardless of what you choose to do, make sure you have a good support team, like a group of friends, a religious or nonreligious community, or an emotional support group.

◇◇

Chapter Takeaways

You have been developing the insight and skills to intentionally grow and foster longevity in your relationships. Even as you envision the best outcome for your work on your relationships, you have also considered when and how to end a relationship. In this chapter, you:

- ✓ Created a vision for your relationships
- ✓ Recognized why it is important to let go of the "perfect" relationship ideal
- ✓ Learned the telltale signs that a relationship is ending
- ✓ Explored the pros and cons of cutoff, as well as bridging a cutoff

On the next page, we offer some final thoughts and well-wishes as you continue on your journey.

◇◇

FINAL THOUGHTS

We hope that by reading this book, you have discovered relationship tools that you can take along as you continue to learn and grow throughout your life. Relationships require work, but if you approach this work intentionally and do a little each day, you will develop into the person you want to be in any relationship.

Nothing that is truly fulfilling is easy all the time. We all have fantasies about how relationships should be, but that is seldom reality. Relationships can be complicated, and they rarely meet our expectations of perfection. No one person will meet all of our needs and desires, much less heal our childhood traumas or resolve our emotional attachments. This is work we must do on our own and through the many relationships we have. Instead of focusing on the difficulties of this work, we encourage you to look at what you stand to gain from it—relationships that are loving, supportive, and empowering, where you feel safe and free to express your true self while still connecting deeply with your loved one.

Even though you have completed this book, this is not the end of your journey in improving your relationships. Rather, you have chosen a worthwhile roadmap to follow, one that allows you to live mindfully and from an authentic place centered on your values and beliefs. Living focused on yourself, in touch with who you are and what you have control over, is an empowering and flexible life. It is, and always has been, within your power to change the next chapter of your story. By consciously living this way, you can lead by example and create a template for all your relationships to flourish.

REFERENCES

Ainsworth, M. D. S., Blehar, M. C., Waters, E., & Wall, S. (1978). *Patterns of attachment: A psychological study of the strange situation*. Lawrence Erlbaum.

The Bowen Center for the Study of the Family. (2023). *Emotional cutoff.* https://www.thebowencenter.org/emotional-cutoff

Bowen, M. (1978). *Family therapy in clinical practice*. Jason Aronson.

Bowlby, J. (1973). *Attachment and loss. Vol. 2: Separation: Anxiety and anger*. Basic Books.

Brown, B. (2012). *Daring greatly: How the courage to be vulnerable transforms the way we live, love, parent, and lead*. Avery.

Curtin, M. (2017, February 27). This 75-year Harvard study found the 1 secret to leading a fulfilling life. *Inc.* https://www.inc.com/melanie-curtin/want-a-life-of -fulfillment-a-75-year-harvard-study-says-to-prioritize-this-one-t.html

Goleman, D. (2020). *Emotional intelligence: Why it can matter more than IQ* (25th anniversary ed.). Bantam Books. (Original work published 1995).

The Gottman Institute. (2022). *The Gottman method.* https://www.gottman.com /about/the-gottman-method

Gottman, J. M., & DeClaire, J. (2001). *The relationship cure: A five-step guide to strengthening your marriage, family, and friendships*. Three Rivers Press.

Jacobson, N., & Gottman, J. (1998). *When men batter women: New insights into ending abusive relationships*. Simon & Schuster.

Johnson, S. M., & Greenberg, L. S. (1992). Emotionally focused therapy: Restructuring attachment. In S. H. Budman, M. F. Hoyt, & S. Friedman (Eds.), *The first session in brief therapy* (pp. 204–224). Guilford Press.

Kerr, M. E., & Bowen, M. (1988). *Family evaluation: An approach based on Bowen theory*. Norton.

Lerner, H. (2014). *The dance of anger: A woman's guide to changing the patterns of intimate relationships*. HarperCollins.

Lisitsa, E. (2023). The four horsemen: Criticism, contempt, defensiveness, and stonewalling. *The Gottman Institute*. https://www.gottman.com/blog/the-four-horsemen-recognizing-criticism-contempt-defensiveness-and-stonewalling

Main, M., & Solomon, J. (1990). Procedures for identifying infants as disorganized/disoriented during the Ainsworth strange situation. In M. T. Greenberg, D. Cicchetti, & E. M. Cummings (Eds.), *Attachment in the preschool years: Theory, research, and intervention* (pp. 121–160). The University of Chicago Press.

Manson, M. (2023). *Vulnerability: The key to better relationships*. https://markmanson.net/vulnerability-in-relationships

Noone, R. J., & Papero, D.V. (2015). *The family emotional system: An integrative concept for theory, science, and practice*. Lexington Books.

Pillemer, K. (2020). *Fault lines: Fractured families and how to mend them*. Penguin Random House.

Vangelisti, A. (Ed.). (2004). *Handbook of family communication*. Lawrence Erlbaum Associates.

Walsch, N. D. (1995). *Conversations with God: An uncommon dialogue*. Berkley Books.

ACKNOWLEDGMENTS

The world can continue to become a better place thanks to people taking the time to develop personally and foster self-awareness. When you work on yourself and your level of maturity, you are not only growing but also giving others a gift to become better versions of themselves. As we wrote this book, we spent some time considering how to help others learn the process of creating solid and fulfilling relationships like we have built our friendship over the last decade-plus. We are both thankful for each other and our ability to keep growing together as friends and colleagues.

We are also grateful to our family and friends for being supportive and encouraging us along the way so we could write. We are appreciative of the PESI team for their professionalism and work ethic.

Finally, we want to thank our clients for sharing their stories with us and allowing us to be a part of their growth and development.